T0287747

MONMOUTH
COURT HOUSE

MONMOUTH COURT HOUSE

THE BATTLE THAT MADE THE AMERICAN ARMY

Joseph G. Bilby

and

Katherine Bilby Jenkins

WESTHOLME

Yardley

First Westholme paperback 2018

Frontispiece: "Washington at Monmouth," an engraving by George
R. Hall, 1858. (*Library of Congress*)

Copyright © 2010 Joseph G. Bilby and Katherine Bilby Jenkins
Maps © 2010 Westholme Publishing, LLC
Maps by Tracy Dungan

Westholme Publishing, LLC
904 Edgewood Road
Yardley, Pennsylvania 19067
Visit our Web site at www.westholmepublishing.com

ISBN: 978-1-59416-319-7

Printed in United States of America.

To Patricia Ann Bilby and Geoffrey Jenkins

Philippe and Jodie Lepine of Neuilly-Plaisance,
in commemoration of the French intervention that made the
battle possible

Pfc. Samuel J. Bilby, U.S. Army Artillery, 1943–1946
"Lafayette, we came back."

CONTENTS

six

"The mystic chords of memory"

The Battle in Legend and History   237

List of Maps

PREFACE

THE OFTEN-OVERLOOKED BATTLE of June 28, 1778, at Monmouth Court House, New Jersey, is among the most important clashes in the history of the United States Army. Perhaps best known in popular history and folklore is the origin of the "Molly Pitcher" story. Monmouth's greater significance is that on that stifling summer day, George Washington's army, which had mixed, modest successes with decisive defeats over the previous three years of war, finally came into its own as a fighting force that could stand up to the best soldiers in the British army.[1]

In June 1778, British Lieutenant General Sir Henry Clinton's army evacuated Philadelphia and struck out across "the Jerseys" on its way back to New York City, a move forced on Clinton by the changing fortunes of war rooted in the French intervention on the side of the rebellious colonists. The Continental army, its ranks bolstered with a growing confidence based on two years of combat experience, enduring the Valley Forge winter and the training received from a German "baron" of dubious provenance who proved a drillmaster without equal, marched in pursuit. On June 28, the armies clashed at Monmouth Court House, midway across the state (just west of the modern town of Freehold, better known today as the birthplace of Bruce Springsteen), some fifty miles south of New York City, in the last major Revolutionary War battle in the north. Although the fighting ended in a tactical draw, Monmouth marked the first time in the war that Washington's Continentals were left in possession of the field following a major battle. The events at Monmouth Court House, coupled with the entire wartime experience in New Jersey between 1776 and 1778, provided solid, if initially unrecognized, evidence that the British could never win the American War for Independence. In that sense, Monmouth was indeed an American victory.

This work attempts to tell the story of the Battle of Monmouth Court House in a holistic manner. It sets the climactic fight west of Freehold within the larger context of the American Revolution and the civil war between Loyalist and patriot forces that erupted within it, particularly in Monmouth County, New Jersey, where the battle took place. In addition to a narrative of the campaign and battle itself, the book provides an analysis of the commanders, personnel, organization, training, tactics and weapons of both armies, and includes an epilogue addressing the story of the real Molly Pitcher and the historical role commemorations of the battle subsequently played, shedding light on their own eras as much, if not more, than the struggles of the eighteenth century.

one

"Many people here were plundered":

NEW JERSEY AT WAR, 1775–1778

THE RIBBON ROAD RAN WHITE through scrub oak and pine, the moon reflecting its cold November light off the sand. It ran through the position Lieutenant Barnes Smock had staked out for his company and then beyond, straight downhill to Raritan Bay. The young officer had deployed his troopers well, for at twenty-six years of age he was a soldier grown old with this war.

Smock surveyed his men as he waited. There were the old militia hands, some who served their alternate months of duty out of a sense of obligation and patriotism, and others who were in the ranks as paid substitutes for those whose fear or greed or indolence or desire to hold themselves apart from this war had kept them from shouldering a musket. Many of these semipermanent militiamen were landless, and soldiering was a damn sight better than pushing someone else's plow. Some of them had done nine-month duty stints as draftees or substitutes with the Jersey Continentals, and they were the best—steady under fire and good men with a bayonet when they could get one. And then there were the young ones—out for a lark with pa's fowling piece. He generally left them back at Monmouth Court House, guarding prisoners. But tonight he might need every man. Raiding parties down from Refugeetown were abroad.[1]

Sergeant Covenhoven broke the lieutenant's reverie by tugging at his sleeve and pointing down the trail to the horizon that crested a small rise fifty yards away. As they came over the hillock, Smock counted them—six. And he had twenty-five. It would be easy if done right.

They were sloppy tonight; bunched up, bent over with loot and talking, their muskets slung carelessly. They could smell the saltwater and hear its rush and thought themselves safe.

As a shadowy form came within feet of him, Smock ordered "fire." The flash of musketry lit dark into day for a moment, and he saw the face of the man in front of him go red with blood. In the black aftermath of the blinding volley there was silence, broken first by a few soft moans, punctuated by a single answering shot and the whiz of a ball overhead and a distant thrashing.

Then the air grated with the feverish scrape of ramrods as "Smock's Light Horse" reloaded, some, especially the old Continentals, with hand-rolled paper cartridges pulled from crude cartridge boxes and others with loose powder, wadding, and ball. Private Daniel Denise, who had discharged a load of swan shot atop a musket ball into the Refugee leader's face, pulled the nozzle out of his powder horn with his teeth, quickly primed, and then poured a measure of powder down the barrel of his weapon. He inserted tow wadding in the muzzle, started it with his finger, spit a ball atop it, and then tamped the load down with his ramrod.

As his night vision returned, Smock peered down the path and counted five dark forms on the sand. One had got away. One of the shapes moved, crawling away from the ambush in a curious dragging manner.

"Got him in the hips or spine," offered Sergeant Covenhoven.

One of Smock's young farmer boys broke from the woods and rushed the crawling man, splitting his head open with a small axe, screaming, "Tory bastard!" The militiaman then started down the road, followed by a few others.

"Back here you fools!" Smock commanded, "unless you want done to you what you done to them. Ambushes ain't just somethin' we do."

His troops back in line, the lieutenant walked with his sergeant a few steps to the closest corpse and turned its head with his boot. In the sheltered flicker of Covenhoven's candle lantern he saw the face of a man he knew, a man who had worked his father's farm in the long ago and had taught him how to fish and how to open an oyster—in a world gone forever.

Smock turned to the company.

"Gather up their loot, we've got some goods to return. Let 'em lay here and rot for good example. Applejack's on me at Laird's tomorrow."

The foregoing was fiction. But it could have happened. Similar incidents occurred with regularity in the dark and bloody combat that consumed Monmouth County, New Jersey, during the larger struggle of the American Revolution. Lieutenant Barnes "Leggy" Smock, Sergeant Lewis Covenhoven, and Trooper Daniel Denise were real people, and they battled Loyalist raiders, who were often their former neighbors, for eight long years. In June 1778, they would be called into action alongside George Washington's Continentals, against the best Britain had to offer, as one of the biggest and most important battles of the American Revolution unfolded, quite literally, in their backyards. This is the story of how that battle came to be.

Despite the scenes of violence and civil carnage that came to pass in Monmouth County and elsewhere in New Jersey as the Revolutionary War deepened, most historians have characterized the bulk of the province's population, in dramatic contrast to New Englanders, as somewhat reluctant revolutionaries as the 1770s unfolded. William Franklin, Benjamin's son and the last royal governor, was a popular and clever politician, and continued to fight the growing tide of revolution even after Lexington and Concord, his efforts abetted by a seemingly ambivalent population. While there had been reactions among Jerseyans to increasing British/colonial difficulties in the decade prior to the war, reflected in a stirring of rebellious ardor evident in some quarters

Not all New Jerseyans looked passively on as the events leading up to the Revolution unfolded. The "Tea Burners" monument in Greenwich, New Jersey, erected in 1908 commemorates the "tea party" held there on December 22, 1774. (*New Jersey State Archives*)

of the colony, and even a "Tea Party" in Greenwich, down by Delaware Bay, the depth of such feelings at the outbreak of hostilities in April 1775 is difficult to determine. At least some evolving opposing loyalties, to king or patriot cause, appeared theologically based at first glance, although David J. Fowler reasonably posits that "religion probably 'followed politics rather than leading it.'" In general, however, New Jersey's many Quakers, doctrinal pacifists, tended to remain loyal to the king or adopt a precarious neutrality, while the Dutch Reformed Church, a significant denomination in the northeastern section of the colony, split into pro- and anti-war factions, paralleling the political views of the conservative and progressive wings of the sect. Presbyterians, who had previous conflicts with Franklin, especially regarding governance of the College of New Jersey, were firmly in the patriot camp from the beginning, and were generally supported by Baptists. All of the dissenting doctrines, and by 1770 there was a veritable stew of them in the colony, feared the establishment of the Anglican Church as the official government-supported religion of New Jersey, a policy supported by Governor Franklin, who also backed New Jerseyan Reverend James Odell for the position of first Anglican bishop in America. Needless to say, however, there were other apparent determinants of loyalty to one side or the other, from complex fiscal and political beliefs and local rivalries to the simple application of peer pressure.[2]

Following the outbreak of fighting in Massachusetts in April 1775, most New Jersey Loyalists sought a low profile as patriot forces seized effective political control through local Committees of Safety and the Provincial Congress. That November, in an effort to regain his fast-ebbing authority, Governor Franklin called on the members of the old New Jersey Assembly, in competition for civil authority with the new Provincial Congress, to establish a committee for reconciliation with the king. Franklin further instructed the colony's delegates to the Continental Congress to vote against any proposals for independence. The governor's efforts, marginally influential at best, came to an abrupt end when his report to London on efforts to stifle the course of the revolt in New Jersey was intercepted by patriot forces. The discovery revealed him as an active agent of the king, not the enabler of compromise and potential reconciliation, as he had portrayed himself. The governor was placed under loose house arrest in January 1776 at his residence in Perth Amboy, where he continued a covert correspondence with British officials. After Franklin's failed attempt to call the defunct Assembly back into session in June to consider British peace proposals, the Provincial Congress ordered him to sign a parole promising to cease anti-Revolutionary activity and go into internal exile at his Burlington County estate. The governor refused and was transported to Connecticut, arriving, ironically, on July 4, and was held there as a prisoner of war until exchanged in October 1778. After returning to British-controlled territory in New York City, Franklin plotted revenge on New Jersey's patriots, initially as an organizer of the "Refugee Club" and subsequently as president of the board of directors of the Associated Loyalists, an organization that sponsored raids that ravaged the state, particularly Monmouth County, until the end of the war.[3]

Although Franklin's continuance in office, coupled with his attempts to use the old Assembly as a counterweight to the Provincial Congress, is often cited as evidence that the population of New Jersey was essentially conservative, tending more toward loyalty or, at worst, compromise and reconciliation than rebellion, that view has been challenged by some recent scholarship. Maxine Lurie, for example, points out that whatever the sentiment was prior to the critical year 1776, the Provincial Congress did indeed adopt a radical stance over the course of that year, deposing and arresting Franklin and passing a constitution that

reinforced and institutionalized the concepts of jury trials, equali-
ty, freedom of religion, and separation from royal and
Parliamentary rule. No matter the overall trends in the state,
though, there is no doubt that there were significant strongholds
of Loyalist sympathies in various areas, and that Monmouth
County was one of them. Initial patriot seizure of effective control
in 1775 was, however, facilitated by a combination of effective
political organization and use of the militia coupled with the withdrawal of many whose loyalties were suspect, chiefly Quakers,
from public life and into cautious neutrality. The patriot ascen-
dency created considerable Loyalist resentment, and eventually
elicited a bungled attempt at counterrevolution followed by a
bloody response.[4]

In October 1775, the New Jersey Provincial Congress authorized the raising of two eight-company regiments of Continental or
regular army soldiers for one year of service. The First, or East
Jersey, Regiment was recruited at Elizabethtown and Perth
Amboy with men from Middlesex, Morris, Somerset,
Monmouth, Essex, and Bergen counties in the ranks. The men of
the Second, or West Jersey, Regiment were from Gloucester,
Hunterdon, Burlington, Salem, and Sussex counties and were
mustered into service at Trenton and Burlington. Both regiments
were initially assigned to upstate New York and participated in the
brief and unsuccessful American invasion of Canada. A Third
New Jersey Regiment was authorized in January 1776 and raised
at Elizabethtown between February and May. That unit was dispatched to upstate New York as well, where it spent some time
chasing Loyalists. With the state's regular regiments far away to
the north, New Jersey had to rely on militiamen for its own local
defense needs. Those needs would become a top priority in the
summer and fall of 1776.[5]

In the waning months of 1775, Lieutenant-General Thomas
Gage, then the British commander in America, found himself and
his field army bottled up in Boston following the fights at

Lexington, Concord, and Bunker Hill, and the subsequent siege mounted by the New England militia. It was Gage's intention to remain in the city over the winter while planning a move by sea to attack New York, which he perceived as the critical choke point of a spreading rebellion. Although Major General William Howe replaced Gage in November, the new commander shared his predecessor's ideas for future operations. Howe was, however, in his turn, forced to evacuate Boston when a growing American army under General George Washington seized the strategic high ground of Dorchester Heights in March 1776 and emplaced heavy artillery to dominate the city. In response, Howe withdrew his army, accompanied by local Loyalists, to Halifax, Nova Scotia. By June of 1776, the British commander was ready to resume the offensive with his immediate force combined with a large number of reinforcements, including German mercenaries, who were on their way from England with a fleet under the command of the general's brother Vice Admiral Richard Howe.

On the American side, Washington was well aware that New York was a probable British target for 1776 and ordered Major General Charles Lee to the city to supervise its defense. Although Lee, a former British officer, would gain lasting fame through apparent failure on the Monmouth battlefield in 1778, he was undeniably an experienced soldier and a fairly astute one. Lee's accurate analysis of New York City as a poor potential defensive position was not encouraging. With British command of the sea unquestioned, Manhattan Island, surrounded by navigable water, was extremely vulnerable. In the end, Lee, before he was transferred to bolster the defenses of Charleston, another danger point, attempted to make the best of a bad situation and ordered the American troops in New York to begin digging defensive trenches at likely landing spots around Manhattan. Washington himself directly assumed responsibility for the defense of New York in April 1776, and by the time Howe arrived off Sandy Hook on June 25, the American general had mustered more than twenty thousand soldiers for the defense of the city, although most were inexperienced militiamen.[6]

In an operational style that would become characteristic, Howe took his time before assuming the offensive against the Americans. After landing at Staten Island in early July, a move that caused more than a bit of panic in New Jersey, where frantically digging militiamen could plainly see the enemy across a short span of water, the British commander consolidated his command as reinforcements from England and a failed British expeditionary force to Charleston arrived, until he had a total of 25,000 men fit for action, supported by thirty ships of the line and frigates mounting 1,200 cannons. As the British force grew before their eyes, New Jersey's nervous patriot leaders called for their militia, many of them deployed in the defenses of New York, to return for home defense duty. When the Jersey militiamen marched back to the state, however, many were discharged from any duty at all. By mid-July, a majority of the New Jersey citizen soldiers had been "temporarily excused from service to gather their harvest." Their places in the state's defenses were taken by Pennsylvanians, who presumably were harvest duty free. Subsequent attempts to call the Jerseymen back to duty were met with what has been kindly described as a lethargic response; in fact, none of the 2,000 men called up on July 18 had responded by August 1. Of a total of 3,300 militiamen initially called up in June, only 1,458 were still serving in mid-August, and desertion and insubordination ran rife among those remaining. New Jersey Loyalists observing the events of the summer of 1776 were heartened by both the arrival of overwhelming royal forces and the apparent lack of enthusiasm in patriot ranks and began, here and there, to plan their own counterrebellion.[7]

Loyalist rumblings did not go unnoticed. On June 26, 1776, the Provincial Congress ordered the militia to suppress Tory demonstrators in Hunterdon County and directed the arrest of others in Monmouth County's Upper Freehold and Shrewsbury townships, where Loyalist agents were active and at least somewhat successful in exploiting Quaker ambivalence about the war and translating it into active opposition to the patriot cause. Within weeks of the British arrival off Sandy Hook, some sixty volunteers from Upper Freehold and forty-eight from Perth Amboy, home town of Governor Franklin's attorney general and prominent Tory Cortlandt Skinner, made their way through American lines to offer their services to General Howe. In July, British officers on Staten Island were advised that "there are thousands in the Jerseys will Join us, as soon as we get footing in that province." Under advisement from Washington, New Jersey governor and former militia commander William Livingston ordered a number of Perth Amboy Loyalists detained and moved inland, to prevent them from communicating with the British on nearby Staten Island.[8]

In late August General Howe, finally moved to action, began what would be a series of successful operations by crossing to Long Island and decisively defeating the patriot force there. Despite the American tactical disaster on Long Island, however, the British offensive enabled George Washington to begin building a reputation as an extraordinary and resourceful commander, as he successfully extricated his beaten army through a cover of fog and darkness from Brooklyn to Manhattan under the noses of the enemy.

Manhattan Island, as Lee had perceived, proved to be indefensible, especially with the unseasoned and inadequately trained force of Continentals and militia Washington had at his disposal. Discouraged by defeat on Long Island, many remaining American militiamen began to drift away from the army toward home. The British landing at Kip's Bay on the East River signaled the advent of another series of American tactical setbacks, which accelerated the deterioration of the army. Although continually bested in a series of battles lasting into November that drove his men north and out of Manhattan to White Plains, Washington, aided by Howe's hesitation, managed to preserve a battered but steady core force, which he moved into New Jersey.

Following the fall of Fort Washington on the New York side, the British crossed the North, or Hudson, River, to New Jersey, where they captured Fort Lee on November 18. New Jersey militiamen who witnessed these operations from their position at Powles Hook panicked and took off for Bergen. With the enemy now lodged in a secure New Jersey beachhead, Washington retreated to Newark with part of his main army, about 4,400 men. He ordered the remainder of his active force, about 7,000 additional soldiers, to concentrate near White Plains under General Lee, who had returned from Charleston, as defense against a possible British thrust north up the Hudson, and assigned the Connecticut militia to defend the back door to New England. In the event, Howe dispatched a seaborne force to seize Newport, Rhode Island, and ordered Lieutenant General Charles Lord Cornwallis, with another, relatively small detachment to chase Washington across New Jersey. The American commander successively fell back before Cornwallis through New Brunswick and Princeton to Trenton, where he crossed the Delaware into Pennsylvania. The American "fox," as Cornwallis was apocryphally credited with characterizing the patriot commander, had eluded the British hounds, but many on the British side, including prominent Pennsylvania Tory Joseph Galloway, felt the dogs had been leashed, and that Howe had not pursued the American army with the persistence and force he could have, a policy the British commander perhaps arrived at in light of his belief that the American army was truly a broken force, coupled with his overall desire to come to a reasonable peace and reconciliation agreement. No matter the rationale, it was a decision that Howe would soon come to rue.[9]

On November 21, as the main American army withdrew across New Jersey, Governor Livingston issued an order for the militia to rally in support of Washington's strategic retreat and to control potential Loyalist uprisings. The initial response was less than stellar. In early December, militia Brigadier General Matthias Williamson established a headquarters at Morristown, a patriot stronghold securely tucked west of the Watchung mountain ranges from British-controlled eastern New Jersey, and awaited the appearance of the state's citizen army. Early evidence suggested that Williamson might have a long wait. As of December 8, less than fifty militiamen from Essex County had reported to the general, and only a few more showed up from Sussex. Eventually enough part-time soldiers appeared, however, to provide, as Morristown's Colonel Jacob Ford Jr. noted, an "appearance of defence," which fortunately would not be severely tested. Washington found few Jersey militiamen on hand to support him when his army arrived at Trenton. The Continental commander and his generals let it be widely known that they were disgusted with the New Jersey militia; Major General Nathanael Greene characterized the behavior of the state's citizen soldiers as being "scurvily."[10]

All in all, by early December 1776, New Jersey appeared, as Leonard Lundin has put it, "almost as completely cowed by the deliberate and nearly bloodless advance of the royal army as it would have been had Washington's force been crushed in fierce battle." Several New Jersey legislators and other patriot leaders, including Trenton's Samuel Tucker, president of the Provincial Congress, along with Princeton's Richard Stockton, a signer of the Declaration of Independence, were in British hands. Formerly discreet Loyalists came out into the open and wavering citizens across the state declared publicly for the king; even some Jerseymen who had espoused the patriot cause accepted what seemed to be the new reality and switched sides. Loyalist commissioners appointed by Howe were instructing local citizens to report to towns like Monmouth Court House to sign loyalty oaths. The British were riding high, and General Howe decided to temper might with mercy, at least in principle, issuing "protections" from British army plundering and requisitions to those who signed a loyalty oath. In at least one instance, British supply officers actually issued food to hungry civilians. Major General Charles Lee, dawdling in northern New Jersey rather than rapidly bringing his immediate command to support Washington, was captured by the British at a Basking Ridge hostelry on December 13. The war seemed to be coming to a close.[11]

But things would change, dramatically and rapidly. Just when all appeared lost, the militia began to revive and harass the enemy in small actions across the state. Enough militiamen made it to Morristown by mid-December to blunt the advance of an 800-man British probing force at Hobart's or Springfield Gap beyond the village of Springfield, the most feasible approach across the Watchung mountains, securing Morristown as headquarters for a potential American comeback. As the year came to an end, Washington struck back against British outposts in New Jersey with a brilliant and successful counteroffensive, crossing the Delaware to recapture Trenton, along with most of its Hessian garrison. In the ensuing days he crossed back into Pennsylvania, and then returned to Trenton, fending off an enemy attack along Assunpink Creek before slipping away in the night and marching to Princeton, where he defeated another British detachment. Washington's victories succeeded in tumbling the enemy outpost line back across the state, and the American commander threatened New Brunswick, where a hefty British payroll was reputed to be stored, before deciding the best course was to march his battered little force north into winter quarters at Morristown. There, protected by the hills and surrounded by a loyal patriot population, he began the process of rebuilding the army throughout the winter and into the spring of 1777. Recruits for new Continental regiments came in slowly after the catastrophes of the summer, but when they did they mustered in for three years or the duration of the war, as opposed to the one-year enlistments of the first generation of Continentals. The new regiments would provide a solid basis for the army's future and finally came into their own on the battlefield at Monmouth Court House in the summer of 1778.[12]

Rebel resistance in New Jersey continued to stiffen into the new year, as the militia, buoyed by its own and Washington's successes, began to restore patriot political control. The American revival was also ironically abetted by the enemy. Dispirited Jerseyans had flocked to the seemingly triumphant British as they crossed the state in the autumn of 1776, with, according to British claims, at least 2,500 of them signing General Howe's loyalty oaths. The British army, however, perhaps surprisingly, considering its reputation as a well-drilled and disciplined force, clearly violated what would today be considered the basics of good counterinsurgency policy. Allowing for a measure of patriot propaganda exaggeration, there is no doubt that the British and their German mercenary allies, despite official orders from Howe, who genuinely believed a rapprochement between king and colonists possible, ignored orders to treat the local population well, and reverted to standard European-style eighteenth-century civil-military relations. One British junior officer then serving in New Jersey recalled years later that "there was never a more expert set than the Light Infantry at either grab, lob or gutting a house." The populace was pillaged, regardless of loyalty or proffered paper "protections." Newark Presbyterian pastor Alexander McWhorter noted that "Whig and Tory were all treated in the same manner . . . one Nuttman, who had always been a remarkable Tory, and who met the British troops with huzzas of joy, had his house plundered of almost everything; he himself had his shoes taken off his feet, and threatened to be hanged." Even higher-ranking officers apparently engaged in looting, including Colonel Sir William Erskine, the British Quartermaster General, "who lodged at Daniel Baldwin's [and] had his room furnished from a neighbouring house with mahogany chairs and tables, a considerable part of which was taken away with his baggage when he went to Elizabeth-Town." Other colonels were also accused of looting, including one who allegedly "took away a sick woman's bed." Howe personally promised protec-

Hunterdon County New Jersey Militiaman Asher Hart. Hart served a number of duty tours as a drafted and volunteer militiaman for varying periods from 1776 through 1781, for a total year and a half of active duty. He was present in the Battles of Trenton, Monmouth and Springfield and as pictured here is dressed in his civilian clothes, armed with a musket, cartridge box and bayonet. It is likely that not only militiamen, but many of the nine month "levies" serving in the New Jersey Brigade in the summer of 1778 were similarly armed and clothed. As with most eighteenth century people, there are no existing portraits of Hart, and this reconstruction of what he probably looked like was created by artist Peter Culos using photographs of his nineteenth century descendents. (*Courtesy Kevin Marshall*)

tion to a woman who cooked a meal for his entourage, but had
no sooner left the premises when "his soldiers Come in And plunder[ed] the Woman of Every thing in the house, Breaking And
Destroying what they Could not take Away, they Even tore up the
floor of the house." Some historians considering the British
army's behavior among what were, in reality, its own people,
make favorable comparisons on its conduct compared to the
European military standard of the day, noting, in one case, that
"the forces of George III manifested unusual respect for the persons and property of noncombatants." This clearly does not seem
to have been the case, however.[13]

Such accounts of civilian abuse, coupled with stories of sexual
assaults perpetrated on New Jersey women by Howe's soldiers,
spread like wildfire across the state, with inevitable results. By
early 1777, British and Hessian troops venturing out of their
diminishing chain of New Jersey posts in search of food for themselves and fodder for their animals found their paths barred by
angry men wielding muskets and determined to make their forays
as costly as possible. On January 4, a New Jersey mounted militia
force captured a British supply wagon train in Somerset County.
Sporadic fighting subsequently sputtered in an arc around
Elizabethtown, which was held by Scottish Highlanders and
German mercenaries. A combined British-German foraging force
was crushed at Springfield, with the entire German detachment,
numbering between fifty and sixty men, killed or captured. On
January 6, Howe ordered Elizabethtown abandoned. The town's
garrison fell back to Perth Amboy, losing a hundred men as prisoners and a large amount of supplies to pursuing Jersey militiamen along the way. The British commander soon withdrew all of
his detachments from the state, save those at New Brunswick and
Perth Amboy.[14]

New Jersey's Loyalists, whose future had seemed so bright a
month before, and who had even established their own counter-
revolutionary governments and militias in several areas, including
Monmouth County's Upper Freehold Township, withdrew along
with the regulars or fled on separate paths to New York or into
the Pine Barrens wilderness to the south. In some instances, luke-

warm British sympathizers, resentful at abandonment by their
sworn protectors, professed a new loyalty to the patriots. One
account, perhaps apocryphal, had former Loyalists using their
Howe-issued certificates of loyalty to roll paper musket cartridges
for use against the British. There was definitely some side-switch-
ing, however, as there had been from patriot to Loyalist at the
onset of the initial British invasion. Of thirty-five Tories sentenced
to hang by a Morristown court in January 1777, thirty-three opted
to join the regiments of the Continental army's New Jersey
Brigade when that alternative option to the scaffold was offered
them. The upshot of the British withdrawal from most of New
Jersey was the effective end of any significant Loyalist chance of
seizing political and military control of the state. Instead, the
Loyalists had exposed themselves to defeat and patriot retribution, which resulted in flight and "refugee" status for many and
led to a vicious civil war within the Revolution. By early 1777,
New Jersey Loyalist property was being confiscated by official
state orders and even those who declared themselves neutral
became subjects of suspicion and arrest. Throughout the year,
New Jerseyans who had declared for the Crown when British victory seem inevitable found themselves, and their families, targets
of patriot militia bent on reprisals. In July 1777, militia light horsemen carried off all of the "cattle, Sheep, Hogs and Horses"
belonging to Thomas Crowell of Shrewsbury and told his wife
they were coming back for her furniture and that the Crowell
house and farm would be confiscated and put up for sale.[15]

With Governor Livingston no longer involved in the details of
militia activities, he ordered Colonel Philemon Dickinson, an efficient commander who had initiated the early patriot revival with
an uprising in Hunterdon County prior to the battle of Trenton,
to "compel all such Delinquents" avoiding service to come to the
colors. Dickinson organized and maintained an active citizen-sol-
dier presence in the field by rotating duty stints through the winter. Another key leader in the American counteroffensive was
Continental Brigadier General William "Scotch Willie" Maxwell.
In December 1777, prior to his Trenton triumph, Washington had
assigned Maxwell, a veteran of the ill-fated Canadian expedition

of 1776, to report to the secure American base at Morristown and begin organizing the new New Jersey Continental regiments, as the original battalions approached the end of their one-year enlistments. Maxwell was assigned the additional task of operating alongside the militia with his recruits as part of the continuous harassment campaign against the remaining British garrisons in the state. Scotch Willie, who subsequently established his headquarters on the east side of the Watchungs in Westfield, fulfilled his mission with an enviable competence. Born in 1733, Maxwell was one of the more interesting brigade commanders in the Continental army. A Scotch-Irishman who had emigrated with his family from County Tyrone to Sussex County, New Jersey, in 1747, he fought in the ranks of the "Jersey Blues" volunteer regiment in the French and Indian War. Following that conflict Maxwell served as a "king's commissary," a quasi-military official responsible for supplying British garrisons on what was then the frontier, from Schenectady to Michilimackinac. He was stationed at the latter post, at the juncture of Lakes Huron and Michigan, where he also acquired property and engaged in the Indian trade on his own. Maxwell, a tough frontier trader with a Native-American common-law wife and a reputed fondness for whiskey, was not the type of person one would expect to find serving as a Continental army general. No matter his social class, however, the man would fight without fear, and his particular genius, in that midwinter of 1777, appeared to be the hit-and-run open style of warfare the militia was successfully practicing against the British in New Jersey. Maxwell used his Continental regiments to stiffen the militia at critical junctures, and cooperated with Dickinson in what proved to be a seamless campaign.[16]

While the British garrisons in New Jersey remained beleaguered by a mix of regulars and militiamen, their living conditions were enhanced somewhat after General Cornwallis took command in New Brunswick and improved supplies of food and clothing for his men. The British still had to stage expeditions into the local countryside to acquire forage for their animals, however. Forage was a serious logistical need, equivalent to gasoline for a modern mechanized force, and so the armies continued to brush against each other on a regular basis into the spring. A New York Loyalist observed that "not a stick of wood, a spear of grass or a kernel of corn could the [British] troops in New Jersey procure without fighting for it, unless sent from New York." Colonel Charles Mawhood had more than skirmishing for food on his mind, however, when he led a strong British force on a sortie from Amboy to Rahway on February 23. Maxwell, his men's confidence on the rise, was happy to accommodate the colonel's desire for a fight. Mawhood tried to outflank a line of militiamen with a company of grenadiers from the Forty-second Foot, a highly regarded Scottish Highland regiment, but Scotch Willie had quietly deployed more Jerseymen, who remained unseen, in a position outflanking the Scottish advance. At the appropriate moment, the amateur Jersey soldiers rose and shot the regulars to ribbons and the whole British force fell back toward Amboy, harassed by Continentals and militiamen along the way. Two weeks later, Maxwell repeated his stellar performance against another enemy column. Historian David Hackett Fischer calculates that over the winter, following the battles of Trenton and Princeton, Howe's army lost "more than nine hundred men . . . killed, wounded, captured or missing," in its "Forage War" operations in New Jersey. That damage was inflicted by the aggressiveness and growing military skill of the New Jersey militia and Continentals led by Dickinson and Maxwell.[17]

The *petit guerre* not only battered and bled the British, but provided much needed military experience and confidence to the Americans, both militiamen and newly enlisted Continentals. Howe's officers realized this as fully as did Washington. In March 1777, a British major involved in the New Jersey fighting wrote that the "rebel soldiers from being accustomed to peril in their skirmishes, begin to have more confidence." He added that "although they do not always succeed, following our people as they return . . . wounding and killing many of rearguards, gives them the notion of victory." A colonel worried that the Forage War was creating a more difficult-to-defeat enemy, declaring that the constant skirmishing was "a plan which we ought to avoid most earnestly, since it will certainly make soldiers of the

Americans." If newspaper reports were correct, by spring even New Jersey's ladies had joined the fight. According to one account, a Woodbridge woman, spying a "drunken Hessian" pillaging a house, "went home, dressed herself in man's apparel and armed with an old firelock" took him prisoner and delivered him to one of Maxwell's patrols.[18]

As the spring campaigning season approached, both American and British commanders planned larger operations. Washington had assumed the tactical offensive at Trenton and Princeton and the swift reaction time and combativeness of his available forces, militia and Continental, had been decisive during the winter outpost war. Despite these encouraging signs, however, it was inarguable that General Howe, with his large army centrally located in New York City and command of the seas in American waters, coupled with another British army forming in Canada under Lieutenant General John Burgoyne and poised to move down Lake Champlain to the Hudson, would retain the overall strategic initiative in the spring of 1777. Howe could strike wherever and however he wished. Washington, tasked with the defense of the American capital at Philadelphia and the Continental Congress meeting there, and also committed to holding his Hudson River forts north of New York City, was in a necessarily reactive position.

On November 30, 1776, Howe advised Lord George Germain, Secretary of State for America and a soldier himself, that he intended to decisively crush the rebellion in the forthcoming year. In brief, the plan the British commander outlined involved holding on to his base in New York City, which he realized was the fulcrum of British America, while dispatching his chief subordinate, General Sir Henry Clinton, to land more troops in Rhode Island to expand his foothold in New England prior to moving on Boston. With Rhode Island secure, Howe himself would lead a second large column of troops, perhaps as many as ten thousand men, up the Hudson, to link up with Burgoyne's invasion moving down from Canada. Lastly, he proposed to move eight thousand men into a pacified New Jersey as a diversion to keep the main American army fixed in position (at that point, he hoped, across the river in Pennsylvania), and prevent Washington from sending reinforcements to other threatened areas. The New Jersey invasion force would be also be poised to take advantage of any opportunities that might arise, including making a dash at Philadelphia. In order to accomplish these goals, Howe requested that Germain reinforce him with fifteen thousand additional soldiers. Inexplicably to many of his subordinate officers, however, Howe radically changed his plans within weeks. The general's new idea limited British forces in Rhode Island and the lower Hudson Valley to a static defensive role and switched his major offensive thrust toward Philadelphia.[19]

Historian John W. Jackson traces the dramatic change in Howe's plans to the appearance in New York of a group of Pennsylvania Loyalist refugees led by Joseph Galloway. Galloway, a Philadelphia attorney, was president of the American Philosophical Society and had been a personal friend of Benjamin Franklin. He was also a prominent prewar American politician and member of the First Continental Congress who had once advocated home rule for the colonies, but resisted a decisive break with Britain. Due to his Loyalist prominence and friendship with Ambrose Serle, Howe's secretary, Galloway was able to obtain personal audiences with both the general and his brother, Admiral Richard Howe, where he argued the case for a move on Philadelphia. Galloway posited that the fall of the seat of the Continental Congress would totally demoralize the American rebels. He also believed that "seventy-five to ninety percent of Pennsylvania's citizens were loyal" and would rally to the British once the city fell, assuring a victorious end to the war. The disintegration of the Loyalist uprising in New Jersey over the winter did not seem to cause either Howe or Galloway to consider the possibility that this assertion might not be correct. The story that large numbers of Loyalists in a given area were just awaiting a British army to liberate them, despite the abject failure of that scenario in New Jersey, would become a familiar one and lead to a

THE
PROVINCE of NEW JERSEY,
Divided into
EAST and WEST,
commonly called
THE JERSEYS.

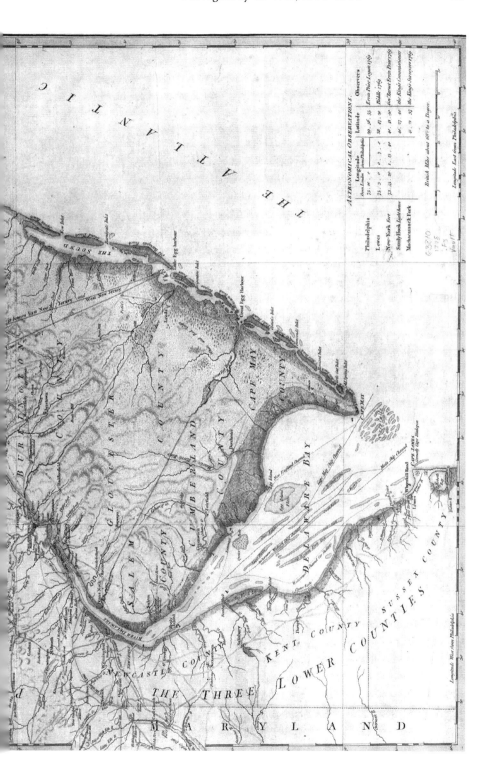

British pursuit of an elusive will-o'-the-wisp of Loyalist sympathizers who would restore their rule, from the Hudson Valley of New
York to the mountains of the Carolinas, that lasted to the end of
the conflict, and Galloway often seemed to be at the center of
such fantasies.[20]

Whether Joseph Galloway was the primary agent influencing
Howe's shift of priorities to the capture of Philadelphia or not, the
commander in chief did advise Germain that he had changed
plans and that the Rebel capital would be his main target for the
forthcoming campaign. Although his subsequent request for reinforcements was not as extensive as in his original plans for 1777,
Howe did ask for additional troops to push up the Hudson for a
possible link with Burgoyne, since the timetable he established for
moving on Philadelphia would limit his ability to support the
Canadian invasion with his current force structure. While this
lack of coordination might seem slipshod and odd to modern
observers, the poor communications of the period made any sort
of detailed advance strategic planning largely moot. Even making
allowances for such difficulties, however, there was a significant
lack of unity of command in the overall British effort in America.
Although Howe was ostensibly commander in chief, he did not
have total control over all of the forces committed, and Germain
and the king were free to dabble wherever they wished, with the
Canadian operation being a prime example. Howe and Germain
both viewed support of Burgoyne as desirable, but not a necessity,
as neither, foolishly as it turned out, had any fear that a small
British army plunging into the wilderness of northern New York
was in any sort of serious danger.[21]

As winter waned, Howe, in keeping with his new plan, began
to strengthen his New Jersey outposts by transferring six battalions of infantry from Rhode Island to Perth Amboy. In February
the British chief made a personal visit to New Brunswick, where
he put out the word, quickly picked up by American spies, that a
Loyalist column was preparing to march into Sussex County and
that British engineers were building a pontoon bridge to cross the
Delaware. Howe's maneuvers and apparent preparations suggested to Washington that the British commander might be ready to

either launch an attack on the main American army, or renew his push across the state to capture Philadelphia. From his Morristown headquarters, the American commander made plans to counter any British moves, but was far from confident, however, that his army, still in the process of rebuilding after the debilitating campaign of 1776, was in any condition to meet the enemy in the open field. Howe may have actually been planning an offensive or his moves may have been simply designed to elicit an American response for intelligence purposes. The latter option seems more likely, as the British troops in New Jersey were not as well supplied as they should have been or in the best physical condition for an aggressive advance as the Americans may have perceived them to be. It is also possible that the fights at Trenton and Princeton, and the subsequent aggressive conduct displayed by American Continentals and militia during the winter forage war, which he witnessed personally during another visit to the New Jersey garrisons in March, may have reinforced Howe's natural caution, leading him to conduct a feint to test the enemy's reaction.[22]

George Washington was cautious as well, despite the fact that his army had been somewhat reconstructed, at least in numbers, over the winter. By May 21, the force under Washington's direct command reported 7,363 officers and men "fit for duty and on duty." Arms and ammunition were arriving in large quantities from France, with nineteen thousand muskets and one thousand barrels of gunpowder imported during the month of March 1777 alone. These facts may have influenced the American commander's decision to push on the enemy's New Jersey lines in hopes of striking a lucky blow and driving the British from the state altogether. In late May, Washington advanced from Morristown toward Howe's garrisons in eastern New Jersey, carefully deploying his main force, reinforced by more than seven hundred militiamen from Elizabethtown and Newark, at Middle Brook, less than ten miles from New Brunswick. The Middle Brook position gave the Americans an interior line vis a vis the enemy, which enabled Washington to move troops on an inside arc quickly to check a British advance from Perth Amboy or New Brunswick, as well as any attempt by Howe to probe up the Hudson River.[23]

Although he realized that Howe had several options, Washington initially assumed that when the British resumed campaigning, they would probably take up where they had left off the previous year and reinitiate their overland advance on Philadelphia. By mid-June, however, that did not appear to be the case. American spies reported a large amount of naval activity in the waters around New York, correctly indicating that Howe was considering some sort of seaborne movement, which could be directed at several possible targets, including Philadelphia and coastal cities to the north and south. In order to confuse the Americans as to his actual intentions, as well as take advantage of any opportunities that might arise to defeat the Continental army in the field, on June 11, Howe advanced eighteen thousand troops into New Jersey in two columns, concentrating them at Somerset and Middlebush in hopes of drawing Washington out of his Middle Brook position, or perhaps cutting off part of the American army under Major General John Sullivan stationed in the vicinity of Princeton. On June 21, after several maneuvers intended to bring the Americans to open battle failed, Howe abandoned his advanced posts and New Brunswick, and withdrew his entire army to Perth Amboy, which he reached by the following evening. The Americans followed carefully, harassing the British as opportunities presented themselves. Mid-June found the British hunkered down in a defensive position at Perth Amboy, with American observation forces concentrated at Quibbletown (New Market in today's Piscataway) and Metuchen.[24]

Despite falling back from their advanced positions in New Jersey, Howe's forces continued to threaten the Americans from Perth Amboy. Although the British commander apparently concluded that an attack on Washington's strong main position at Middle Brook would not be successful, on June 26, he marched two columns out of Perth Amboy in an operation aimed at cutting off and defeating the American force stationed at Metuchen under New Jersey Major General William Alexander, usually referred to as "Lord Stirling" after the Scottish title he laid claim to on rather tenuous grounds. Although initially positioned on good defensive terrain, Alexander, who was outnumbered, aggressively moved his men forward and engaged the advancing British. After his impetuous advance was almost cut off by a flanking movement initiated by Cornwallis, Alexander hastily retreated, losing three artillery pieces and about seventy men as prisoners. Cornwallis followed Alexander's force to Westfield, while Washington fell back with his main army on Bound Brook. Howe declined to mount a general attack, however, and withdrew his army once more to Perth Amboy, from where he began to cross it over to Staten Island, a move completed by June 30. A little known aspect of British operations in New Jersey in June 1777 was that they may have provided the occasion for the first combat use of breech-loading firearms in America. Captain Patrick Ferguson, inventor of a breech-loading flintlock rifle, had arrived in New York on June 1 with a company armed with the experimental weapon, and he and his command participated in Howe's offensive that month.[25]

After concentrating his army on Staten Island, Howe continued his leisurely preparations for the Philadelphia campaign into July. When Sir Henry Clinton arrived from London on July 5 to take charge of the garrison detailed to remain in New York, he was surprised to see his commander had still not initiated field operations against the patriot capital. Clinton was also dismayed when he discovered that Howe planned a seaborne movement against Philadelphia, rather than an overland one, which would, Clinton believed, help defend the British position in New York by screening that city from American attack. Howe, who harbored a personal dislike for Clinton, refused to change his plans and, convinced that both Burgoyne, by mid-July approaching Fort Ticonderoga, and Clinton's New York City garrison were in no danger from any American forces, he finally initiated his leisurely campaign to capture Philadelphia.

On July 23, Howe's fifteen-thousand-man expeditionary force weighed anchor off Staten Island and proceeded south in more than 250 ships. As long as the main British field army remained in New York, Washington had been forced to consider four possible enemy action scenarios. These included a British advance up the Hudson, an attempt to recapture Boston, operations against

Charleston–scene of a failed attack the previous year–or a move on Philadelphia by land or sea. As American scouts informed him that Howe's fleet had rounded Sandy Hook, those possibilities were reduced to Charleston or Philadelphia. Leaving a force behind to counter Clinton, the Americans marched south, across New Jersey, camping at Neshaminy, Pennsylvania, on August 10. When the British fleet appeared, then disappeared, from Delaware Bay, the consensus of a council of war was that Howe was headed for Charleston, but when the enemy was once again located, sailing north in Chesapeake Bay, that possibility was eliminated. Howe had actually considered using the most obvious approach to Philadelphia from the sea, up the Delaware River, but dismissed it because of potential difficulties involved in fighting past American fortifications on a narrowing river. His eventual landing at Head of Elk, Maryland, in the upper Chesapeake, however, clearly confirmed to Washington that the British objective was Philadelphia. The American commander marched his eleven thousand men south, parading directly through the capital city to boost patriot morale. Congressman John Adams for one, was impressed, and wrote his wife that the Continentals appeared "an army well appointed," despite the fact that "they don't step exactly in time."[26]

On arrival at Wilmington, Delaware, Washington halted his main army to await developments, and decided to push forward a small elite force to make contact with the advancing British, observe and report on enemy activities and movements, and engage in limited combat when appropriate. The most likely American detachment for this type of assignment, Colonel Daniel Morgan's riflemen, had marched north to reinforce Major General Horatio Gates's army against Burgoyne. To replace them, Washington created a special light infantry battalion of "picked men" for the forthcoming campaign, a practice he would continue for the remainder of the war. The general ordered each of his seven best brigades to detail one hundred men, along with commissioned and noncommissioned officers to command them, to the battalion. These soldiers were armed with smoothbore muskets, rather than the more accurate rifles carried by Morgan's men, but Washington still specified that commanders select their best marksmen for the battalion. In addition to good shots, the general specified that men who "may be depended on" and were physically fit and taller than average soldiers be assigned to the light infantry. Choosing a qualified officer to command the battalion proved a simple task. As senior brigadier general with the army, William Maxwell had a claim on the position and had also proved a master of the *petit guerre* during the previous winter in New Jersey. A natural choice, Maxwell was assigned to the position on August 30. Washington cautioned him to "be watchful and guarded on all the roads," to "annoy" the enemy "whenever possible," and to be careful when and where he fought, only engaging the British when he had a good chance of success.[27]

While the light infantry, reinforced by Pennsylvania and Delaware militia, moved south, with the main American army cautiously following, Howe dispatched several supply ships back to Delaware Bay with orders to establish a forward base at Newcastle. The initial party was later joined by the army's sick, and all supplies not portable enough to be carried overland. Howe then marched north in two columns, one commanded by General Cornwallis and the other by Hessian Major General Wilhelm von Knyphausen. The slow and deliberate British advance was preceded by a screen of light infantry units of regular soldiers and rifle-armed German jaegers, including a company under the command of the highly observant Captain Johann von Ewald.[28]

After halting his main army at Red Clay Creek, Washington ordered Maxwell to directly confront the British advance guard. On September 2, Maxwell deployed his battalion in the vicinity of Cooch's Bridge, which crossed Christiania Creek. The Jersey general established a defensive line extending from the creek bridge on his left along the front of Iron Hill, then sent most of his men forward down the Aiken's Tavern Road, which he perceived would be the main axis of the British advance, ordering them to fire on the enemy and fall back toward the main position. The Americans made contact with jaegers and light infantrymen under the command of Lieutenant Colonel Ludwig von Wurmb early the following morning.

Maxwell's Continentals conducted a two-mile fighting withdrawal against Wurmb to the Cooch's Bridge line, made a short stand and then retreated again, through woods and across fields and up the slope of Iron Hill itself. At that point General Howe personally appeared on the field, reinforced Wurmb with the Queen's Rangers, an elite Loyalist unit led by Major John Graves Simcoe, as well as artillery, and ordered a rapid bayonet charge on the American position. The British bayonet charge, a tactic effectively used against the Americans on Long Island, was designed more to rattle an enemy defensive line so that it broke and ran rather than actually close and fight hand to hand with bayonets. It succeeded. Maxwell's outgunned and outnumbered light infantry, which had battled the British advance for seven hours, rapidly fled the field, some men tossing away their blankets and muskets. Unlike his actions in New Jersey, Maxwell's conduct of the operation drew mixed reviews. The young and inexperienced Marquis de Lafayette caustically and presumptuously condemned the Jersey general's conduct and characterized him as "the most inept brigadier general in the army." General Washington, however, who along with Lafayette witnessed the last stages of what had been a long and grueling fight, concluded that Maxwell had done a good job until he "had to retreat" due to overwhelming odds.[29]

Skirmishing continued as Howe moved north and Washington redeployed his eleven thousand men, first north of Red Clay Creek and then along the north bank of Brandywine Creek, adjusting as Howe concentrated at nearby Kennett Square along the main route to Philadelphia (approximating today's U.S. Route 1). Although it seemed a barrier at first glance, the Brandywine, which divided into West and East branches beyond the American right flank, was crossable by troops at a number of locations, including seven official fords, a fact that proved detrimental to the Americans. On September 11, Washington placed his best units in a position to contest a British crossing of the Brandywine in the vicinity of Chadds Ford, then strung out militia to protect his left and covered his right flank with a light cavalry screen, a few infantry detachments, and some more militiamen. On arrival at Kennett Square, where the road forked, Howe ordered

Knyphausen's column of around five thousand men to advance along the Nottingham Road and engage the Americans at the ford, while Cornwallis maneuvered another seventy-five hundred soldiers up the Great Valley Road against the Rebel right rear.[30]

Knyphausen's advance, which stepped off at 8:00 a.m., was led by the Queen's Rangers, supplemented by Patrick Ferguson's riflemen, the latter armed with the captain's breech-loading rifles. The force was promptly ambushed by Maxwell's men and "nearly half of the two corps was either killed or wounded." Ferguson subsequently claimed that the fact that his men were armed with breechloaders, more easily loaded by soldiers lying on the ground, saved his unit from suffering more casualties, although the British advance lost almost a hundred men, including thirty killed. The Americans had already handled Ferguson's company roughly on the road to Brandywine, and one writer estimates he had "only some 24 to 30 men" left in action by the time the actual battle began to unfold. Despite the setback, Knyphausen ordered more men to the front and gradually drove the American light infantrymen, who were supplemented by a detachment of local militia, back in a running fight to a rise near the banks of the Brandywine, where the Americans took shelter behind some quickly erected field fortifications. As at Cooch's Bridge, the British brought up artillery to shell Maxwell's position and filtered around his flanks until he withdrew across the creek. Ferguson stated that he had shouldered a rifle himself and joined his men in the front line, later claiming he passed up a shot at Washington, who was observing the fighting.[31]

Knyphausen halted, and spent much of the rest of the day engaged in skirmishing and a desultory artillery duel with the Americans across the Brandywine, which provided a distraction to cover the upstream outflanking maneuver. By late afternoon, Cornwallis was heading for the American rear, replicating the successful British operations on Long Island the previous year. Although Washington had been notified by midmorning that an enemy column was marching north, he believed Cornwallis to be further upstream than he actually was, and considered attacking Knyphausen in an attempt to defeat the British in detail. Before

he could implement this plan, however, the American commander discovered to his chagrin that the enemy had successfully
crossed Trimbles' and Jeffries' Fords and was posing a serious
threat to his right. In response, he ordered troops to move from
the Chadds Ford line and confront Cornwallis. The Americans
rushed to engage the enemy flanking force and soon there was
heavy fighting around Birmingham Meeting House. As the tide
of battle on the right began to turn against his men, Washington
left Chadds Ford with reinforcements to take personal command
of the growing fight. With opposing forces to his front thus weakened, Knyphausen launched his own attack, spearheaded by
German jaegers, the remains of Captain Ferguson's riflemen and
Major Simcoe's Queen's Rangers, who splashed across the
Brandywine under heavy fire and then pushed up the hill on the
other side, capturing an American battery, but losing Ferguson,
who was put out of action when a musket ball broke his right
arm. By 7:00 p.m., the Americans were driven from the entire
field in heavy fighting, leaving the way to Philadelphia open to
Howe. Although beaten, Washington's army once again escaped
destruction, and fell back to Chester to reorganize. The
Americans reportedly suffered around twelve hundred casualties,
including killed, wounded, and missing or captured; the British
about half as many.[32]

In the aftermath of his Brandywine victory, General Howe
assigned British light infantry and cavalry under Major General
James Grant to maintain contact with and shadow the Americans,
while he evacuated his sick and wounded through Wilmington in
preparation for a final advance on Philadelphia. The opposing
armies had no major contact during this period, although
Brigadier General Anthony Wayne's fifteen hundred-man division, tasked with ambushing the British baggage train, was surprised itself at Paoli. In a daring night bayonet attack ordered by
Major General Charles Grey who, by ordering his men to take
the flints out of their guns so that troops firing in the dark could
be immediately identified as Americans, earned the nickname
"No Flint Grey," the British wiped out at least 10 percent of
Wayne's force. What the Americans quickly dubbed a "massacre"

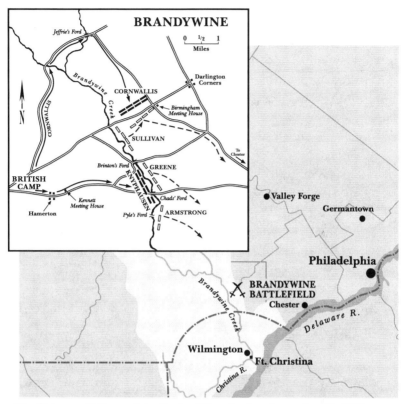

The Delaware Valley and the Battle of Brandywine, September 11, 1777.

appears to have simply been a well-executed surprise attack, as half of their casualties were prisoners. While the British advanced, Pennsylvania militia scoured the countryside picking up American deserters and returning them to their units, as Washington's army continued to regroup, with an eye toward taking the offensive at the earliest possible opportunity.[33]

The American commander had been easily outmaneuvered by Howe at Brandywine, embarrassingly so considering that Howe was simply repeating his successful Long Island tactical scenario of the previous year. As in 1776, however, Washington managed to extricate his army from the British trap in reasonably good order. In the long run, this fact would prove critical to the survival of the Revolution, but the immediate picture was not encouraging. Although the Rebel army survived, its defeat at Brandywine guaranteed that Philadelphia would fall to the enemy. As Howe

advanced on the city, congressmen took to their heels, but not
before ordering the arrest of a number of prominent accused
Loyalists, many of them Quakers. Those arrested who would not
agree to comply with a series of restrictions were packed off to
imprisonment in Virginia. Military supplies, government paper-
work and money were rapidly evacuated from the capital before
the British marched in on September 26, 1777. In a seeming vali-
dation of Galloway's prediction, they were greeted by large numbers of apparent Loyalists lining the streets, although at least one
British officer was cynically suspicious of the timing of the apparent popular support. The British army had not gained any local
sympathy after Brandywine, when pillaging the local farms, as
had been the case in New Jersey the previous year, became the
order of the day. According to a local doctor, "the officers sent
their servants round among the farmers of the vicinity to collect
poultry and other provender for their own tables. These maraud-
ers regarded as lawful plunder everything they could lay their
hands upon and deemed worth carrying away." Personal property
was plundered as well, including "clocks, spice boxes, and looking
glasses." Birmingham, Kennett, Pennsbury, Thornbury, and
Westtown townships subsequently filed claims totaling 8,602
pounds or $333,227 in 2001 dollars; and Birmingham Township
alone filed claims worth 5,844 pounds or $226,117 in 2001 dol-
lars in stolen property.[34]

Although Philadelphia was won, the campaign was not yet
over. While he attended to occupying Philadelphia, Howe had stationed nine thousand men at Germantown to occupy the attention of the main American field force, which continued to hover
within striking distance of the city, and dispatched his remaining
troops to accomplish other vital tasks, including securing his overland supply line back to Delaware. While Howe consolidated,
however, Washington was not idle. After rallying his beaten army
and supplementing it with several thousand militiamen, the
American commander decided to strike at the British in
Germantown in early October. Pulling a leaf out of Howe's tactical book (as well as his own successful offensive at Trenton),
Washington launched his attack by dividing his army, with one

force fixing the enemy's attention while other troops worked their way around the British flanks. Washington's plan at Germantown was actually more complex than either his own previous efforts or Howe's maneuvers at Long Island or Brandywine, as he advanced forces on both flanks in an attempted double envelopment. This was a tricky move with well-trained troops, made much more so when attempted with militia and half-trained Continentals. To complicate matters, as the Americans approached the British positions on the early morning of October 4, a dense fog set in. Although it initially provided cover for the Continentals' advance, and first contact resulted in a confused British retreat, the fog also created numerous subsequent coordination problems. Things began to fall apart as the main column was held up by a small British force holed up in the Chew House. Although the Americans, including Maxwell's New Jersey Brigade, bounced thousands of musket balls off the brick building, the British inside held on. As the attack stalled, one of the American flanking divisions fired on the main column in the haze and precipitated a panicky retreat. Although Washington and his officers eventually got their retreating men under control, and the British pursuit was not aggressive, the American commander realized that the battle was lost and ordered a general withdrawal. American casualties, including around four hundred men captured, mostly from one Virginia regiment, totaled about a thousand, with British losses roughly half as many. Although Washington was defeated, his ambitious Germantown offensive almost succeeded, which was recognized by the troops themselves, and the fact that the American army yet again survived potential disaster intact and was able to withdraw to fight another day was a significant morale booster. In the wake of the battle, Washington remained outside Philadelphia, and his outposts continued to spar with Howe's patrols into the countryside.[35]

Washington's failure at Germantown and the subsequent stalemate left one final act to be played out in the Philadelphia drama, as the British addressed American control of the lower Delaware River. Prior to the campaign, the Americans deployed ships, strung underwater obstructions, and built forts on both banks of the Delaware south of Philadelphia to hinder a British attack up the river. Even with Philadelphia lost, these defenses still served to block British access to the city via sea. In order to assemble enough troops to clear the Delaware so that he could abandon his tenuous and inadequate overland supply line to Wilmington for a more secure waterborne route, Howe contracted his lines outside Philadelphia and constructed a series of defensive redoubts before moving on Fort Mifflin on the Pennsylvania side and Fort Mercer on the New Jersey side of the river. Although it was impossible for the Americans to hold the forts indefinitely, Washington, the pressure on his main army relieved by the enemy's shift of forces, dispatched reinforcements to the river defenders and moved closer to Philadelphia with his main army. When the British finally attacked Forts Mifflin and Mercer, the Americans exacted a heavy price, particularly at Mercer, where a landing force of Hessians was shot to ribbons by the defenders. The British army in Philadelphia suffered from a severe lack of supplies and warm clothing until both forts were evacuated in November, and the American river defense fleet was abandoned and burned. While this operation was ongoing, Washington, on the lookout for opportunities to successfully bring on a battle with the enemy, kept his increasingly ragged army in the field near Philadelphia at Whitemarsh until mid-December. Reinforcements that he requested from General Gates, who had bagged Burgoyne's invading northern army at Saratoga on October 17, were slow in coming, although Colonel Morgan's riflemen, followed by three infantry brigades, arrived in November.[36]

As the weather worsened in December, and it became apparent that the American army needed to go into winter quarters soon, Washington had to fend off yet one more British advance. Informed that the enemy was marching out of Philadelphia, he deployed the bulk of his men in strong defensive positions. Although Howe's light infantrymen had some success skirmishing with American riflemen and militia at the outset of their advance, when they came upon the main American line on December 5, the British, no doubt recalling Bunker Hill, and perhaps Fort Mercer, declined to attack. Howe withdrew to Philadelphia on December 8, leaving the next move to Washington. The American commander chose to march away from Whitemarsh on December 11, crossing the Schuylkill River and skirmishing with a strong British foraging force along the way.[37]

After considering several sites, including Wilmington, Delaware, which was dismissed as being too far south of Philadelphia, Washington decided on Valley Forge as his army's winter campground. About eighteen miles away from Philadelphia alongside the Schuylkill at its intersection with Valley Creek, Valley Forge was well situated in fairly good defensive terrain with an abundant supply of wood and water nearby. At Valley Forge, the American army was well positioned tactically to cover Philadelphia and also fulfilled the political priority of providing a protective roadblock against any British expedition that might be launched to capture the Continental Congress, which was then meeting at York. Unfortunately, the location's good features as an encampment could not compensate for the fact that many men were still residing in canvas tents as late as February, and only left them for poorly constructed and unsanitary huts, where they lived in increasing misery as the American logistical system collapsed over the winter.[38]

During the course of the winter of 1777–78, some twelve thousand troops were quartered at Valley Forge at one time or another, and as many as three thousand of them died there. The deaths were not the result, as legend might have it, of severe weather conditions, but were due to malnutrition and disease. Although supplies of food and clothing were available elsewhere in Pennsylvania and neighboring states, the army's supply system, crippled by corruption, administrative incompetence, and poor roads, proved totally ineffective. In February 1778, for example, the roads were so bad that no supply wagons at all reached the camp. To make matters worse, while the American soldiers suffered, nearby Pennsylvania and New Jersey farmers sold food to the British garrison of Philadelphia. Salem County, New Jersey residents, some of them previous patriots, supplied the British in exchange for "specie coin, as well as sugar, tea, syrup and strong liquors, which are much used here." In addition to the travails of the Continental army's enlisted men, the morale of the officer corps was seriously damaged by a number of quarrels, based on professional rivalries, political intrigue, and bruised egos.[39]

Despite its tribulations, Washington's army emerged from the Valley Forge winter as a more capable force than it had been the previous year. The belated appointment in March of Nathanael Greene as Quartermaster General, replacing Major General Thomas Mifflin, who had resigned with no successor the previous October, eventually improved the supply system, while the arrival of Baron Friedrich Wilhelm Augustus von Steuben and his institution of a uniform training regimen dramatically improved the discipline and drill of the soldiers. Steuben was born in Magdeburg, Prussia, in 1730, the son of a Prussian army officer. At the age of seventeen he joined the Prussian army, eventually rising to the rank of captain and serving as a staff officer. Discharged as the Prussian military downsized in 1763 at the end of the Seven Years' War, Steuben found subsequent employment at the court of another German principality, was terminated, some say for homosexual activity, and then moved to France. Along the way he began to style himself as "Baron von Steuben." The ersatz baron was down and out in Paris and living on a shoe-string budget when the American War for Independence broke out. After a meeting with Benjamin Franklin, in which he apparently considerably impressed Franklin by exaggerating his former level of command responsibility, he was accepted as a volunteer by Congress. Posing as a former lieutenant general, Steuben traveled to America in December 1777, and arrived at Washington's headquarters at Valley Forge in February 1778.[40]

Steuben could not speak English, and the American commander neither German nor French, but francophone Lieutenant Colonel John Laurens of Washington's staff was on hand to serve as interpreter, and Steuben impressed the American commander in his initial interview. Although he had a great deal of respect for

Washington's abilities as a commander, and thought the Americans fine "raw material," the German officer was not impressed with the Continental army itself. After a few days of observations, he correctly perceived that the army's chief problem, aside from a lack of food and clothing, was its poor marching and maneuvering ability. Inability to move in a rapid and disciplined manner was essential to an eighteenth-century army, and the lack of these skills had demonstrably hindered the army's performance in its fights from Long Island to Germantown. Steuben's approach to solving the problem was to create an entirely new drill manual combining and simplifying British, Prussian, and American ideas, and then establish a cadre system of training to instill its lessons throughout the army. The Prussian personally instructed selected officers and enlisted men from different units in the new drill, and then sent them back to their units to train their comrades. Swearing and yelling in various languages, with an interpreter close at hand, Steuben shouldered a musket himself and drilled his Continental charges into the spring. The Prussian's manual proved so effective that it endured long after the Revolution as the standard drill text of the American army. Perhaps never before in history has an army progressed so far in so short a time as the Continentals under Steuben's tutelage. Washington recommended the Prussian be awarded a major general's commission and be appointed inspector general of the army. Congress approved on May 5, 1778.[41]

Although nowhere near as severe, there were supply problems in occupied Philadelphia as well, complicated by British behavior. While General Howe tried to make provisions for assisting impoverished civilians in the city, many of his troops looted the inhabitants. Howe preferred to use Loyalist units for foraging expeditions into the countryside, even though his attempts to recruit soldiers from among loyal Pennsylvanians failed to live up to expectations. Some of these organizations were little more than bandits, who "live[d] from pillage." While Steuben trained the Continentals—Americans, mostly militiamen—made contact with the enemy, skirmishing with Howe's foragers in Delaware, Pennsylvania, and New Jersey throughout the winter as both armies scoured the surrounding countryside for food and fodder. In February 1778, General Wayne led an American foraging force through the Swedish settlements along the New Jersey side of the Delaware. According to Reverend Nicholas Collin, pastor of the Swedish Lutheran Church at Penn's Neck, some of Wayne's men marching past his parsonage were "without boots, others without socks." The Americans, who quickly moved on, were hotly pursued by a British force that scattered the local Swedesboro militia. Although a neutral with an innate tendency to sympathize with established authority, Collin reported that "many people here were plundered," as "the English soldiers are undisciplined and cannot always be controlled." The conduct was a replication of British behavior in northern New Jersey in 1776–77, and Collin wrote that "often both friend and foe were robbed in the most despicable manner, and sometimes with the permission of the officers." Throughout the winter and into spring, southwestern New Jersey was subjected to wholesale theft, raids, kidnappings, and random violence perpetrated by regular and militia forces of both sides.[42]

Perhaps the most egregious New Jersey raid was that conducted by a party of Howe's Loyalists, including Simcoe's Queen's Rangers and the New Jersey Volunteers. On March 17, 1778, a foraging force under Colonel Mawhood landed on the Jersey shore in Salem County and pushed inland, luring an American militia detachment into an ambush at Quinton's Bridge. Mawhood, who held a grudge against militiamen from the previous year's Forage War and considered them an inferior species, assigned Major Simcoe to remove another perceived threat to his rear, the militia guarding Hancock's Bridge on Alloways Creek. On the night of March 20–21, Simcoe's Loyalists conducted a surprise attack on the Hancock's Bridge garrison, killing everyone they could find in the vicinity, including men they encountered along the road, twenty to thirty militiamen sleeping in the Hancock house, and the house's owner, Judge William Hancock, and his brother, who happened to be noted local Loyalists. Following the massacre, Mawhood threatened to use local Loyalists to "attack all such of the Militia who remain in Arms, burn and destroy their Houses and other Property, and reduce them, their unfortunate Wives and Children, to Beggary and Distress." In response to such British incursions in Salem County, Washington had dispatched Colonel Israel Shreve's Second New Jersey Regiment from Valley Forge to the state. Mawhood tried to bag Shreve's regiment at Haddonfield, but the colonel slipped away to Mount Holly. When Mawhood returned to Pennsylvania on March 31, the

William Hancock house in Salem County, New Jersey, the site of a massacre of New Jersey militamen by Simcoe's Queen's Rangers in March 1778. (*Library of Congress*)

Second remained in New Jersey. After the war, Simcoe bragged about the massacre of the militiamen at Hancock's Bridge as a stellar surprise operation, but expressed sorrow at the "unfortunate circumstances" of the accidental skewering of the Loyalist judge and his brother, stating that "events like these are the real miseries of war."[43]

The incident at Hancock's Bridge was but one glaring example of the brutality visited upon each side by the other in the Philadelphia hinterlands of New Jersey that winter. Although British newspapers in Philadelphia argued that Mawhood's expedition actually won over a populace that "lamented much that the army was to depart and leave them again to the tyranny of the rebel faction," it seems more likely that it merely elevated the general climate of sociopathic chaos in the area. The violence created a situation that Reverend Collin described as a climate of "distrust, fear, hatred and abominable selfishness" and spawned, not for the first or last time in Revolutionary War New Jersey, a civil war within the context of the general war. The struggle in the lower Delaware Valley led "parents and children, brothers and sisters, wife and husband" to become "enemies to one another," Collin recalled. The minister wrote that "militia and some regular troops on one side and refugees with the Englishmen on the other were constantly roving about in smaller or great numbers, plundering and destroying everything in a barbarous manner."[44]

To add to the confusion, a number of Jerseymen switched sides, often for economic reasons. One Isaac Josten, "a Swede" from Salem County who had been a "strong Republican and officer in the militia" went over to the British "after he had begun to trade [with them]." Fickle loyalties were also apparent in both field armies, with desertions fairly common. Unsurprisingly, considering the situation at Valley Forge, where soldiers were poorly clothed and fed and sporadically paid, some two thousand Americans took unauthorized leave or deserted over the winter, either heading for home or to the British lines around Philadelphia. Less understandably, considering their superior logistical position, Hessians often deserted from Howe's redoubt ring. Eleven British and German deserters entered the American lines at Valley Forge on one day, December 30, 1777.[45]

As if Washington did not have enough problems over the Valley Forge winter, some of his officers tried to undermine him in what became known as the "Conway Cabal" after one of its principals, Thomas Conway, an Irish-born French army officer currently serving in the Continental army. Conway's letters to the Continental Congress criticizing the American commander served as a pretext for some to demand Washington's removal and his replacement by General Gates, the late victor of Saratoga. Although the plot failed to materialize, it took Washington's mind off of more important matters.[46]

As winter wore on, it seemed that General Howe did not have any intention of ever leaving Philadelphia, and had no plans to even actively harass the Americans outside the city with operations aside from foraging missions, although some historians have suggested that the dismal condition of Washington's army on some occasions at Valley Forge would have made a British victory a foregone conclusion. Howe's relative torpor suggested that he knew his days as commander of the British forces in America were numbered. He did. The general had submitted his resignation to Lord Germain in December, although, due to the communications vagaries of the era, he did not receive orders to turn his army over to General Clinton and return home until April. The British commander believed he had been shortchanged by his government's failure to send the reinforcements he requested prior to the campaign, and that Germain had paid more attention to Burgoyne's ultimately disastrous northern efforts than his own advance on Philadelphia. Conversely, Germain thought Howe had conducted the Philadelphia campaign in a desultory and lack-luster manner and was frustrated that it had not produced any sort of decisive result. The American army had indeed been defeated but was still intact. The Rebel capital had been captured, but Congress had merely adjourned to a new location further west, and, after the initial self-interest-inspired rush in occupied Philadelphia, Joseph Galloway's stampede of Pennsylvania Loyalists had failed to materialize. In addition to those failures, it seemed likely to many that Burgoyne's fate was a result of Howe's mistaken priorities and strategic shortcomings, a reasonable conclusion considering the evidence.[47]

In the spring of 1778, the course of the war took a dramatically different turn. The American victory at Saratoga in October 1777 led to French recognition of American independence in December. In March 1778, the British were advised of a forthcoming French alliance with the United States, which was formally approved by the Continental Congress on May 5. Although spurred by a chance at revenge against the British for previous humiliations rather than the altruistic idealism of individual French volunteers like Lafayette, the intervention proved a decisive event. It created a new military reality that dramatically changed the American strategic chessboard. British troops and ships had to be detailed to defend against potential French offensive moves against Britain's West Indian possessions, which had more commercial value than the mainland colonies, as well as to initiate their own offensive operations against French islands in the West Indies. These priorities necessarily led to a scaling down of operations in the Middle Atlantic region. The consolidation needed to provide troops for other tasks required that the main British army in America move from Philadelphia back to New York, and Clinton was ordered to initiate this change of base as soon as possible.[48]

On April 20, General Washington, not privy to the British strategy, convened a council of his generals to ponder his initial moves for the 1778 campaign season. There were three options on the table: attacking or besieging Philadelphia, moving north against New York, or remaining at Valley Forge and continuing to train and strengthen the army. Although some generals wanted to pursue a more aggressive policy elsewhere, the final conclusion, reached on May 8, was that recovery of Philadelphia was the most important item on the American agenda, and that Washington should keep a close watch on British activity in and around the city and continue to strengthen the Continentals. The army's morale continued to improve, especially after word of the French entry into the war arrived at the end of April. On May 6, following a rollicking May Day celebration in which the men of Maxwell's New Jersey Brigade, some dressed as Indians and well fortified with whiskey, marched, their hats adorned with cherry blossoms, with "mirth and Jollity" in honor of "King Tammany," the whole army gathered for a formal announcement of the French alliance, followed by salutes of cannon fire and a musketry "*feu de joie.*"[49]

On May 8, Washington launched a twenty-two hundred-man expeditionary force of Continentals and militiamen supported by five artillery pieces across the Schuylkill under the Marquis de Lafayette. Leading his first independent command, the young Frenchman was ordered to disrupt British foraging parties and gather intelligence on the enemy's intentions for the forthcoming campaign season. Lafayette camped at Barren Hill, where he deployed his force in a defensive position, and Howe, in a last effort before turning over formal command to General Clinton, decided to try to bag the entire American force. He ordered Clinton to move out of Philadelphia with twelve thousand men in three columns intended to converge on Lafayette in a complicated tactical scenario. It proved too complex a task, and was undone by the alertness of the Americans and coordination failures on the part of the British. The Barren Hill affair was Howe's last official act as army commander, and symbolic, in its outcome, of his entire American effort. Beloved by his subordinates, however, Howe would depart in grand style. British officers in Philadelphia staged an elaborate going away party on May 18–the "Meschianza." The event, described as an extravaganza that "had no peers in eighteenth-century America," involved "a procession of decorated watercraft . . . along the waterfront . . . a joust of tournament of knights, followed by an elaborate banquet, dancing and a colorful display of fireworks." As one of his final acts, the general sold some of his private provision trove to Clinton, including a thirty-eight pound wheel of Parmesan cheese. Whatever else one could say about him, Howe was always a paragon of good taste.[50]

Washington's conclusion soon proved to be the correct one, as British evacuation plans were indeed in process as the Americans deliberated. Ideally, Clinton, now charged with effecting the pull-out, would have withdrawn by ship down the Delaware River, through the bay, around Cape May and north to New York. The fact that the French fleet was at sea, its location unknown, made such a course potentially dangerous, however. In addition, the available shipping would have made it necessary to move the British army and its entourage, which included some three thousand panicked Loyalists eager to leave town before the Americans arrived, in relays, making the operation even more vulnerable to interdiction. In the event, Clinton decided to load his heavy gear and baggage aboard ship, along with all of his sick and disabled soldiers and the frightened Tories, then march across "the Jerseys" with his able-bodied troops and the remainder of his supplies and equipment, the latter hauled in some fifteen hundred wagons.[51]

By mid-May, with British raiders aggressively crossing the Delaware more frequently, Washington responded by dispatching a mobile force of New Jersey Continentals under General Maxwell to harass them should they choose to march across the state. It was becoming apparent to the American commander that

the enemy was going to be moving soon. Maxwell's brigade, reinforced by nine-month service draftees and supported by militiamen under General Dickinson, took up a position at Mount
Holly and awaited developments. The Jersey general had had a
few rough spots over the winter; he was found innocent at a
court-martial accusing him of being drunk during the
Brandywine fight and survived lobbying by some of his officers
to have him removed from command. With the arrival of the
campaign season, however, "Scotch Willie" was ready for
action.[52]

In the middle of the growing military activity, a peace delegation from England headed by Frederick Howard, 5th Earl of
Carlisle, arrived in Philadelphia. Concerned about the Franco-
American coalition, the British government empowered the
Carlisle Parliamentary Peace Commission to present a possible
settlement to Congress, granting all American demands save actu-
al independence, should they opt out of the alliance. Congress
turned down the offer, and although the commissioners remained
in America through November, first in Philadelphia and then in
New York, the entire effort proved a fiasco. One member, George
Johnstone, was apparently caught trying to bribe members of
Congress, and Carlisle himself was challenged to a duel by
Lafayette for insulting France. The time for such offers to be
taken seriously was long past.[53]

By early June, Hessian Captain Ewald noted that terrified
Tories were "packing up and fleeing [Philadelphia] before the
wrath of Congress," as British troops in small numbers began to
permanently cross the Delaware into New Jersey. In the early
morning hours of June 16, Clinton removed his artillery from the
redoubts Howe had built to defend Philadelphia and began to
march his army down to the river. Within two days, the entire
British force had crossed and the huge baggage train was well on
its way to Haddonfield. The British left behind a city in shambles,
including battered and broken houses and the floors of the
Pennsylvania statehouse, where Congress once met, littered with
the results of a winter's worth of defecation. Once aware that
Clinton had evacuated Philadelphia, Washington began to move

his own army from Valley Forge, heading northeast to Coryell's Ferry (present-day New Hope/Lambertville) to cross the river to New Jersey. The Americans marched swiftly and efficiently, by divisions, revealing the professionalism that had permeated their ranks over the winter at Valley Forge.[54]

The game was afoot.

two

"The enemy amongst us":

REVOLUTION AS CIVIL WAR IN

MONMOUTH COUNTY, 1776–1783

TWO COMMON PERCEPTIONS DOMINATE the average read-er's thoughts about Loyalist Americans during the Revolution: first, that Loyalists were almost always members of the elite attempting to salvage a corrupt system from which they benefited; and second, that Loyalists always comprised a small percentage of the general population. The first assumption is incorrect—adher-ence to the Crown often crossed class lines, and many members of the colonial elite harboring anxieties about the mob turned up as leaders in the patriot camp. The second assumption, however, is all too true. Many Loyalists, Joseph Galloway being a prime exam-ple, deluded themselves into thinking that the majority of Americans, either intimidated or simply misled by a handful of crazed patriot leaders, could be easily returned to loyalty by a brief show of British force. In reality, most Americans, including a lot of initially ambivalent New Jerseyans, had independently and fully committed themselves to the cause of independence by 1778, whether through ideology or pragmatism. This reality notwith-standing, some colonial regions became hotbeds of Loyalist activ-ity and subsequent civil war, and thus serious political anomalies. Monmouth County, New Jersey, scene of what would be the war's climactic battle in the north, was one such anomaly.

In 1665, a group of twelve Baptists and Quakers from Long Island and New England was granted the Monmouth Patent in the English colony of East New Jersey by Governor Richard Nicolls. This document secured their right to settle around present-day Middletown, located in eastern-central New Jersey in an area originally inhabited by Leni-Lenape Indians. By 1683, the settlement had expanded to become Monmouth County, one of the original four counties in East Jersey. In 1693, the county was composed of three major townships: Middletown, Shrewsbury, and Freehold. Freehold, which became the seat of county government, gained a second name as Monmouth Court House in 1715. By the time of the Revolution, much of Monmouth County's economy revolved around agriculture and trade, owing to the area's rich farmland and proximity to the ports of Philadelphia and New York, while the coastline was sparsely inhabited by subsistence farmers, fishermen, and boat builders. It was home not only to English and Scottish settlers of Quaker, Presbyterian, Methodist, and Anglican religious adherence, but also held a significant Dutch community, as well as a large African American slave population.[1]

Fighting in Monmouth County went on before, during, and after the pitched battle that would forever bear its name, in a retaliatory cycle of violence that turned the Revolution into a bloody civil war. Several case studies of this struggle highlight the intense divisiveness which characterized war in Monmouth: the 1776 Quaker-led Loyalist uprising in Upper Freehold Township; the raids of "Colonel Tye," an escaped Monmouth County slave, and the Tories of his Loyalist Black Brigade, as well as other members of former Governor Franklin's New York-based Tory organization; Colonel David Forman's Association for Retaliation, which waged guerrilla warfare on suspected Tories for both vengeance and profit; and the 1782 execution of Captain Joshua Huddy, a brutal incident which took place after the cease-fire, and which graphically illustrates the deeply personal and enduring nature of the Revolution in Monmouth, and the power of a cycle of retaliation.[2]

As early as 1776, the Revolutionary War in Monmouth County had taken on the characteristics of a civil war, one that often had much less to do with political principles than with cultural disparities, personal enmities, and general self-interest. As the war wound down, life in Monmouth was still characterized by a numbing violence that had become so pervasive, it continued well after the formal cessation of hostilities. The story of Monmouth County is the story of the Revolution's seamy side; traditional stereotypes of the war as a unified struggle for liberty from a tyrannical authority shatter in the face of a much more grounded struggle, in which both parties behaved badly. Comprehension of Monmouth County's experience is important to a fuller understanding of the Revolutionary War as a whole—it encompasses the serious human failings and troublesome complexities many Americans would rather erase from our Revolutionary mythology, and did for many generations.

The large number of Quakers in Monmouth County during the Revolutionary era contributed significantly to the strength of Loyalist sentiment there. Avowed pacifists, many Quakers simply refused to take up arms as participants in the patriot cause. Early in the war, the colonel commanding a militia unit in the Quaker stronghold of Shrewsbury resigned his commission, complaining that "few [of the residents] are likely to turn out (hiding themselves and deserting their houses) whenever he marches to defend the shores." However studiously neutral Quakers may have attempted to be, a "with us or against us" mentality on the patriot side often turned these neutral parties into default Loyalists. As such, they eventually became fair game for retaliatory raids made by vigilante groups, most prominently David Forman's Retaliators. The victimization of the truly neutral and the "mildly" disaffected—that is, those whose personal views tended toward Loyalism, but who made no serious efforts in support of the Loyalist cause—only furthered unrest in the county, turning likely fence-sitters into serious Loyalists.[3]

Within the Quaker community, there were always exceptions to the prescribed pacifist stance; some did march off to join either patriot or Loyalist forces. The Quaker Woodward family of Upper Freehold Township came down firmly on the Loyalist side. As a religious minority, colonial Quakers sometimes felt vulnerable and exposed. The Woodwards would act on their fears of the local Presbyterian and largely patriot majority by siding with the British Empire, hoping to preserve the protection they had thus far enjoyed in New Jersey under the royal authority personified by William Franklin. In June of 1776, as Franklin fell from power, the New Jersey Provincial Congress ordered that Anthony Woodward Jr., otherwise known as "Little Anthony," and his cousin Thomas Lewis Woodward, be taken into custody along with other seemingly "disaffected persons." Anthony apparently escaped capture, because on July 17, his brother George presented a petition to the legislature asking that his brother be allowed to return to his home and reintegrate himself into the community. The legislature's response was to inventory Woodward's estate in anticipation of its confiscation, and to fine his cousin Thomas as well as two other Quakers, Moses Ivins and Richard Robbins, as punishment for their perceived offenses.[4]

Prosperous and well established, the Woodwards of Upper Freehold were descended from Englishman Anthony Woodward, who emigrated from Long Island to the Quaker settlement at Crosswicks, New Jersey, around 1686. He amassed huge tracts of land in both East and West New Jersey and was a prominent member of the Chesterfield Meeting. Little Anthony and other members of the third generation of Woodwards in the area had continued to build on their grandfather's success. According to the 1778 tax ratable for Upper Freehold Township, taken before the confiscation of their estates, Little Anthony held 600 acres; Jesse, 200 acres; Anthony "Black Nat," 300 acres; Thomas Lewis, 200 acres; and Thomas, 400 acres. All held significant herds of livestock as well.[5]

With property and status at stake, the most obvious course of action for the Woodwards would have been quiet acquiescence to patriot demands, at least for as long as they retained control of the state. Why would well-established persons with much to lose so blatantly align themselves against the current authority? There are several probable answers to that question. First, as prominent members of the community, the Woodwards had an investment in the status quo; in 1776 and 1777, there was really no telling what the new self-declared government had in store for the colonies, particularly once Committees of Safety began to scrutinize the local populace for signs of disaffection. Ironically, considering the popular modern view of many, one prominent lament of many Loyalists in various pamphlets, tracts, and petitions was the lack of respect the new government institutions afforded to traditional British rights such as privacy and freedom of speech.

Many Loyalists feared that the fledgling government of the United States, which would go on to become synonymous with the inalienable rights of man, was prepared to stomp upon the traditional rights of British citizens in the name of self-preservation. At a local meeting of similarly concerned citizens in the summer of 1776, Anthony Woodward Jr. articulated this anxiety when he voiced the complaint that "'the Non Associators [those who refused to sign on to the Continental Association] had no vote.' As they viewed the insurrection unfolding before their eyes, many Loyalists saw what modern eyes must strain to see: a frightening descent into political anarchy, in which the civil rights guaranteed by British tradition would be lost and the protection of life and property could not be promised." As Woodward pontificated, a number of Upper Freehold men voted with their feet and stole away to join the British army on Staten Island.[6]

Second, the British army under General Howe appeared invulnerable prior to the battles of Trenton and Princeton. New Jersey had never been a leader in the movement for independence, and, although the patriot forces seized control from Franklin in 1776, fewer New Jersey voices were raised in support of rebellion during 1775 and early 1776 than in other states. New Jersey was heavily dependent upon New York and Pennsylvania both culturally and commercially, however, and followed them into revolt. As if to underscore New Jersey's ambivalence about independence, the Continental army was driven back across the state and finally out

of it into Pennsylvania as the British and their Hessian allies settled in at Trenton for Christmas of 1776. During this period,
active Loyalist behavior was not only possible, it was advisable.
More than one New Jersey resident signed one of General Howe's
oaths of loyalty to the king during the fall and early winter of 1776
out of sincerity, but many did so out of pure pragmatism.[7]

Third, the Loyalism of the Woodwards and their compatriots
may have been rooted in various motives, but their status as
Quakers was clearly an important, albeit not the only, impetus.
There was no love lost between them and the largely Presbyterian
patriot or "Whig" element in western Monmouth, an outgrowth
of prewar theological and political differences. As a minority,
Quakers would likely have been wary of dominance by a larger,
more powerful religious community. Richard Robbins, a leader
amongst the Woodward insurgents, accused Presbyterian Whigs
of being "the cause of all this bloodshed." This was a common
view. Presbyterians in New Jersey and elsewhere were widely
viewed by Quakers and other religious minorities, such as the
Anglicans and many Methodists, as key fomenters of colonial
unrest. In New Jersey, their dominance within the patriot war
effort is clear—more than half of General George Washington's
New Jersey Continentals were Scotch-Irish Presbyterians, and
most Presbyterian ministers became vocal supporters of the
Revolution.[8]

Within the generally moderate social and cultural dynamics of
New Jersey, Anglican Loyalism seems to have been rooted in that
religion's dependence on the Crown for its *raison d'être*, and some
Methodists remained loyal to the king out of ingrained conser-
vatism. Quakers followed a somewhat different logic. Their aver-
sion to both war and the forcible removal of governments, made
evident by Quakers' studious avoidance of the political turmoil
leading up to and during the English Civil War of the previous
century, meant that their cries of protest ceased as soon as the first
shots rang out. Most felt called by their personal doctrine to
remain neutral during the Revolution, no matter what other
course of action their personal finances or inclinations might dic-
tate.[9]

Neutrality was the Quakers' religious ideal. The majority of Quakers adhered to it at great cost; their refusal to claim allegiance was often interpreted as closet Loyalism. A notable minority, however, was unable to sit idly by and suggested that a defensive war was justifiable though an offensive one was not; a Quaker named James Logan was the most vocal proponent of this approach, and he attracted a following among younger members of the Philadelphia Meeting.[10]

The meeting at Waln's Mill in May or June of 1776, at which Little Anthony voiced his concerns over the vote being denied to "Non Associators," marks the beginning of the Woodward insurrection in Upper Freehold. Richard Waln, the Quaker owner of the mill and member of a prominent family in the county, was known to be partial to the Crown. Little dramatic action would be taken, however, until military events turned in the Loyalists' favor during the late summer. Encouraged by the spectacular patriot defeat at the Battle of Long Island on August 27, 1776, Little Anthony returned to Upper Freehold from behind the safety of the British lines. He set about recruiting more locals to join the Woodward group, making vague allusions to guarantees by General Howe that loyal subjects would be justly rewarded.[11]

Taken in by this talk was Thomas Fowler, a land-poor local man, whose eventual testimony against his fellow raiders provides the narrative of their development. In a society where real property was the basis of wealth, it is not hard to imagine that the promise of land grants would seduce men into the service of the Crown, especially those already distrustful of the new patriot regime. The new government had already begun seizing and selling off the estates of "Refugees," or Loyalists who had fled their homes for fear of reprisal. It was reasonable to assume that the British, once they gained control of New Jersey, would provide for Loyalists in a similar manner.[12]

By mid-December, at the nadir for the patriot cause, Continental troops had essentially vacated the state. At this point, those Loyalists who had been dragged before the legislature and asked to prove their loyalty, and who had suffered serious economic losses and harassment when they could or would not, had the upper hand. One can imagine the tumult in communities across the state as the tables turned. In Loyalist-heavy Monmouth, the blood was particularly bad. It is reasonable to assume that many disaffected persons came to the attention of the authorities, not so much because they blatantly advertised their political opinions, but because their erstwhile friends and neighbors turned them in. The motivations for such actions could range from sincere patriotism and devotion to the revolutionary cause, to old prewar rivalries and bitterness, to simple lust for the suspect's material goods, which would most likely be confiscated by the government and sold at auction. It should be noted that at this time there was no British army presence in Monmouth to either rally Loyalists or, by indiscriminate looting of the populace, turn the ambivalent against the king.

During December 1776, the Woodwards and other Loyalist parties roamed the county, however, impressing men, horses, wagons, and other supplies in the name of the Crown. In one notable incident, the Woodward boys, led by Little Anthony's cousins Jesse and Anthony "Black Nat," took prominent Monmouth Whig Thomas Forman captive while he was visiting William Hendrickson's house. Forman was a relation of the later-to-be infamous David Forman, the shady figure who led the Monmouth County Association for Retaliation to greater and greater heights of radicalism after the Battle of Monmouth, and who made a brief appearance on the battlefield as a guide for Charles Lee's lead element on the morning of June 28, 1778.[13]

The party confiscated a musket belonging to Hendrickson. They then accompanied Forman to his own home where they again searched for weapons, shot, and powder. At that point they insisted that Forman accompany them to Lawrence Taylor's tavern, threatening to deliver him to the Hessian garrison at Trenton if he refused. On their way they met up with another group of Tory insurgents. Once at the tavern the men condemned Congress, accusing its members of enriching themselves through the confiscation of Loyalist estates and the exchange of worthless Continental money for gold and silver. Drunkenness led to bravado, and the party commissioned Black Nat Woodward to obtain

aid from British regular forces for an assault upon patriot militiamen gathering at Monmouth Court House. At the end of the
evening, the group let Forman go but made him promise to deliver his musket to Black Nat the next day.[14]

This anecdote is both amusing and illuminating. Although the
members of the Woodward gang embraced theft and, apparently,
alcohol-induced absurdity, their behavior exhibits none of the
startling violence that would characterize later raiding parties in
the county. At this early stage, the Woodward band and other
Tory groups may have felt confident in British success, and therefore had not yet resorted to the violent acts committed by desperate and vengeful men. Their anger at Congress also indicates that
many of them felt economically vulnerable and unrepresented by
the new government. At this stage of the conflict, they were on top
of their game and hopeful about their future prospects. It was not
to last.

But while it lasted, the Tory resurgence in Monmouth, as elsewhere in the state, crushed patriot morale. Other Loyalist captives
in Monmouth County included Richard Stockton, New Jersey
signer of the Declaration of Independence, who was captured
with his friend John Covenhoven, a member of the state legislature, at the latter's home in Monmouth County. These men and
others, including Samuel Tucker, were handed over to the British
and roughly handled, and both signed loyalty oaths to the king.
Eventually exchanged, both men signed new oaths of "abjuration
and allegiance" to the United States, but their health, fortunes,
and reputations had been ruined by the experience. Stockton died
of cancer in 1781.[15]

The Woodward boys continued their visitations through the
end of December, impressing men and goods and enjoying their
success. Loyalists posted notices boldly ordering the Monmouth
County militia to assemble at Monmouth Court House on
December 30 to take a loyalty oath to the king. Unfortunately for
them and other Tories, the British withdrew their lines to New
Brunswick in Middlesex County after their disastrous defeats at
Trenton and Princeton in late December and early January. This
retreat left Monmouth's Tories, particularly high-profile ones such

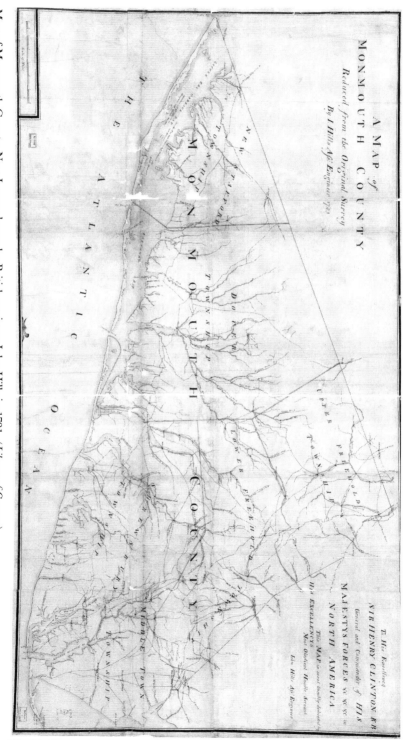

Map of Monmouth County, New Jersey, drawn by British engineer John Hills in 1781. (*Library of Congress*)

as the Woodwards, extremely vulnerable. Sensing that the jig was up, the Woodward band scattered and went into hiding. The difference of a few weeks meant the disparity between holding forth in county taverns, plunder in hand, and hiding out in the empty hunters' cabins and caves of the Pine Barrens forest to the south. Jesse Woodward, for example, split his time between a cabin in the pine woods and one near Waln's Mill, the initial gathering place for the Woodward gang, although he sometimes returned home to collect supplies and to hear the latest news.[16]

In March of 1777, gang members Nicholas Williams and the aforementioned Thomas Fowler decided out of apparent desperation to attack Lewis Bestedo, a former victim who was rumored to be searching the woods for them. Their incompetent attempt to ambush him on the road to Crosswicks failed miserably, and resulted in the death of Williams and the single-handed capture of Fowler by Bestedo, who was alone at the time. Days later, Fowler testified to the gang's history and activity before a newly formed Council of Safety; the level of Loyalist activity in the state had been deemed serious enough to warrant a special council mandated to investigate treason. His testimony, combined with the testimony of victims against the gang's ringleaders, sent several to jail. These included Richard Robbins, who had previously returned home and submitted a bond guaranteeing his good behavior, and Jesse Woodward, who had been captured during Bestedo's manhunt.[17]

This sudden outburst of violence on the part of the Woodwards says something about the changing face of the war in Monmouth County during 1777. Loyalists, who for a brief period controlled the county, were now on the run. Although some members of the Woodward gang managed to conceal themselves in areas close to their homes, most Tories of any note were forced to flee the state entirely. Their property and belongings were often confiscated in their absence. Their underdog status, combined with serious economic losses, made many Tories into desperate, angry men. Once Tory raiding parties took on a truly malicious tone, it was only a matter of time before patriot organizations responded in kind.

The Council of Safety investigation signaled the end of the Woodward gang as a functional entity. Most of the ringleaders remained jailed until January 1778, when they were tried during a special session of the Court of Oyer and Terminer, assigned fines, and jailed again until the fines could be paid. Little Anthony had escaped capture, probably having made his way to British lines. He would fall in and out of patriot hands for the duration of the war as he continued to aid the British as a guerrilla and raider. In 1783, Little Anthony, Jesse, Black Nat, John, and Samuel Woodward all relocated to Canada, as did Richard Robbins. In the late 1780s, however, Little Anthony and Black Nat returned home and managed to reintegrate themselves into the community at Upper Freehold, probably owing to their extensive kinship network in the area.[18]

The behavior of the Woodward clan and those they recruited during the summer, fall, and early winter of 1776 illustrates the difficulty in ascribing moral supremacy to either the patriot or Loyalist faction in Monmouth County or, for that matter, New Jersey. Although Loyalists endured notable depredations at the hands of patriot forces and vigilantes, it is clear that they also scrambled to manipulate what power they had when they had it. When Washington's troops had temporarily abandoned New Jersey, and British military presence was strong in the state, the Woodwards and others harassed and assaulted proven and suspected patriots, robbing them of provisions and farm animals to be donated to the British service, and even forcibly impressing the men themselves.[19]

What primary impulse drove the Woodwards and their brethren? A sincere religious belief that defensive war was called for in the face of an unnatural political insurrection? A fear of and desire for control over local Presbyterians whose dominance had unsettled them for decades? A desire for economic reward? Or was it even baser than that, a chance to exact revenge for offenses now lost to history, the stealing of a hog or refusal of a right of way? Given the complexity of all human motivations, it seems safe to conclude that the Loyalists in Upper Freehold were driven by some combination of all these things. It would seem, however,

that the glee these men felt in turning the tables suggests the presence of old local conflicts within the mix. The religious and economic tensions, which propelled the Woodward family and its
supporters, buttress the concept that the Revolution in
Monmouth, and by evidence and implication other areas of New
Jersey, was a war possibly shaped in some measure by of preex-
isting social discord.

The Quakers were one significant minority in revolutionary
Monmouth County; slaves and free blacks were another. The
farm owners in the largely rural county found slavery an economically viable alternative to hired farm hands and house servants.
In East Jersey as a whole, the black population is estimated to
have remained somewhere between 10 and 20 percent of the general population throughout the eighteenth century, and in some
communities it exceeded 20 percent. Freehold and Shrewsbury
townships in Monmouth are examples of agricultural areas containing a notably large black population, almost all of them slaves.
As important as their numbers was their attitude; documentary
evidence indicates that again and again, enslaved blacks exhibited
insubordinate, even reckless behavior, and many were ready to
risk all for freedom. The American Revolution came along at a
time when black restlessness was reaching a high point, and provided a perfect avenue for both escape and revenge.[20]

Slaves in eighteenth-century Monmouth lived under conditions very different from those commonly perceived as common
to slavery in today's popular imagination. Although their lives
were by no means easy, in general, Monmouth County slaves
enjoyed a far greater degree of material comfort, independence,
and integration with life outside the homestead than Southern
plantation slaves harvesting and processing tobacco, rice, and
indigo. Rather than living in quarters situated far from the main
farmhouse, slaves lived in nearby outbuildings or, even more
commonly, attic rooms or areas off the kitchen in their masters'
home. Their workdays were long, but the farming and household

activities they undertook were preferable to the incredibly grueling work of plantation agriculture. In some instances, slaves
developed a comfort level with their owner's family equivalent to
that of a white servant. For example, British officer Alexander
Graydon reported that a slave belonging to the household in
which he was quartered "took a post in the chimney-corner with
his hat on and occasionally joined in the conversation." Such a
casual, even friendly relationship between master and slave seems
incongruous, and is surprising to the modern reader. Sometimes
relations were even closer, and one 1777 traveler through central
New Jersey recalled that he "saw a Child, the Son of a Negro
Woman but of a white Father, who could not be distinguished
either by his Color, Skin or Hair from the Children of white
Parents; in short, he appeared to house nothing of the Negro in
his Composition."[21]

Of course, it is likely that while many white masters read genuine affection and loyalty into their interactions with their slaves,
the slaves themselves were largely playing a role necessary to their
comfortable survival as enslaved people. The small liberties that
slaves enjoyed, such as leisure time on holidays and the ability to
travel unencumbered through the countryside on errands, however, merely intensified their desire to be fully free, no matter how
their masters rationalized.

Therefore, the coming of the Revolution to Monmouth raised
fears within the slaveholding community. Although some slaves,
such as the one witnessed by Alexander Graydon, joined in conversation at their master's table, still others stole, displayed what
was termed "impudence," or ran away, given the opportunity.
One such slave was Titus, the bondsman of Quaker John Corlies,
a member of the Shrewsbury Meeting.[22]

In 1758, the progressive Philadelphia Meeting had voted
against slavery and embraced abolitionism. East Jersey Quakers,
however, under the influence of the more conservative New York
Meeting, stalled for years on the matter of manumission. By 1775,
as war broke out, members of the Shrewsbury Meeting were finally making a concerted effort to wipe out slaveholding within the
Society of Friends. That year, a delegation of Quakers traveled to

Corlies' homestead, hoping to persuade him and his mother Zilpha to free their six slaves.[23]

Titus must have been well aware of why the delegation had come; he had probably seen Quaker parties visit Corlies before on the same mission. Knowing that his stubborn master continued to reject entreaties to free his slaves, even as other local Quakers made it policy to free theirs (usually upon the individual slave's twenty-first birthday), Titus likely realized his only hope for freedom lay in his own hands. So, like so many Monmouth County slaves before and after, he ran away. Titus escaped on November 8, 1775, just one day after the royal governor of Virginia, John Murray, 4th Earl of Dunmore, bestowed freedom to all slaves willing to join the British war effort. This declaration further inflamed white distress in eastern New Jersey, where the problem of insolent and deceptive slaves had steadily intensified in the years leading up to the outbreak of hostilities with Britain. Many stole liquor and foodstuffs, then sneaked away at night, or blatantly alluded to their anticipated liberty in conversation with their owners. Increasingly frequent Quaker petitions to the provincial authority calling for manumission did nothing to calm slaveholders' nerves.[24]

A prewar anti-manumission petition from residents of Shrewsbury to the General Assembly dated February 2, 1774, articulates local anxiety about disobedient slaves.

> The Petition of Sundrie of the Inhabitants Freeholders and Owners of Negroes in Shrewsbury in the County of Monmouth and Colony aforesaid Humbly Informe you that in the Abovesaid Township there is a Great Number of Negroes, Men Women and Children Being Slaves and Daily Increasing in Number and Impudence that we find Them Very Troublesome by Runing about all Times of the Night Stealing and Taking and Riding Peoples Horses and Other Mischiefs in a Great Degree Owing to Having a Correspondence and Recourse to the Houses of Them Already Freed and Being Informed that there have Been Sent into your House Great Numbers of Petitions for the More Easey Freeing of Slaves.[25]

This petition reveals both the abundance of slaveholders in the county (another petition with identical language was also sent to the assembly, and both feature several pages of signers) and their feeling even before the war that the system of slavery was not firmly in their control. The slaves described in the petition not only blatantly disobey their masters, apparently without too much fear of the consequences, but they also gather in the houses of former slaves and free African Americans. This combination of mobility, a degree of privacy, and intense dissatisfaction in the lives of Monmouth County slaves gave their masters good reason to be concerned.

Although fear of insurrection haunted Monmouth County slaveholders, enslaved men and women within the county proved themselves to be more interested in long-term freedom than short-lived revenge. Many took advantage of the opportunity to flee when General Howe's troops swept across eastern Jersey in the fall and winter of 1776, joining British forces to serve as soldiers, laborers, domestic workers, and in other capacities. Even after the abrupt British retreat across the state in early 1777 following the military defeats at Trenton and Princeton, slaves still fled to British-held areas surrounding New York City. The close proximity of the British, especially at Sandy Hook, for the duration of the war, provided a more than decent chance for success in escaping. Furthermore, British presence and influence were never formally restricted to the city itself; the so-called neutral ground, comprised of parts of New Jersey adjacent to New York and Staten Island, facilitated the largely unimpeded comings and goings of many Loyalists, British military units, and illicit traders throughout the war. [26]

Many escaped slaves made new homes for themselves within British-controlled territory, arranging for family members and friends to join them when they could. Some escaped slaves banded together to create an ad hoc unit that local patriots referred to disparagingly as a "motley crew," an organization of black and white Tory raiders who terrorized Monmouth under the leadership of one "Colonel" Tye (the rank was an honorific). Tye was none other than John Corlies' escaped slave Titus. He was to become one of the most feared and also one of the most respected Loyalist militants in the state.

Tye first appears as a Loyalist combatant in June 1778, around the time of the Battle of Monmouth, when he was alleged to have orchestrated the capture of Monmouth County militia captain Elisha Shepard. Tye's proven competence caught the eye of his superiors early on, and in 1779 he was hired on as a raider by the Associated Loyalists, former Royal Governor Franklin's vehicle of personal revenge against the New Jersey revolutionaries.

And so began a year-long period of brutal raids on Monmouth County patriots by Tye and his irregulars, who were paid on what could be considered a commission basis, according to the value of the materials they confiscated. They also tended to specifically target patriot slave owners, including former masters of band members. Admittedly, this targeting required little extra effort; it was simply a fact that many prominent, well-established county patriots also owned slaves. Typically, Tye and his multiracial band would descend upon the household of a known patriot, kill or capture any military men who happened to be present, and gather up valuables, livestock, and foodstuffs that were then turned over to the British army.

Following a raid, the Loyalists would retreat to "Refugeetown," a fortified community located at the northern tip of Sandy Hook that had been established by Tories who fled their homes in other parts of the county fearing patriot reprisal. Adding to the settlement's free white population were many escaped slaves. Most residents did not cower in Refugeetown awaiting the end of armed conflict; it became a base of operations for those who saw an opportunity to exact revenge and pocket a profit at the same time, by joining Tye or making their own excursions in entrepreneurial war.[27]

Tye's raids did not only entail property loss. The Revolution in Monmouth had become much nastier since the Woodward boys led off their neighbors' cattle in the name of the king and the major British and American armies fought it out at Monmouth Court House. On March 30, 1780, Tye and his band looted and burned the home of patriot John Russell, reviled for his raids on

Staten Island, and then killed him and wounded his son (the son would later famously take revenge on Tye's associate Philip White). In June 1780, Tye's men murdered militiaman Joseph Murray, another patriot detested for his swift summary executions of captured Tories. Just a few days later, Tye boldly attacked the home of militia light horse commander Barnes Smock. Although Smock and his comrades fought valiantly, the end of the day saw the capture of Smock himself, as well as twelve other patriot leaders.[28]

Throughout the month of June 1780, Tye and his crew wreaked havoc on Monmouth County's patriot population, not only striking economic blows but also depriving them of leadership. Many residents began to panic and frantically petitioned Governor Livingston for some sort of intervention. Although Livingston established martial law in the county, there were few available men to enforce it; militia recruiting was often problematic in Monmouth, and most farmers with patriot leanings were more interested in tending to the planting season than policing far and wide.[29]

Finally, in August of 1780, Tye embarked on a spectacular raid that would become his most famous endeavor and also provide his undoing. He and his men, accompanied by a detachment of regular Loyalist troops, made an attempt to capture prominent patriot Captain Joshua Huddy in his Colt's Neck home. Huddy held off the small army for hours by running from one window of the home to another firing off shots as his only other companion, a woman named Lucretia Emmons, reloaded muskets for him. The illusion that the Tory and British forces were facing down a house full of armed patriots was sustained until they managed to set fire to the house and finally flush out its two occupants, making the captain a prisoner.

The commotion at Huddy's had, however, aroused neighborhood patriots, and militiamen caught up with Tye as he was attempting to convey Huddy out to Sandy Hook by longboat. As shots were fired, Huddy made his escape by jumping overboard and swimming ashore in the dark, calling out "I am Huddy!" just in time as his friends trained their weapons on him. Although the captain would fight another day, the rare good luck that saved Joshua Huddy during Tye's raid would not endure to the end of the war.[30]

As for Tye himself, a bullet wound to the wrist, perhaps from a buckshot, suffered during the raid, which at first seemed minor, quickly became infected and led to his death, apparently from tetanus, within days. Although Stephen Blucke would replace Tye as leader of black and white Tory raiders, Tye remained the most effective and legendary black Loyalist military leader. The *New Jersey Gazette* referred to "the famous negro Tye" in an April 1782 article detailing the subsequent execution of Joshua Huddy, judging him "justly much more to be feared and respected, as an enemy, than any of his brethren of the fairer complexion."[31]

Tye's story provides a glimpse of the potential rewards of loyalty to the Crown for colonial slaves. It is unlikely that many British policy makers were sincere abolitionists, and their attempts to lure slaves away from patriot masters were surely self-interested and even cynical. Perhaps, though, the motives do not matter as much as the results. British policy gave hundreds of Monmouth County slaves an undreamed of opportunity to make a life for themselves out from under the weight of human bondage, and in many cases to exact retribution from those who had kept them in that bondage. A popular tune of the day, "The World Turned Upside Down," surely must have run through more than one patriot's head as his own escaped slave led him off to confinement in New York's infamous Sugar House prison, or one of the "prison hulk" ships floating off Manhattan. The vicious, personal tone of Revolutionary violence in Monmouth had many origins, but one important contributing factor was certainly the rage of the oppressed toward the oppressor, and the outlet Tye's group gave to such sentiments.

The adventures of Tye and his men also reveal something about the changing nature of the Revolution in Monmouth County after the brief period of Tory ascendancy in 1776. Lacking the support of a controlling British military presence once British lines had been withdrawn to the area immediately surrounding New York and Sandy Hook, many Loyalist adherents left their homes and banded together to form guerrilla forces geared toward lightning-style raids. Conflict quickly moved from the battlefields of Trenton, Princeton, and Monmouth and into people's very homes. Although the tendency of eighteenth-century armies to engage in pillage and other generally bad behavior toward non-combatants while "foraging," had always meant that distance from the front lines, garrison towns, or an army on the march such as Clinton's in June 1778, did not guarantee complete safety from the ravages of war, such losses were unlucky matters of happenstance. British army excesses, while they turned many ambivalent New Jerseyans against the Crown in 1776, were geographically limited, although the patriot propaganda they fed magnified their effect. With the advent of the partisan raiding parties, however, homesteads across a widespread area were transformed from a convenient source of material goods, food, and livestock into potential military targets. Now, residents of Monmouth County had to deal with paramilitary units for whom specific rather than generic pillage and kidnapping was a goal.

Whether they were looking for revenge, financial gain, or a mixture of both, Tye and his ilk engaged in behavior that invited retribution by Monmouth County patriots. The retribution would come, leading to an almost unstoppable cycle of vengeance. Most of Tye's high-profile targets were well known for executing captured Tories without even the pretense of a trial. The "eye for an eye" philosophy at work helps to explain why the civil war in Monmouth continued even after the surrender at Yorktown. It also makes it difficult to either condemn or praise either faction. The organized guerrilla warfare that exiled Tories inflicted upon the county was bound to find an answer, of course. That answer came in the form of the Monmouth County Association for Retaliation, which created its own fair share of cruelty and mayhem under the leadership of controversial county leader David Forman.

Following the brief period of so-called Tory Ascendancy during the summer, fall, and early winter of 1776, most overt militant Monmouth Loyalist adherents, including the Woodward gang, had been driven underground or out of the county. The era of organized Loyalist insurrection in Monmouth was at an end; the county's problems with violence, however, were far from over, as the Refugee community set up bases deep within the wooded areas to the south and behind British lines at Sandy Hook and New York. From these strongholds, Tory bands led by Tye and others began striking out in lightning raids across the county. By the time of the Battle of Monmouth in the summer of 1778, their raids were beginning to become common occurrences. In the aftermath of the battle they would intensify.

Regular Continental troops could do little to combat Tory raiders. Monmouth County's expansive shoreline was impossible to effectively control, and the Continental army had bigger fish to fry with Howe and then Clinton and could not waste manpower on what were essentially police duties, although Continental troops were occasionally stationed at particular points within the county. In addition, militia organization, recruiting, and conscription were often less successful than they should have been, especially in the war's early years. On July 9, 1776, even as state patriot leadership under Governor Livingston overcame the Franklin regime, Colonel Breese of the Monmouth County militia tendered his resignation, citing the "great backwardness of the people" and stating that he was "so indifferently attended on field days, and so few ready to turn out, hiding themselves and deserting their houses, when called upon to defend the shore."[32]

Throughout the conflict, infuriated Monmouth County patriots sought legal sanction from the state legislature for retaliatory acts against Loyalists. In September 1779, a proposal to compensate victims of Tory raids directly from the estates of Loyalist refugees who had fled the county was defeated by a margin of thirty to six; despite its general unpopularity, all three Monmouth representatives supported the bill. Patriotic Monmouth men were obviously feeling the pressure created by frequent raids by various parties—Colonel Tye's multiracial force struck all along the eastern shore, bands of horse thieves were active in the northern part of the county, and Refugees and robbers infested the Pine Barrens region to the south.[33]

To complicate things further, many otherwise law-abiding county residents traveled frequently between New Jersey and British-occupied New York City and Staten Island for various personal and economic reasons. Although official passes were ostensibly required for such travel, Governor Livingston's policy was to avoid granting them in excess. Most New Jerseyans chose to avoid the bureaucratic tangle and took their chances making the journey without official leave. Some were simply checking on family members, but many were looking to turn a profit. Many people in central coastal New Jersey became dependent on illegal trade with British forces during the course of the war, in a similar manner to that carried on by Salem County residents during the enemy occupation of Philadelphia. In January of 1779, William Davis, John Thalman, and John Purtle were all charged with "voluntarily, maliciously, advisedly, unlawfully, and seditiously" going over to New York City, "which said City of New York was then in the possession of the Enemy, to wit, of the Army of the said King of Great Britain, without any Leave . . . or Passport previously obtained from any competent Authority." In 1781, a woman named Elizabeth Newell was condemned in strong terms for conveying a calf to Staten Island with the purpose of selling it. She is described in court records as "not having any Regard for the duty of her Allegiance and withdrawing that Cordial Love, and that true and one Obedience and Fidelity which every subject of this State ought to bear." A review of Monmouth County court records for the period revealed that the only charge competing in numbers with trading with the enemy was that of fornication.[34]

It seems that the county suffered to various degrees from the actions of violent Loyalist raiders, traders who consistently abetted the enemy, and a significant portion of the populace that tended to disregard lawful procedure. Officials in the state government, however, refrained from allowing Monmouth patriots to adopt an official policy of retaliation. Perhaps they feared it would only intensify the cycle of violence and increase disaffection within the county. This lack of official support did not stall efforts by patriots in Monmouth County to give as good as they got; in early 1780, a group of Monmouth leaders came together in order to form the Association for Retaliation. This extra-legal group was convened with the sole purpose of harassing known local Loyalists and suspected sympathizers using many of the same tactics employed by Tory refugee groups: violence, theft, and murder. The participants drafted a document to be circulated for signing titled "The Articles of Association for Purposes of Retaliation." This document clearly articulates the Association's goals, which exemplify the "eye for an eye" attitude.

> Whereas from then frequent incursions and depredations of the Enemy (and more particularly the Refugees) in the county, whereby not only the lives, but the liberty and property of every determined Whig are endangered, They, upon every such incursion either burning or destroying houses, making prisoners and most inhumanly treating aged and peaceable inhabitants, and plundering them of all portable property; it has become essentially necessary to take some different and more effectual measures to check the said practices that have been taken; and it is a fact notorious to everyone that these depredations have always been committed by the Refugees (either Black or White) that have left this county, or by their influence or procurement; many of whom have near relations and friends that have, in general, been suffered to reside unmolested amongst us, members of which, we have full reason to believe, are aiding and accessory to these detestable practices.[35]

The Articles cite relatives, friends, and other suspected "co-conspirators" of Loyalist Refugees as fair targets for the Association's enforcers. Lacking easy access to the actual Refugees, these unfortunate individuals would become the most common vigilante victims. Unless ambushed by militia, which occasionally happened, the raiding parties that inflicted damage to Monmouth County homesteads melted back into the safety of the

Pine Barrens or the British lines soon after their attacks; therefore, it was extremely difficult to track down and attack them in kind. It was very easy, however, to strike back at county residents who had proven, or even assumed, connections to known Tory dissidents. By proceeding in this manner, members of the Association did little to affect the actual perpetrators of Tory violence in Monmouth County; they did, however, contribute heavily to the near-anarchic level of violence there during the final years of the war following the Battle of Monmouth Court House.

The Retaliators did not keep minutes of their meetings, preferring to maintain the secretive posture natural to an organization operating outside the boundaries of the law. It is clear from their behavior, however, that they remained true to their vow to revenge the wrongs of Monmouth County patriots by targeting "suspicious" local figures. The Retaliators were also not overly concerned with a record of formal charges against the people they harassed. Samuel Bard, a Shrewsbury physician rumored to have harbored Loyalist raiders but never charged with such an offense, was victimized by the Association twice in the middle of 1780. He eventually fled to Staten Island with his family. Joseph Wood, a captured Tory refugee, later died in the custody of Retaliators near Colt's Neck. Wood had never been officially charged with any crime.[36]

The Retaliators and like-minded Whigs were attempting to reestablish control of the county at any cost, and the result was a petty tyranny with the Retaliators at its head. News of the troubles in Monmouth reached as far as Philadelphia, where French diplomat Conrad Alexandre Gérard wrote of Tories who "infest their [the Whigs'] roads with robbery," and of vengeful Whigs who "seize property all over, where they drag them [suspected Tories] before juries of their choice and assume the rights of the entire body of people; they pronounce them guilty and enforce their sentences immediately without due processes, and confiscate their goods." Gerard wearily concluded, "If such exercises are the good fruits of Democracy, this is a fruit people should not wish on their enemies."[37]

Monmouth County in 1780 was certainly a poor showcase for the "fruits of Democracy." The Revolution had degenerated into a bitter civil war whose participants' political agendas were underpinned by desires for primal revenge and economic opportunity. The Retaliators were at the center of this maelstrom, and despite the questionable nature of their actions they continued to seek official recognition from the state, petitioning the legislature in June 1780 to recognize them as a legal entity. The language of the petition underscores the Retaliators' belief that Loyalist enemies not only hid within the Pine Barrens and the environs of New York City, but also lived their daily lives in plain sight everywhere within the county: "The enemy amongst us, who not only conceal the plunderers, but, we believe, give information as to most of our movements, and are so crafty that we are not able to bring lawful accusations against them, although there is great reason to think them active as aforesaid."[38]

Although the above statement carries more than a whiff of paranoia about it, the Retaliators were surely justified in suspecting that locals sympathized with and even sheltered and aided Loyalist raiders or known refugees trying to make their way unnoticed through the county, for whatever reason. One must question, however, how many innocent individuals may have been caught up in the Retaliators' net when their standards for targeting an individual were no real standards at all. Perhaps locals who were so "crafty" in their activities that no evidence could be brought against them were simply uninvolved. The evidence acted on by the Retaliators would often have been, by their own admission, based mostly on rumor and innuendo. Their rejection of hard evidence as unnecessary or impossible to obtain and the fact that they did not, as an extra-legal body, feel compelled to draw up official charges or offer their victims due process meant that almost any excuse could become a good enough reason to raid someone's farmhouse—even if the real motive was, perhaps, an old prewar grudge or jealousy, or the very present desire for valuable plundered goods.

The Retaliators did not wait for a response from the state government, however, before shedding some of their secretive tactics by holding their first public meeting on July 1, 1780. During this meeting, they elected former militia Brigadier General David Forman, an active Whig from a prominent Freehold Township family, to serve as chairman of their nine-man board. Forman's increasingly controversial status would dash any chances the Retaliators may have had of achieving official status for the Association.[39]

The election of Forman to the chairmanship would lead to a split between the more restrained and the more active members of the Association. He had been stripped of his militia rank (he retained a commission as a colonel in the Continental army) by the state legislature over accusations of rigging elections, plundering suspected Tories without proof of any wrongdoing, and prizing his own economic interest above other concerns. Several of Forman's relatives held positions of significant power within the county, including sheriff, justices of the peace, judges, and officers in both the Continental army and the county militia. Forman, known as "Black David" and "Devil Dave" by those who incurred his wrath, was himself a judge for both the Court of Oyer and Terminer and the Court of Common Pleas during the Revolutionary period.[40]

Forman, who appeared during the opening phase of the Battle of Monmouth only to fade from view once the action got hot, was known to turn his various titles to his own personal advantage whenever possible. One famous instance had to do with the Union Salt Works on the Manasquan River in what is now Brielle, in which Forman had a personal stake. While the battles of Trenton and Princeton raged in late December 1776 and early January 1777, Forman declined to join in the action, preferring to use soldiers under his command to guard his salt works. Salt was an extremely important strategic commodity in the eighteenth century, used in the preservation of meat. In October 1776, the New Jersey legislature encouraged private individuals to erect salt-making establishments along the coast, distilling the product from ocean water, and a year later planned for a state salt works. The latter idea was abandoned when it became clear that private efforts would suffice. Although Washington at first consented to this use of the troops, assured as he was by Forman that his salt works would soon be producing salt for military use, it was soon revealed that recruits for a Continental army regiment he was authorized to raise were also busy building the works and making salt for Forman's for-profit enterprise. In this role they provided free labor for Forman, but were of little advantage to an army that needed them. Following an investigation by the state Council of Safety, Washington requested the troops be reassigned to the main army, although some apparently remained up to seven months later.[41]

Forman thus brought extensive baggage with him to the chairmanship. He was, however, also charismatic and well connected. The Retaliators likely sought to gain status and clout from Forman's position in the local establishment, but his soured relationship with the state legislature assured that the Association would remain an extra-legal organization. Furthermore, Forman's polarizing effect eventually drove off many moderate Retaliators who were genuinely interested in self-defense, creating a group more focused on aggression and plunder than ever before.

The Retaliators continued to play a double game, simultaneously petitioning the New Jersey legislature for recognition and carrying out unapproved vigilantism behind its back. In September 1780, the legislature convened a committee to examine the situation in Monmouth and consider the petitions of the Association. Their final report recognized the vulnerability of the county to Tory raids and recommended that more militia and semiregular state troops be assigned to active duty in the area. The committee did not view the Association for Retaliation as making a positive contribution to local security. The report condemned the Retaliators as a subversive, terroristic group and advised that captured Loyalist plunderers were most effectively dealt with through traditional legal channels. The legislature stopped short, however, of explicitly banning the group. Its members likely recognized their inability to enforce a moratorium of the Association's activities. [42]

Not only had the Association failed to significantly improve safety and security in the county, but many of its members had also begun to exhibit a clear preference for extreme methods. The reaction of many Retaliators to the kidnapping of militia captain Hendrick Smock by Tories is a prime example. A moderate who resisted concentrating too much power in the hands of elected leaders, Smock was a member of the Association and had even been elected to its board of directors. Upon hearing of Smock's predicament, fellow militia officer Colonel Asher Holmes, another moderate voice amongst the Retaliators, paroled a Loyalist prisoner of war, John Williams. Williams then set off toward New York to negotiate a prisoner exchange. This system of parole and exchange was commonly used during the Revolution; officers, considered worthy of the privilege and trusted not to impugn their own honor, were routinely freed to negotiate their own exchanges and expected to return if no deal could be arrived at. Even before exchanges could be procured, many lived comfortably in quarters of their own choosing within enemy territory. Enlisted men, needless to say, were not afforded this privilege; many local patriots ended up in New York's Sugar House prison or the dreaded prison ships anchored in New York Harbor, while British regulars and Loyalist volunteers languished in the dismal prison mine at Simsbury, Connecticut.[43]

The Association for Retaliation immediately sent Holmes a written admonishment, reminding him that the Association supported acts of retaliation, not conciliatory prisoner exchanges, when it came to dealing with the British military and associated forces. In the same letter, they pressed him as to why he had not appeared before the board of directors to explain his role in the prisoner exchange.

> We are sorry to learn of your refusal to attend, after first a verbal request from a member, and afterward a note from the Chairman, without assigning any particular reason. Given the attending members' real concern–we do therefore again request your attendance, or that you assign the particular reason for refusing.[44]

Although the tone of the missive is restrained, it evidences a threatening undercurrent and indicates the emergence of a serious division within the Association. Clearly, many Retaliators insisted on adhering to their system of vigilante justice and extra-legal action, despite the fact that it had done little to control violence in the county; if anything, it had probably increased it. Others, including Colonel Holmes, saw no reason not to engage regular channels when possible, and regretted the direction David Forman was taking the Association in. It seems likely that the more moderate members of the Association had signed the initial Articles and perhaps attended meetings, but remained far less active in the group than others who personally engaged in retaliatory violence to vent frustration and acquire plunder.

Forman, as leader and official voice of the Association, had condemned the prisoner exchange of John Williams for Hendrick Smock. This meant that to Forman and other like-minded Retaliators, uncompromising, violent retaliation stood as the only acceptable way to combat Loyalist guerrillas and British support forces. An extreme stance, it likely startled many more moderate Retaliators out of inaction. On May 10, 1781, a group of Monmouth County patriots formed the Whig Society of Monmouth County. The society pledged to preserve the value of Continental currency and shame those who refused to accept it. Essentially, the Whig Society sought to undercut Loyalist activity in the county through legal, economically focused means.[45]

Competition from the Whig Society and its very different approach to combating Loyalist sympathizers inspired another flurry of activity on the part of the Retaliators geared toward official recognition of their activities. Once again their petitions to Trenton were unsuccessful, and once again the Retaliators continued to pursue their course of action regardless of outcome. Their behavior during the latter half of 1781 was so egregious that it inspired several petitions to the legislature signed by local citizens who had been abused by Retaliator bands. One petition complained that of the Retaliators' victims: "Some they have Imprisoned, from some they have Taken Money, and goods from Others and when these Injured persons have attempted to rite themselves by a Course of Law they have been abused their lives threatened and some unmercifully beaten by those persons who took their property."[46]

Not only were the Retaliators acting outside the boundaries of the law, they were actively operating against it by abusing their positions as office holders to deny wronged individuals legal recourse and by intimidating voters at the polls. In the eyes of many, the Retaliators had become almost as much of a threat to peace, safety, and justice in Monmouth County as the Tory raiders and Loyalist conspirators they claimed to work against. It would be expected that disaffected individuals, such as relatives of known Loyalists and Quakers, would sign anti-Retaliator petitions, as many did. They were joined, however, by moderate Whigs, such as former assemblymen James Mott and Joseph Holmes. The Association for Retaliation's outrageous disregard for the rule of law had driven middle-of-the-road Whigs and the mildly disaffected into an alliance against extremism.[47]

The Retaliators would not yet be quelled, however, and the intense enmity that motivated both them and their Refugee foes would carry the violence in Monmouth far past the general cessation of hostilities that followed the Yorktown surrender in 1781. The famous murders of Philip White and Joshua Huddy in 1782 are emblematic of both the generally disastrous effects of a retaliatory military policy and the particularly virulent ill will that characterized the war in Monmouth, so much so that not even the effective end of the war could still the rage of the county's former neighbors against one another. Throughout 1782 and 1783, the Retaliators continued their old patterns. In May and June 1782, David Forman, as a judge for the Court of Common Pleas, issued orders empowering militia officers to impress the horses of several suspected but uncharged Loyalist sympathizers. In July 1783 at Sandy Hook, even though the war was effectively over, a band of Retaliators fell upon, captured, and severely beat three sailors from the British ship HMS *Vixen* as they completed a routine mission to collect freshwater from a well. It was not until the British evacuation of New York in the fall of 1783 that the Retaliators, somewhat surprisingly, finally quietly faded away. They were replaced, in some sense, by the Association to Oppose the Return of Tories. This group exploited local animosities toward Tories but vowed to conduct itself moderately, utilizing legal channels, and apparently provided a political home for many former Retaliators in the postwar era.[48]

Although the Retaliators always maintained that their goal was the defense of Monmouth County, it seems clear that they were also strongly motivated by a thirst for vengeance and the potential for economic gain. The Retaliators' actions did little to bolster the county's defenses, as evidenced by the fact that Tory raiders continued to terrorize locals long after the Association came into existence. Furthermore, the Retaliators rarely ended up confronting the raiders (or British support forces) themselves, because they inconveniently disappeared into their woodland hideouts or behind the protection of the British lines. Consequently, the Retaliators were left for the most part to vent their frustrations on "suspicious" locals who may or may not have had anything to do with Loyalist military ventures in the area. Whatever their personal sentiments or the actions of their kin, these individuals were clearly noncombatants and therefore inappropriate targets. If anything, the Retaliator's eye-for-an-eye policy made the situation in Monmouth worse by increasing local animosities and making it that much more difficult for Monmouth County to let go of the bitterness of the war after Yorktown.

By April 12, 1782, the Revolutionary War was, for most Americans, a finished affair. The surrender of General Cornwallis's army had occurred at Yorktown months before, and though the war had not officially drawn to a close, the writing was clearly on every wall. Yet for residents of Monmouth County, New Jersey, the bitterness and personal enmity that had turned the Revolution into a ruthless civil war could not be stopped in its tracks. A brief note found pinned to the body of a hanged man in Monmouth County on that April day encapsulates the anger that defined the Revolution in Monmouth and spurred Loyalist and patriot conflict on.

We the Reffugees having with Grief long beheld the Cruel Murders of our Brethren and finding Nothing but such Measures Daily Carrying into Execution.

We therefore Determine not to suffer without taking Veangeance for numerous Cruelties and thus begin and have made use of Capt. Huddy as the first Object to present to your Veiws, and further Determine to Hang man for man as long as a Reffugee is left Existing.

UP GOES HUDDY for PHILLIP WHITE[49]

The hanged man, Captain Joshua Huddy, was a famous patriot in Monmouth County. He had led his militia company in a daring attack on the British baggage train during the Battle of Monmouth and escaped the clutches of the much feared Colonel Tye, but was most famous to Tories for his zealous pursuit of known Loyalists. Huddy was hanged at the order of Captain Richard Lippincott, a Monmouth County refugee, in retaliation for the murder of Philip White. White was an infamous Loyalist raider, who was captured along with his brother Aaron on March 30, 1782. Unfortunately for White, a member of the militia named John Russell was charged with guarding him during a prison transfer. The prisoner had been involved in a dramatic raid in which Russell's father was killed and he himself was wounded. As related in a nineteenth-century local history, the raid itself certainly seems terrible. Russell's father was killed and Russell himself was wounded and feigned death, while in the midst of their plundering, one of the raiders supposedly fired into a bed in an attempt to frighten the child cowering in it, badly wounding him. Afterward, Russell reportedly got up and said to his wife, in truly stoic fashion, "Ducky, bring me a glass of whiskey; I'll come out all right yet."[50]

It's impossible to establish the veracity of a story so steeped in local folklore, but if Russell's experience at all resembled the tale that was passed down, one would expect him to be vengeful toward Tory raiders. To have in his hands one of the very men who ransacked his home was certainly an irresistible temptation. Officially, Philip White was killed while trying to escape as he was

Memorials from both sides of the American Revolution. Left, a plaque marking the place where patriot Joshua Huddy was hanged by loyalists. Right, monument erected in 1927 on New Jersey State Highway 70, just north of the Manasquan River, by the descendants of one Samuel Allen, commemorating his summary execution of "six Tories and their chief" during the civil war within the Revolutionary War in Monmouth County. (*Joseph Bilby*)

being transferred to the Monmouth Court House jail. Although White ran from his captors, under what duress it is easy to guess. His body exhibited at least one saber cut, a nasty and unusually close-quarters wound for an escapee who could just as easily have been brought down with a shot.[51]

Personal enmity and revenge seem to have played a part in the killing of Philip White, just as it had in hundreds of other atrocities in Monmouth during the course of the war. Now the cycle of violence would consume Joshua Huddy, captured during a raid on Toms River, where he was commanding a garrison of state troops and held as a prisoner in New York for some three weeks before White's killing. William Franklin's Board of Associated Loyalists, which was, in effect, the Loyalist version of the Monmouth County Association for Retaliation, arranged for the summary execution of Huddy as a specific act of revenge.

Like the Association for Retaliation, the Board of Associated Loyalists functioned on its own terms without an official mandate from the British high command. In fact, Huddy's execution would shock and dismay the British authorities as the scandal surrounding it snowballed, eventually jeopardizing the Paris peace talks. The *New Jersey Gazette* for April 24, 1782, reported Huddy's killing with outrage, using language ominously colored by retaliatory fervor: "Is it not high time seriously to enquire whether these refugees are owned by, and under the direction of, the British commander at New York? If so, and he should refuse to deliver up the wicked perpetrators of the above murder, ought we not to treat his officers in the same manner until satisfaction can be obtained?"[52]

The trouble had worsened considerably by mid-May, when British commander-in-chief Sir Henry Clinton received an angry missive from George Washington regarding the Huddy affair. Washington demanded that Richard Lippincott or the officer who commanded the execution be given over to the Continental army. He did not mince words: "Candour obliges me to be explicit;–to save the innocent I demand the guilty."[53] In other words, if Washington could not punish the authors of the crime, he would substitute one of their brothers in arms already in American custody.

The Board of Associated Loyalists was soon on the defensive. William Franklin initially claimed that Huddy had been among the party responsible for White's death. Although the execution of a militia officer without trial was still unacceptable military practice, connecting Huddy to White's murder would have taken some of the pressure off Franklin and Lippincott. It was quickly proved, however, that Huddy had been imprisoned in New York for four days at the time of White's capture. Franklin had failed to do his homework when concocting the story. Clinton took Lippincott into custody pending a court-martial. Meanwhile, the former royal governor fired off a snippy missive to Clinton, perhaps figuring the best defense would be a good offense.

> "I am desired by the Board [of Associated Loyalists] to inform you that the three prisoners . . . delivered to Captain Lippincott on the 8th Instant were not exchanged according to the Intentions of the Board, but that they were nevertheless disposed of in a Manner which the Board are clearly of Opinion was highly justifiable from the general Principles of Necessity and the peculiar nature and circumstances of the Case . . .

"Randolph and Fleming were both exchanged for
Captn. Tilton. Captn. Lippincott . . . mentioned verbally
that Huddy was exchanged for Philip White . . .

Your Excellency will please to excuse the freedom of
these Observations."[54]

Clinton was not persuaded by Franklin's arrogant and peevish
communication, and cracked down on the board's activities,
ordering that no further expeditions against area patriots take
place without his express command. Lippincott was subsequently
acquitted of any wrongdoing under the pretense that he was "just
following orders," in this case given by Franklin and the Board of
Associated Loyalists. Perhaps leery of what the judgment of the
court-martial would portend, Franklin made his way to England
in September 1782, before the trial had even ended. He never
returned to New Jersey, and, despite a meeting in 1784, remained
permanently estranged from his patriot father, as well as his son
Temple. William Franklin, judged by many as New Jersey's best
royal governor, died in England an alienated, exiled, and embittered old man on November 16, 1813.[55]

Clinton refused to relinquish Lippincott to the Continentals on
the grounds that he had been cleared by a jury of his peers; meanwhile, the truly culpable individual, Franklin, had left America for
good and in any event was too important a figure to be made into
an offering. Yet the public clamored for justice, or the next best
thing, retaliation. When Lippincott could not be had, Washington
ordered a British prisoner of war to be selected at random for execution in his place. This terrible fate fell upon nineteen-year-old
Captain Charles Asgill.

It appears that Washington began to regret his decision almost
immediately. He feared Asgill would play the role of martyr perfectly, thus turning the retaliatory execution from an act of justice
into an ugly crime. These fears would prove well founded. The
only son of an English baronet, Asgill was a handsome and well-
bred aristocrat as well as a charming, generous, well-liked figure.
His personal conduct was impossible to impugn. In many ways he
echoed the unfortunate Major John Andre, a Battle of Monmouth

veteran and another young and likable British officer who had become an American prisoner of war. Andre's execution went forward despite the protestations of both his British compatriots and the many Continental officers who had been impressed by his stoicism and social grace. Andre, however, had been caught red-handed acting as a spy. He was intercepted riding through the woods of upstate New York in civilian clothing with documents related to Benedict Arnold's planned defection on his person. Asgill had done nothing to warrant execution or punishment of any kind.[56]

When the news of Asgill's looming execution broke in Europe, it caused a sensation. Asgill became the subject of plays, poetry, and pamphlets. His distraught mother, a French Huguenot by birth, wrote to Louis XVI's foreign minister the Comte de Vergennes, pleading for his intervention. Vergennes himself contacted Washington, delicately but insistently demanding the pardon of Asgill and the end to retaliation. This pressure from the French court gave Washington the out he desperately needed. He turned the matter over to Congress, where it was unanimously decided on November 7, 1782, to spare Asgill's life "as a compliment to the King of France." Washington subsequently wrote to Asgill describing his happiness at having been able to save an innocent individual from the dismal fate of a scapegoat. Asgill did not reply, although one cannot fault him much for being miffed.[57]

Although the end of the Huddy-Asgill debacle was not the absolute end of all Revolutionary-inspired violence in Monmouth County, it does represent the last great scandalous horror to emerge from the county's terrible wartime history. It also represents at least one instance where retaliatory violence was stopped by individuals more driven by common sense and empathy than frustration and anger. As the fresh wounds of the war faded away and the anti-Tory societies grew more lax, many Loyalists would manage to reintegrate themselves into county communities that had been shattered by the war. In the new postwar Monmouth County of the late 1780s and 1790s, even the infamous Woodward clan could return home to the forests and streams of Upper Freehold, as if the conflict they sacrificed so much in had never happened. Perhaps it is a credit to the triumph of common sense that Monmouth County was able to recover so rapidly from the anarchic violence that had plagued it for years. Or perhaps it is a testament to the human desire to forget the ugliness of the past.

During the Revolutionary War, Monmouth County, New Jersey, suffered an extremely high level of routine violence, much of it having very little to do with standard military maneuvers like the great battle that took place within its borders. The heterogeneous makeup of the county, which included significant slave and Quaker minorities, contributed to high levels of Loyalism there; slaves sought the freedom promised them by joining the British war effort, while Quakers reacted against feared Presbyterian domination or became vilified as Loyalists while maintaining the strict neutrality their religion required. The violence of 1776 escalated into a retaliatory cycle between Tory raiders and the Association for Retaliation that led to an international incident and did not burn itself out until 1783.

By June 1778, the Monmouth County cauldron of violence was simmering, so perhaps it was fitting that in that month the longest battle of the Revolutionary War, foretelling the inevitable outcome of the struggle, occurred within the county's boundaries, in the fields beyond the little county seat where "Devil Dave" Forman and his cronies held forth. Forman and his militiamen had already extinguished the spark of Loyalism that had flashed so brightly in Monmouth in 1776 with the Woodwards' attempt at counter-revolution, but raiders like Colonel Tye were beginning to ply their trade within its borders. There would be no Loyalist welcome for Henry Clinton's army as it struggled across Monmouth toward Sandy Hook.

three

"The rattle of the drum and the power of the spoken word, lavishly supported with drink":

THE ARMIES AND THE ROAD UP

TO MONMOUTH

ALTHOUGH THE BRITISH ARMY THAT LEFT Philadelphia in June 1778 was marching under a new commander, he was far from unknown to its officers and men. Born in 1730, Henry Clinton joined the British army in 1751 as a junior officer in the First Foot Guards, and then served in the German army of Field Marshall Ferdinand, Duke of Brunswick-Lüneburg, from 1760 to 1762, where he became a personal aide to Ferdinand. As a member of an influential family, Clinton's path into political life was considerably eased, and he entered Parliament after his return to Britain. Commissioned a major general in 1772, he was assigned to Boston in 1775, just as the American Revolution began. Clinton was involved in the battle of Bunker Hill—although the disastrous frontal assault was not his idea—and then assigned as second in command to Sir William Howe when Howe became the British commander in America. The relationship between Clinton and Howe was rocky from the start, and steadily deteriorated.

Howe grew to detest Clinton, gave him assignments away from the main army whenever possible, and constantly lobbied to have him transferred. Howe was not alone in his feelings toward Clinton. As one historian noted, "He [Clinton] was not a winning person; his friends were few and his enemies legion."[1]

In the spring of 1776, Howe ordered Clinton to open up a southern front in conjunction with British naval forces and new troops expected from England. Although the reinforcements showed up two months late at a rendezvous point on the Cape Fear River in North Carolina, Clinton decided to try to capture Charleston. When the operation failed dismally following a poorly planned and executed attack on Sullivan's Island, a defensive bastion protecting Charleston Harbor, Clinton abandoned the southern effort and sailed north to join Howe at New York. He planned and led the successful outflanking attack on the Americans at Long Island, which redeemed his reputation as an astute field commander. Clinton continued to urge bold moves against the retreating Americans, but was ignored by the cautious Howe as the campaign continued. When Cornwallis pursued Washington across New Jersey in the fall of 1776, Clinton led a force that captured territory in Rhode Island for a British naval base and then returned to England on leave. Although publicly blamed for the Charleston fiasco, Clinton's later successes gained him a promotion to lieutenant general and a knighthood. Turning down an opportunity to lead an invasion force from Canada in favor of Burgoyne, Clinton returned to New York in the summer of 1777, where he vainly argued that the main British army should march up the Hudson to rendezvous with Burgoyne rather than sail off to capture Philadelphia. Howe ignored that advice, and left his chief subordinate behind as commander in New York. Clinton later attempted to relieve the pressure on Burgoyne as that commander and his ill-fated force plunged into the wilderness by marching an expeditionary force up the lower Hudson, but to no avail.[2]

Generally thought to be lacking in charisma and tactical dash as well (although he personally led an aggressive attack at Monmouth Court House), Clinton is credited with having a sound strategic sense. According to one historian, he "understood that large-scale Loyalist support required a permanent military presence." That perception at once put him light years ahead of Howe and politicians like Joseph Galloway in his understanding of counterinsurgency operations. Howe and Galloway were of the opinion that a British military victory over the main American field army would generate a Loyalist military and political revival that would be self-sustaining. Clinton's more realistic view should have

Henry Clinton (1730–1795) became British Commander-in-Chief, North America, in May 1778. (*National Army Museum*)

persuaded him that suppressing the Americans was an exercise in futility, and there is evidence it may have after Monmouth, but he kept it largely to himself. Clinton would continue to present grand plans, although he consistently tried to transfer any responsibility for their potential failure to his political leadership, a not uncommon characteristic of generals, then or now. Grand plans of any sort, from any quarter, were especially unrealistic by 1778, since there were considerably fewer resources available with which to accomplish them than there had been the year before. Clinton lost a full third of his manpower to operations in the West Indies due to the French entry into the war. Considering the British strategic situation in America, the withdrawal of the main British army to New York that led to Clinton's march across New Jersey in the summer of 1778 was not an option, but an absolute necessity.[3]

Naturally argumentative and brimming over with self-regard, Clinton, who commanded the British army in North America through his 1782 resignation following the Yorktown disaster of the previous October, continued to disagree frequently with subordinates and superiors alike. Combined with his other shortcomings, this disputatious reputation assured he would never be assessed among the great commanders of the eighteenth century.

In his defense, however, it must be said that he was indeed dealt a losing hand from the outset of his tenure as commander, a hand no one else available likely could have played any better. Nevertheless, an ungrateful British political establishment blamed Clinton for Cornwallis's defeat, and he subsequently lost his seat in Parliament. The general later recovered his reputation, place in Parliament, and military position, however, dying as governor of Gibraltar in 1794.

Charles Cornwallis, who served Clinton as a division commander at Monmouth, was born in 1738. Of noble ancestry, he possessed a birthright entrée to high command. After attending Eton College, receiving private tutoring by a Prussian officer, and studying at an Italian military academy in Turin, Cornwallis joined the First Foot Guards as a junior officer. Appointed aide-de-camp to the king in 1765, and then "lord of the bedchamber," he inherited the title of earl and a seat in the House of Lords on his father's death. At the outbreak of the American war he held the rank of major general.[4]

Although philosophically opposed to the Parliamentary policies that sparked the Revolution, Cornwallis traveled to America with reinforcements for Clinton to aid that general's ill-fated Charleston expedition of 1776. After moving north, he served under Howe, and scored significant tactical successes on Long Island and in subsequent actions in New York. Cornwallis allowed Washington to escape with the remains of his army across New Jersey, however, and was subsequently somewhat embarrassed by the American commander's successful Trenton and Princeton campaign. He and other British generals managed to reduce the sting by transferring the blame to the Hessians they had placed in an untenable position. Cornwallis returned to England for the winter, but came back to America in the spring of 1777 to take part in the Philadelphia campaign, where he led the outflanking force that defeated the American army at Brandywine and then led the British army into Philadelphia. When the

Americans feinted at his position during the battle of Germantown, he was not deceived and rushed troops to aid Howe's repulse of the main American force. After supervising the operation that opened the Delaware River to British shipping, Cornwallis returned to England on leave in December with a solid reputation as a competent and tactically aggressive field commander.[5]

Charles Cornwallis, 1738–1805, served as General Clinton's division commander at Monmouth. (*National Portrait Gallery*)

While home in England, Cornwallis was attacked by politicians unhappy with Howe's performance, squabbled with government officials on the course of the war, and privately expressed his growing feeling that the British effort in America would be "frittered away." When he returned to Philadelphia in the spring he held a "dormant commission," which would place him in command of the army in America should something happen to Clinton, who had been appointed to succeed Howe. On the day the British army evacuated Philadelphia, Cornwallis, ever more convinced of the growing futility of the war, given British strategic moves, penned a letter requesting permission to return to England.

Despite his overall misgivings and his increasing differences with Clinton, Cornwallis was entrusted with command of the army's elite units on the march across New Jersey, and he would play a crucial role at Monmouth Court House. In November 1778, Cornwallis, whose role in the Monmouth fighting was publicly praised by Clinton, returned once more to England, reported on the campaign, and resigned his commission. Distraught and at loose ends after his wife's death in February 1779, however, he returned to the army and America, although conceding privately that "nothing brilliant can be expected in that quarter." Indeed that proved to be the case as, after breaking with Clinton's more cautious approach to the southern theater of war, he led an expedition through the Carolinas and into Virginia that ended in a humiliating surrender at Yorktown in October 1781. Paroled after his surrender, Cornwallis immediately initiated a successful political campaign to shift responsibility for the Yorktown outcome, largely due to his own errors, to Clinton's lack of proper support. It worked; the British government and public ultimately blamed the disaster on Clinton, and Cornwallis emerged the unlikely hero of the affair.[6]

Like Clinton, and most high-ranking generals throughout history, Cornwallis never suffered from a lack of artful self-promotion, although he was characterized by one of Clinton's aides, who of course was not entirely unbiased, as "the worst officer (but in personal courage) under the crown." One historian ventures that Cornwallis's erratic military actions after 1779 were affected by the death of his wife, claiming that he "was far stricter about plundering and other acts of indiscipline—by officers and men" prior to that date. This interpretation does not seem to take into account the looting and abuse of New Jerseyans by troops under his command in 1776 and again in 1778, although it could plausibly be argued that his erratic behavior, poor judgment, and disregard of basic military maxims in the Southern campaign could have been a result of his personal tragedy. In the postwar era, Cornwallis built a reputation as an excellent administrator in India and was elevated to the status of marquis in 1793. Appointed governor-general and commander in chief in Ireland in 1794, he served in that role during the unsuccessful 1798 rebellion and returned to India in 1805, where he died that year.[7]

General Wilhelm von Knyphausen was born in 1716, the son of an army officer, and had forty-two years of military service and experience under his belt when he arrived in America as commander of Hessian troops in October 1776. He was appointed commander in chief of German troops in America, replacing Leopold Philip von Heister, with whom Howe had a number of disagreements and who served as a scapegoat for the Trenton defeat. An experienced and competent commander, completely divorced from British army and home front politics, Knyphausen was entrusted by Howe with important tactical tasks, including fixing the American army's attention while Cornwallis maneuvered around Washington's flank at Brandywine, and commanding a division of the army that marched out of Philadelphia. Knyphausen's main task on the march across New Jersey was to protect the British baggage from capture, and he completely succeeded in that mission. Remarkably, considering the bad roads and harassing attacks by both militia and Continental detachments, the Americans failed to seriously interdict the baggage train. Although caricatured by American propagandists as fat and boorish, he was a consummate professional soldier. Knyphausen returned home to Germany in 1782 due to failing health, including blindness in one of his eyes. After the war he had a cordial meeting with the Marquis de Lafayette, in which both men reminisced about the war, and no doubt the Battle of Monmouth. Knyphausen, a solid soldier with none of the prima donna instincts of many of his fellow officers in the British forces in America, died of natural causes in 1800.[8]

The American leadership began with George Washington. Experienced and tested by three years of command, General George Washington faced the campaign season of 1778 a far better leader than he had been three years earlier. Washington had assumed command of the Continental army encamped around Boston in 1775 on the basis of a minimal military resume combined with good geographical qualifications. As a Virginian leading a largely New England army, Washington provided a living symbol of colonial unity. He would prove to be much more than a symbol.

Fortunately for the American cause, Washington far exceeded his apparent potential, surpassing all expectations as an administrator, field commander, and judge of men. There was a learning curve to be surmounted, to be sure, but he managed to create a national army out of a hodgepodge of local militiamen, keep that army together through the defeats in New York and a demoralizing retreat across New Jersey, execute the comeback victories of Trenton and Princeton, and then raise a whole new army in Morristown while keeping the British army in eastern New Jersey on the defensive. Defeated at Brandywine and Germantown by Howe during the Philadelphia campaign of 1777, he still managed to extricate his army intact and nurse it through the Valley Forge winter.

In the spring of 1778, Washington, who had spent the previous months justifying his actions in the field during the 1777 campaign to Congress, dealing with the Valley Forge administrative supply system nightmare, and fending off the clumsy quasi-coup of the Conway Cabal, had to address the newly developing strategic and tactical situations created by the French entry into the war and the British evacuation of Philadelphia. He would soon demonstrate again, as he had in the past, that he was a flexible leader able to rise to the challenge of command.

Even his enemies reluctantly and backhandedly conceded that George Washington was a remarkable figure. The month after the Battle of Monmouth, an anonymous contributor to a British magazine noted that, "it should not be denied . . . that all things considered, [Washington] really has performed wonders. That he is alive to command an army, or that an army is left to him to command, might be sufficient to insure him the reputation of a great General." Although the author's intent was a sarcastic slap at General Howe for not defeating such an amateur, the writer inadvertently penned the truth. Washington also had another important attribute defining a great commander. He was lucky. Napoleon is alleged to have said that he preferred lucky generals to skillful ones; George Washington, while certainly not without fault, combined both attributes in enough measure to win a struggle that started with an unlikely chance of success. In the summer of 1778 he would gain an army to match his skills.

Aside from Henry Clinton, Washington's chief problem during the Monmouth campaign would be his chief subordinate, Charles Lee. At the outset of the Revolutionary War, the Continental army could only claim the services of three professional officers, all with British army experience: Richard Montgomery, Horatio Gates, and Charles Lee. Montgomery was killed leading a New Year's Eve 1775 attack on Quebec. Gates basked in glory after his Saratoga triumph and was touted by some for overall command, but his career would end prematurely in disastrous defeat at Camden, South Carolina, in 1780. Charles Lee reached his military apogee on the morning of June 28, 1778, at Monmouth Court House. Born in England in 1731, Lee joined the British army as a junior officer at the age of thirteen after a stint in a Swiss military school. He served in the French and Indian War in America, was badly wounded at the failed attack on Fort Carillon (the future Fort Ticonderoga) in 1758, and subsequently fought at Fort Niagara and the capture of Montreal. He went on to fight in Portugal and then, after his regiment was disbanded and he retired on half pay at the end of the Seven Years' War, joined the Polish army as an aide to King Stanislaus II. Lee became a Polish major general and led troops against the Turks. Throughout his continental adventures, he retained his British commission and rose to the rank of lieutenant colonel on the retired list by 1772.[9]

Lee immigrated to America in 1773 and settled in Virginia. Of a somewhat radical political persuasion, he offered his services to Congress in 1775 and was commissioned a general after resigning his British commission. Miffed by losing the overall command he thought he deserved to Washington, Lee served in the Siege of Boston, then constructed defenses for both New York City and Charleston, returning to New York in time to fight at White Plains, and then retreat north with his command instead of joining his hard-pressed commander, who was falling back across central New Jersey in late 1776. Lee explained his failure to rejoin the main army by bloviating about how he was going to commit a "brave, virtuous type of treason" and "reconquer the Jersies" with a newly raised militia army backed by Continentals. Actually, as was often the case with Lee, there was some merit to his idea, and a similar strategy implemented by Washington and Maxwell proved successful in the Forage War of early 1777.[10]

Instead of reconquering the Jerseys in December 1775, however, Lee was ignominiously captured by a British cavalry patrol at an inn in Basking Ridge. Surprised away from his main force without any troops save a small bodyguard to protect him, Lee's carelessness and lack of appreciation of basic security on this occasion does not reflect well on his reputation. Although there was some talk in British circles of court-martialing him for desertion from the British army as well as treason, his formal resignation saved him from that fate, and he spent a relatively pleasant captivity in New York, much of it apparently dedicated to explaining his analysis of the weaknesses of the American army and its commander to his captors. Perhaps to ingratiate, or simply to self-promote his own genius, he also returned to the reconquest business, offering himself this time, however, as a consultant to the British. Written evidence uncovered in the nineteenth century revealed that Lee actually proposed a somewhat detailed plan to defeat the Americans to General Howe. The proposal, in his handwriting, was based on the not unfamiliar concept of seizing coastal cities and rallying the Loyalists, and Lee was apparently never taken seriously. When discovered, the plan was seen as ex post facto proof of his treason, long suspected by his detractors. The general's posthumous defenders have suggested, however, that it was merely a ruse to trick the British into initiating an untenable plan. Considering Lee's overall character, which was, above all, dedicated to promoting Charles Lee and impressing as many people as possible with his abilities, the truth probably lies somewhere in the middle.[11]

Exchanged in May 1778, Lee rejoined the army at Valley Forge just prior to the beginning of the Monmouth campaign, which would be his last. Aware that Lee held him in little regard, Washington still staged a grand reception for the returning general, who promptly left the army to lobby Congress on his own behalf. No doubt sensing the experienced and capable Steuben as a potential competitor in the "most valuable foreign born officer" category, Lee dismissed attempts to turn the Continentals into a truly trained force, characterizing any attempts to do so as futile. "If the Americans are servilely kept to the European Plan," he contended, "they will make an Awkward Figure, be laugh'd at as a bad Army by their Enemy, and defeated in every Rencontre which depends on Manoeuvres." To Lee, planning for a decisive battle, or, for that matter, advocating any stand-up fights with the British army, was "talking Nonsense," which fit in with his view of the Continental army's lack of ability. According to Lee's new grand plan, the Americans, inherently unable to confront the disciplined British, should withdraw altogeth-

A contemporary caricature of Charles Lee which was said to look remarkably like him. He was not a handsome man. (*Library of Congress*)

er from populated areas to the frontier and conduct guerrilla-type operations from there, while the French assumed the main combat role in the war. Washington wisely disregarded Lee's advice, which would have conceded the bulk of the American population to British and Loyalist rule, for a more flexible and nuanced strategic vision that combined well-drilled Continentals, who would face the main British army prudently but with discipline, alongside a strong militia that would exercise political and social population control, and act as a military asset to the main American army when need and opportunity arose. As the British moved into New Jersey in 1778, Washington had other things on his mind than the harebrained schemes and possible personality disorders of Charles Lee. Unfortunately, Lee's mercurial characteristics would soon come front and center on the battlefield and lead to a confrontation that would, in its aftermath, end the general's career. Latter-day attempts to rehabilitate Lee's reputation are not convincing. Although not the cartoon villain he has sometimes been portrayed as, Lee was a problematic commander and an unreliable subordinate who brought much of his trouble upon himself, and left a written record to judge him by.[12]

The men the commanders of both sides led across New Jersey were a diverse lot of veterans. In 1775, the entire British army mustered a total of 48,647 men, spread around the globe from India to America. The onset of war led to an intense domestic recruiting campaign, and the army was quickly expanded to meet its new responsibilities. Although enlisted into an existing organization with a specified training regimen, many of the British army's new recruits, lacking militia experience, actually began their military careers at a lower theoretical baseline than many of their American opponents. The structured unit training programs in British regiments, and the government's hiring of disciplined German mercenaries, offset this problem somewhat.

By 1781 the British army, not counting its mercenary auxiliaries, had more than doubled to a force of some 110,000 men, 56,000 of them stationed in the American theater of war. This figure does not convey an accurate total of men who actually served during the conflict, including those who were invalided out of service, died of wounds or disease or deserted. The unpopularity of the war in Britain led to recruiting difficulties from the conflict's outset, and as early as the end of 1775, one recruiter was calling his task "sad work" in "damned times." Invalids and pensioned soldiers were reenlisted into line regiments, and Germans were recruited directly into British service as individuals, as well as in whole leased units. One recruiter had enlisted almost 2,000 men from various German states to serve in British army regiments by February 1776. That summer, two British line regiments in America reported that 9 percent of their soldiers were Germans. British recruiting headhunters fanned out all across Europe, and enlisted men from the Dutch Republic and as far away as Hungary and Poland. A failed attempt was made to contract for the service of 20,000 Russians. Impoverished Ireland and Scotland proved a more fertile field for recruiters than England, as the ban on Catholics serving in the ranks was lifted—opening the Irish manpower pool—and enterprising Scots joined up with the thought of gaining land in America should the British army prevail. "Raising for rank" or the creation of new units by wealthy individuals, who, along with their relatives, would receive commissions as officers, became common in Scotland. Still, despite all these measures, enlistments lagged. Beginning in May 1778, the "Press Acts" forced into service "all such able bodied, idle, and disorderly persons who cannot upon examination prove themselves to exercise and industriously follow some lawful trade or employment." This attempt at wholesale involuntary impressment of men, which often led to violence and self-mutilation to avoid service, actually seems to have spurred voluntary enlistments somewhat.[13]

Even the volunteers were often coerced, however. As historian Richard Holmes notes, "Many were offered the choice of serving the monarch in a military rather than a penal capacity." Included among these would be "John Quinn an Irish American" convicted of robbing fruit from an English orchard in September 1777, who agreed to enlistment over imprisonment. In 1778, a Berkshire undersheriff assured a recruiter that his jail was filled with horse thieves and highwaymen awaiting death sentences who were, nonetheless, "exceedingly proper Fellows either for the Land or the Sea Service." Of course not all the British army's recruits, nor even a majority, were enlisted under such circumstances, and it is unfair to tar the entire force with such a broad brush. Many men were attracted to the military life because of patriotic impulses, the promise of glamour and excitement over a humdrum daily existence, or the possibility of a secure job in hard times, which arrived often in an erratic economy. Hard as an army life might appear to the modern sensibility, in the eighteenth century, it provided a sense of security and less difficult physical labor than most employment available in the civilian economy for the average worker. "The rattle of the drum and the power of the spoken word, lavishly supported with drink," often provided a convincing show at agricultural hiring fairs in the 1770s, especially when combined with a promised bounty that significantly exceeded the traditional "king's shilling." The only physical requirements for enlistment in the British army were that the recruit be at least five feet six inches tall with no noticeable disabilities. In addition, he had to swear before a local magistrate that there were no other bars to his enlistment. Among the latter, until the manpower shortage of 1775, was being a Roman Catholic.[14]

Once sworn in, the recruit was forwarded to his regiment, or, if the regiment was on active service in America, to a replacement depot run by the unit, for initial training. If the training took place at a regimental depot, the new soldier was subsequently grouped with a "draft" of other recruits and then sent to his unit in the field. In addition to paying bounty fees to motivate recruiters, the government provided negative incentives for them to be as selective as possible. If a recruit proved unfit for service at any stage from taking the king's shilling to finally joining his regiment, the recruiter who enlisted him would lose his fee and be held personally responsible for all government expenses incurred from the date of the man's initial enlistment.

The regiment the new recruit joined served as his new home and surrogate family and was the basic building block of the British army. The cream of the army were the elite "Household" or "Guard" regiments, including the Grenadier, Coldstream, and Scots "Foot Guards," all infantry organizations, and three regiments of Horse Guards cavalry. The Guard regiments were considered the personal guardians of the king, but fifteen men from each of the sixty-four foot guards infantry companies were formed into a special "Brigade of Foot Guards" for service in America, a unit which would fight at Monmouth.

Ordinary or "line" regiments were assigned numerical designations (although they often also bore informal names referring to geographic recruiting areas or commanders), ranging from one to seventy in the infantry, and one through eighteen in the cavalry in 1775, with additional regiments raised as the army expanded. The average strength of an English infantry regiment at the outset of the war was supposed to be 477 officers and men organized into ten companies, which included eight line companies, a grenadier company, and a light infantry company, although field

Private of the Fifteenth Regiment of Foot, 1777. His "slop" or combat duty uniform heavily modified with a "roundabout" jacket, breeches and a "cap-hat," this
soldier provides a generalized view of British infantrymen as they might have
looked at Monmouth Court House. Following the campaign the Fifteenth was
sent to the West Indies, when the grand army Howe had assembled was dispersed as a result of the French entry into the war. (*Painting by Don Troiani
www.historicalartprints.com*)

strength usually lagged, sometimes considerably, below authorized strength. The term regiment and battalion were usually inter-
changeable, as most, but not all, regiments were one battalion

unit, although some regiments had as many as three battalions. General Howe wrote from Halifax in May 1776 that the average strength of his eight-company battalions, after detaching the light infantry and grenadier companies to create special service units, was a mere 220 men. Along with its privates, each company included a captain in command, assisted by a lieutenant, an ensign, three sergeants, and two corporals. The grenadier company had its origins in a unit composed of strong, tall men who were capable of tossing hand grenades longer distances than the average soldiers in a regiment. By the time of the Revolution, the hand grenade was temporarily out of style as a field weapon, and the grenadiers were selected from the steadiest and most experienced soldiers in the regiment. The men of the light infantry company, a more recent category of elite troops, were supposed to be chosen for their intelligence and agility, and were expected to move quickly and independently to engage the enemy in advance of the main line of battle as skirmishers. On campaign, the elite companies were usually detached from their regiments and served with other grenadier and light infantry companies in ad hoc tactical battalions. Cavalry regiments were significantly smaller than their infantry counterparts and usually numbered around 231 men, although at least one regiment destined for American service was reinforced to a strength of 288 troopers, who were organized into six troops. Cavalry proved of minimal use in much of the fighting in America, and the two mounted regiments stationed in Philadelphia during the occupation of 1777–78, the Sixteenth and Seventeenth Light Dragoons, were largely used for reconnaissance missions, as couriers and for other special duties. The organization of these regiments was modified in American service, so that they became "Legion" type combined arms units mixing mounted and dismounted men like Simcoe's Queen's Rangers. Dragoons were expected to fight dismounted or mounted, so were better fitted for this role than light cavalry, who were intended to fight only on horseback. In the summer of 1778, both regiments were considerably under their authorized strength, and, although not capable of turning the tide of battle in any general engagement, they provided good flank security for Clinton's column crossing New Jersey, and even engaged in a formal charge at Monmouth.[15]

British artillerymen were all classified as members of one regiment, which in 1775 was composed of four battalions of eight companies each, with each company theoretically mustering 116 officers and men. The enlisted men included gunners, who aimed and supervised the loading and firing of each gun and "matrosses," who maneuvered the guns into position, carried ammunition, and performed other less skilled tasks. Drivers for the horses pulling the guns were not enlisted soldiers, but civilians hired for the campaign. Clinton's artillery at the outset of the Monmouth campaign was twelve companies strong, but with each company mustering only around fifty men. Since a certain number of soldiers were absolutely necessary to move and service each gun, these companies had to be kept at a reasonable effective strength, and the matrosses who serviced the guns under the direction of gunners and officers, were often supplemented with infantrymen detailed from Loyalist infantry battalions.

Officer of Simcoe's Queen's Rangers. (*Peter Culos*)

No matter his branch of service, much of the British soldier's minimal pay was allocated to pay back the government for feeding and clothing him. Part of his "subsistence" was subject to deduction for any additional clothing beyond a once–year issue. In England, a soldier often received some of this in cash specifically to pay for his personal food, purchased on the civilian economy. If rations were supplied by the government, this pay was "stopped," or deducted from the money theoretically due him. In some circumstances, soldiers sold their issued rations to civilians and used the money to unofficially buy more desirable food at the local market. Actual pay beyond the subsistence was termed "off reckonings." This money was supposed to be paid to the soldier on a bimonthly basis, but was apparently dispensed on an irregular schedule. Individual men, with their obligations totaled up by a "pay sergeant," often found themselves in debt to their regiment. There was widespread belief, with evidence, that much money was stolen, sometimes by the unit's commanding officer. Some soldiers would take clothing against their pay, and then sell it on the civilian market to get cash. Such a chaotic compensation system no doubt added to the incentive of British soldiers to rummage through farmsteads and loot local private property, Loyalist or patriot, in New Jersey.[16]

While stationed in the British Isles, soldiers were quartered in barracks when available, but, with barracks being scarce, troops were often housed among the civilian population, usually in local taverns or inns. In America, where the quartering of soldiers on the civilian sector was a contentious issue, the British built barracks in various colonial cities around the time of the French and Indian War. During the Revolution, these buildings proved too few and far between to house the large British army, which was often on the move, so that the king's soldiers, when stationed at a fixed location for a period of time, commandeered public and private buildings. In Philadelphia in 1777, British and Hessian soldiers built temporary makeshift shelters for themselves, often using the property of local citizens for the raw material, yet another practice not calculated to endear them to an already disaffected or at least cynical public. Fortunately, there were enough commercial buildings and homes abandoned by fleeing patriots to house much of Howe's army once it went into formal winter quarters.[17]

The previously noted lack of enlistment enthusiasm displayed by Englishmen led to the Crown leasing whole foreign units from German principalities to assist the British army. Although the most famous of these contingents, the "Hessians," came from Hesse-Kassel, other small German states also supplied troops to the British. Perhaps the most useful of the Germans were the jaegers, who could shoot as accurately as American riflemen. On some battlefields during the war, most notably Hubbardton, Vermont, there were no American riflemen present, and the only troops on the field armed with rifles were Germans in British employ. The occupation army in Philadelphia included German soldiers from two kingdoms, Hesse-Kassel and Anspach-Bayreuth. Jaeger Captain Ewald thought the soldiers of two new Anspach regiments arriving in Philadelphia, just as the evacuation of the city was underway, "handsome and well drilled people." The Anspachers were sent to New York by ship, however, due to fears they would desert on the march. Individual replacements for German regiments in the field arrived in America sporadically as well. The captain noted that of the 14,000 Hessians who had landed in 1776, some 2,210 had either died or deserted by 1778. To remedy these losses in the short term, some German regiments apparently enlisted Americans, with at least one racially integrating its ranks by recruiting escaped African American slaves. An officer noted that "in order to fill its vacancies as far as possible, the Erb Prinz Regiment has enlisted negroes. Some of them have run away, and others have been claimed by their owners."[18]

Enlisting Americans was only an emergency measure for the Germans, however. Although many of their recruits were experienced soldiers, Captain Ewald questioned the quality of some, as well as their motives and origins. In May 1778, around the same time the Anspach units landed, 300 recruits for the Hessian regiments already in service arrived by ship from Europe. Ewald noted that "the most remarkable person among these people was a man of fifty years [of age] named Leonhard. He had served in the Hessian army as captain in the Seven Years' War until 1760, deserted because of debts, served with several potentates as a common hussar, enlisted again in Hesse, and was sent to America

A *Jaeger* of Captain Ewald's Company, dressed in green coat with his short German made rifle. Ewald's men were detailed to skirmish with the New Jersey militiamen and Continentals who harassed Clinton's column across the state in the summer of 1778. (*Painting by Don Troiani www.historicalartprints.com*)

as a private. The remainder consisted of nothing but foreigners of all classes and the scum of the human race." A month after the army reached New York, another shipload of replacements arrived. Ewald recalled that

> on the 29th [August 1778] three hundred Hessian recruits arrived, consisting of all classes of human beings, of which a part had rebelled against their officers on the ships. Twelve of them were roughly handled, who were said to be court-martialed. Among these people were many nobles who had been officers; among others a Frenchman named Detroit who had been a gendarme and had served with the French legion in the Polish war. He was recruited as a corporal and had very good recommendations from Poland.[19]

The British also enlisted a number of Loyalist soldiers after their arrival in America, with New Jersey contributing a significant percentage of the total. These men were not integrated into existing units, but organized into both formal and informal units. Although initially hesitant to turn the Revolution into a civil war because it would complicate any possible reconciliation process, the numerous New Jerseyans led into his lines by Cortlandt Skinner as soon as he made landfall in New York in 1776 quickly led General Howe to change his mind. He subsequently organized these volunteers into "Provincial" regiments, a process that continued with the occupation of Philadelphia, where a number of local Tories offered their military services to the Crown. One estimate is that 10 percent of Clinton's army crossing New Jersey in the summer of 1778 was composed of Loyalists. The principal Loyalist units on the march were Skinner's New Jersey Volunteers, the "Guides and Pioneers," a hodgepodge aggregation of scouts, demolition men and engineers, and Simcoe's Queen's Rangers, perpetrators of the Hancock's Bridge massacre. Simcoe's unit, a legion, was the most useful of these, combining infantry, light infantry, some of whom carried rifles, and a troop of mounted "hussars." Aside from Simcoe's men, who often took the advance on the march, and the reliable New Jersey Volunteers, most Loyalist units recently recruited in the Philadelphia area were assigned to less demanding tasks than Clinton's regular forces.

Eighteenth-century armies were unusual by later military standards in often trailing a large entourage of women and children. Each British company was allowed by regulation to carry six soldiers' wives and their children on the rolls, but there is evidence these instructions were not strictly adhered to. In addition, there were apparently a significant number of other, informal, camp followers who became attached to each unit. One study concludes that "between one eighth and one quarter of the people considered a part of a regiment were women and children," and some estimates are even higher. In exchange for work, including washing and mending clothing and nursing when necessary, the official women and children of the regiment were entitled to be

Women and children were an integral part of Revolutionary War armies, providing nursing services and a touch of home for troops in the field. (*Peter Culos*)

fed and housed, although not paid a salary. Some were allowed to be sutlers, or vendors of provisions, especially liquor, beyond the army ration. When a unit was shipped overseas to America on troop transports, it was easier to limit the followers to the officially accepted number, but even then exceptions were made, with one ten-company regiment recorded as boarding 105 women rather than the 60 authorized.

Once in America, soldiers, and even officers, often acquired wives or more informal female companionship, like Patrick Ferguson did with a woman known as "Virginia Sal," from among the local population, and bigamy was not unheard of. Sometimes commanders tried, or claimed, to limit the number of women on campaign with their armies, to no avail. Although he denied it, General Burgoyne's army apparently mustered "some 2,000 women" when he marched down from Canada to the debacle at Saratoga, and Burgoyne himself, like Howe, took the wife of one his subordinates as a mistress. German regiments also carried official females on their rolls, usually at a rate of 6 per company. Perhaps surprisingly, French armies of the era, although there is evidence of "camp followers" in their European campaigns, had no provision for maintaining women or children with the troops, and there were few if any in French ranks when they landed in America later in the war. Records of rations issued, or "victualing" records, for June 27 and 28, 1778, at Monmouth Court House reveal that Clinton's army fed 357 women. The overall number may have been reduced by transporting some dependents by ship from Philadelphia to New York.[20]

In addition to the large numbers of women attached to combat forces, one of the most interesting social aspects of Revolutionary War armies on both sides, considering their nineteenth-century successors, is widespread racial integration, at least on the lower levels. Some slaves took advantage of wartime confusion to seize their freedom. When a "certain Negro Fellow named Jack" emancipated himself from Ogden Furnace, New Jersey, early in the war, he took with him "his master's Gun and a Grenadier's Sword with Brass Mountings." Jack may well have put his newly acquired ordnance to service in Loyalist ranks.[21]

Jack would not have been the only black soldier in the British army. Word of the November 1775 proclamation of Lord Dunmore, the royal governor of Virginia, promising freedom to slaves who joined the British in his proposed "Ethiopian Regiment," traveled fast through the African American grapevine. Dunmore's pledge proved a powerful incentive to many slaves, and, although the special regiment was never organized, some escaped slaves who responded to his offer fought alongside the British against the American army at the battle of Long Island in 1776. In response to such unanticipated African American attempts toward self-emancipation, local New Jersey patriot officials imposed travel and gathering restrictions on slaves in late 1775. In addition, the Shrewsbury Committee of Safety in Monmouth County ordered the confiscation of firearms and ammunition in the possession of African Americans "until the present troubles are settled."[22]

Offers of freedom to runaway slaves were spurred more by a desire to weaken the American war effort than by abolitionist idealism, however, and the buying and selling of slaves continued behind British lines. Slaves who did not run away from their patriot owners, but were captured by the British in the course of military operations, were often classified as legitimate war booty, and simply continued their servitude under new ownership. The proximity of a British garrison, including numerous black Loyalists, in New York between 1776 and 1783, however, provided a haven for escaping New Jersey slaves, many of whom found civilian and military work for the British. Some were recaptured attempting to reach New York, and at least one such fugitive was confined to stocks in New Brunswick as punishment.[23]

Enlistment in British line units was limited to white soldiers only, and black Loyalists were more likely to fight in irregular organizations, although one British enlistment roll from early in the war identified a recruit as having a "Brown" complexion. The members of a unit dubbed the "Black Pioneers," organized in Philadelphia and paid, armed, uniformed, and supplied as a British army formation, performed many critical military tasks for the British, including building fortifications, conducting guerrilla raids, and acting as spies. A Black Pioneer spy captured by patriots at Cranbury, New Jersey, was hanged, but cut down by British rescuers. He survived the war. Pioneers were considered utility troops by the British, however, and often engaged in less romantic work than raiding and spying. In 1778, the British occupiers of Philadelphia used a Black Pioneer unit as street cleaners.[24]

Other ad hoc black Loyalist units included the "Black Brigade," "Followers of the Army and Flag," and "Black Shot." Titus, the Shrewsbury slave who ran away from his master, John Corlies, in early November 1775 and eventually joined the Loyalist forces, provides an example of the membership in these units. "Colonel Tye," whose exploits are related in the previous chapter, gained a reputation as a brave and resourceful guerrilla leader operating against targets in Monmouth County from New York and Sandy Hook until his death following a gunshot wound in November 1780.[25]

As described earlier in this work, the Revolutionary War in New Jersey and Monmouth County was a particularly bitter and internecine conflict, and continued apace long after the war began to wind down elsewhere in the country. As late as June 5, 1782, the "Armed Boat Company," an eighty-man unit of black and white Loyalists, ravaged Forked River and captured Joshua Huddy at Toms River, which led to the international incident that followed Huddy's subsequent lynching. Similar mixed-race freelance privateer outfits raided the Connecticut coast. Rather than be returned as patriot "property" at the end of the war, more than three thousand African American Loyalists, many, but by no means all from the New York and New Jersey area, fled New York City to Nova Scotia, England, and elsewhere in 1783. Many ended up in Sierra Leone, Africa.[26]

The army that George Washington marched out of Valley Forge was not the same force he started the war with. The Continental army's command and administrative staff structure, initially created during the 1775 Siege of Boston, was based on that of the British army, unsurprising considering that some of its original higher-ranking officers, like Generals Gates and Lee, were veteran British army officers, and most of its middle-ranking commanders gained their military experience within the British system during the French and Indian War. Individual regiments, raised directly from the militia and each bearing a number and colony (later state) designation, averaged 474 rank and file each. They were formed directly from the New England militia and organized into brigades, which were formed into divisions. A force of riflemen from Pennsylvania and Virginia, specialists armed with more accurate guns than the common musket, remained outside the divisional structure.[27]

Washington's first reorganization of the army, which raised regiments for one year's service beginning in December 1775, assigned troop quotas to each colony and structured the regiments to provide more firepower than their British counterparts, but differed from British regiments in lacking grenadier and light infantry companies. Theoretically, an American regiment had a broader frontage than the British, since it deployed in two ranks instead of three, although the British usually dispensed with the third rank in America. In spite of being raised locally, the new regiments continued the previous militia army system with "Continental" numerical and colony designations.[28]

Even though British military thought infused the organization of the Continental army, the whole idea of creating a "standing army" like those of European powers ran counter to the political ideology of the Revolution. After the events of 1776, however,

Congress conceded that a longer-term force was indeed necessary, and the new army Washington raised over the winter of 1776–77 reflected that idea. The men of the Continental regiments of 1775, with which the American commander had lost New York and New Jersey, and then regained much of New Jersey due to his victories at Trenton and Princeton, had been enlisted for one year's service, and were discharged by early 1777. Some of the old soldiers reenlisted, but many returned home, available for militia duty but believing that they had fulfilled any obligation to national service. The new army's units, again organized as eight-company regiments, rendezvoused at Morristown, and also at Ticonderoga and Peekskill, New York. As before, quotas were assessed, with most regiments assigned numerical and state designations, but with some "additional regiments" known by their commanders' names.[29]

The new longer-service Continental army's infantry gained valuable combat experience in the campaigns of 1777. Washington had experimented with his tactical structure, making use of special temporary light infantry formations of elite picked men, like Maxwell's battalion at Brandywine, as an equivalent to the detached light infantry and grenadier battalions in British service. The arrival of Steuben and his training techniques, along with an ample supply of French muskets, did much to refine and standardize drill and weaponry in the army, although uniforms were still in short supply. While some historians have questioned the wisdom of using picked men from various regiments, since it put them into combat in ad hoc units they had no experience maneuvering with, and under officers they might not have been familiar with, the Steuben drill did give them a common grounding in maneuver practices. In the Monmouth campaign, the Continental infantry was supplemented by the New Jersey militia, called out by Governor Livingston to bolster the main army while it was in the field in the state. Livingston's militia was organized into regiments and brigades based on geographical boundaries, and these units had varying levels of strength, training, leadership, and combat capability. In 1778, however, unlike in 1776, New Jersey militiamen were eager to come to grips with the enemy. In addition, the states of Massachusetts, New York, New Jersey, Maryland, and North Carolina had reinforced their Continental regiments serving under Washington with nine-month conscripts from the militia prior to the campaign.[30]

What kind of men served in the ranks of the Continentals and militia? A varied lot, by most accounts. When the new Continental regiments were raised in 1777, it was proposed that enlistments be for the duration of the war. In the face of lagging enthusiasm, however, the states, tasked with recruiting and keeping their regiments in the field up to strength, received permission to enlist men for three-year terms of service. Although states could furnish volunteers or conscript men to fill assigned quotas, the Continental Congress had no real means of enforcing the quotas, so they were often not met. State draftees for terms of service with

Artist's conception of a soldier from the 2nd New Jersey Infantry during the Philadelphia Campaign of 1777. (*Peter Culos*)

the Continentals were given the option of providing substitutes at their own expense, and often did. Volunteering was usually spurred by bounty payments from state and local governments, and the Continental Congress and local officials were rewarded for producing recruits, who were often poor farm laborers and indentured servants. Although Continental army pay was erratic, and often, due to inflation, worthless, recruits were promised land grants upon discharge as an incentive to enlist and stay with the colors.[31]

Continental recruiters were instructed to enlist only men who were "healthy, able-bodied, at least sixteen years old and not under five feet two inches in height." One muster roll perusal, however, uncovered a Pennsylvania recruit who was twelve years old and another who was a three-year veteran at the age of fifteen. Recruiting methods varied as well, from appeals to fight for freedom to the effort of a South Carolinian who "besides treating potential soldiers to wine and grog," served free barbecue at a "Virginia Hop" to potential volunteers and their wives and girlfriends. As the war continued and the recruit pool diminished, British deserters, captured Loyalists, and others "bound to us by no motives of attachment" ended up in the ranks. Despite these drawbacks, the army that marched out of Valley Forge in June 1778 was a solid force, composed for the most part of men loyal to their comrades, regiments, army, and nation, who were well trained and confident in their abilities. And they would do themselves proud that summer.[32]

The American cavalry, authorized as four regiments of light dragoons by Congress, and assembled in a brigade organization in late 1777, had not spent its winter at Valley Forge but at Trenton, New Jersey. Lacking a commander since the resignation of Colonel Casimir Pulaski in March, and short of men and mounts, Washington's horse soldiers did not participate in the Monmouth campaign as a unit, although small detachments were used, along with mounted militiamen, as scouts and couriers. In 1779, the light dragoons were converted into legion-style composite mounted and dismounted organizations.[33]

By 1778, the Continental Artillery had turned into perhaps the most professional branch of the army under capable Brigadier General Henry Knox, who had used the Valley Forge winter to good effect in improving his men's gunnery skills. Knox's artillery was composed of five Continental Artillery regiments of from three to ten companies each. It was tactically integrated into the overall command, with a company manning four brass three-, four-, or six-pounder artillery pieces, assigned to each infantry brigade; an artillery reserve combining light and heavier guns, including two twenty-four-pounders and four twelve-pounders, as well as howitzers, additional unmanned field guns in the army trains; and two siege gun depots at Springfield, Massachusetts, and Carlisle, Pennsylvania. In 1778, the guns were still an eclectic combination of French-, British-, and American-made pieces. Knox was of the opinion that the artillery's main job was to support the infantry by concentrating on advancing foot soldiers before engaging in counterbattery duels with enemy artillery. This philosophy would play out well at Monmouth.[34]

Like the British and Hessian forces, the American army trailed an entourage of noncombatant women and children. In the war's initial stages women were scarce in camp, but by 1776 the army had a significant civilian community attached to it. The presence of women and children could prove a drain on food supplies, a fact recognized by British General Burgoyne in his attempts to limit their presence (apparently unsuccessfully) during his Saratoga campaign. During the Philadelphia campaign, Washington ordered his commanders to "use every reasonable method in their power" to reduce the "multitude" of dependents attached to the army. No one ever suggested actually banishing the women of the army, however, since, as in the British army, they provided essential services not covered by the army itself. An additional uncounted benefit of women serving with the army was the morale-boosting link they provided with normal civil life. Washington eventually relented and provided rations for the "extra women" rather than lose "some of the oldest and best Soldiers in the Service" to desertion. The presence of women with militia units, who operated close to home, was minimal at best, and most distaff campaigners were attached to Continental regiments. One study of the numbers of women officially attached to Continental units early in the war revealed that they composed "three percent of the strength of the unit to which they were attached," or roughly "one woman for every thirty men." Within a year after the Battle of Monmouth, however, the number of women attached to the army had significantly increased, with one Pennsylvania brigade mustering over 10 percent of its strength in female auxiliaries, although it appears to never have approached the 20 percent posited in one study. Women not only provided washing and nursing services for their husbands, but for other soldiers as well. In August 1778, following the Battle of

Monmouth, the colonel of the Second Pennsylvania Regiment ordered that no women attached to the regiment be allowed to draw rations unless "they make use of their endeavors to keep the men clean." Women could earn extra money by doing laundry for soldiers at a fixed rate set by the regiment. The women of the American army, like its men, were a diverse lot. As John Rees notes, "From respected wives to women on the fringes of society, from free white women to enslaved women of color, they all found a place, at one time or another, with the regiments of the Continental Army."[35]

Like some elements of the British army, the American army was integrated. African American men had served in the early American militia, although laws growing out of the formalization of slavery in the late seventeenth century gradually excluded them from bearing arms. As is often the case, however, the exigencies of war superseded law and custom. More than four hundred black men served as combat soldiers in the South Carolina Yamasee Indian War of 1715. As late as 1740, South Carolina still enlisted slaves in its militia. A shortage of willing white manpower led to African American service in both the militia and the regular regiments of the Continental line during the American War for Independence. It is estimated that as many as ten thousand black men served the patriot cause in various military roles in the Revolution. The record indicates that Congress and senior officers waxed hot and cold about allowing either slaves or free black men to bear arms, but pragmatism assured that blacks continued to serve in the army despite all legislative efforts to exclude them. In 1777, a Hessian officer commented that "one sees no [American] regiment in which there are not negroes in abundance, and among them are able-bodied, sturdy fellows." A survey of Washington's army, conducted following the Battle of Monmouth, revealed that seven brigades each had an average of fifty-four African American soldiers in the ranks, including sixty in the First Maryland Brigade and another thirty-five in the Second Maryland Brigade.[36]

Black soldiers were initially banned from serving in many southern units, but the need for troops led to the prohibition being lifted by all states, save South Carolina and Georgia.

Prominent South Carolinian Lieutenant Colonel John Laurens asked that the restriction be abolished by his state, but the idealistic young Laurens, who developed serious doubts about the legitimacy of slavery itself, was ignored by his plantation-owning neighbors. Black soldiers were represented in most if not all northern regiments by the Battle of Monmouth, however. African American combat soldiers were most numerous in New England regiments, but black Pennsylvanians and New Jerseyans also bore arms for their state. In 1777, New Jersey specified that "all able bodied men not being slaves" were eligible to enlist in its Continental regiments as well as active militia units, opening the way for free black men to join the

An African-American reenactor at the 1978 Bicentennial recreation of the Battle of Monmouth. A recent estimate is that around 880 African Americans served in integrated American ranks at Monmouth. (*National Guard Militia Museum of New Jersey*)

ranks. In 1779, the state sought "male free inhabitants" regardless of race, as recruits for its semiregular state troops. Later laws simply required that prospective soldiers be "able bodied effective recruits," or "such inhabitants as are willing." Although servants, minors, and apprentices were officially exempted, slaves were apparently not barred from service under certain conditions, especially in state troop or Continental ranks.[37]

It is estimated that 2 percent of the men who served in New Jersey's "Second Establishment" brigade of Continentals in the Revolutionary War were nonwhite. Although some of these soldiers were Native-Americans, most, like John Evans, who enlisted from Reading Township, were black. The most well-known New Jersey African American Revolutionary War soldier was Oliver Cromwell, a Burlington County man who served in the Continental Line's Second New Jersey Regiment from 1777 to

1783. Cromwell, who apparently shared African, white, and Native-American ancestry, fought in a number of engagements, including the Battle of Monmouth, and lived until 1853. Jacob Francis, a twenty-one-year-old newly freed New Jersey slave, found himself in Massachusetts at the outbreak of the war. Francis served over a year in a Massachusetts Continental Line Regiment, fighting at Long Island and Trenton. When discharged, he returned to his home in Amwell, New Jersey, and served numerous tours of active duty in the militia until the cessation of hostilities. The New Jersey legislature was often inconsistent in its enlistment policies. In 1779, it banned slaves from serving in militia units, but on three occasions it specifically freed slaves owned by Loyalists, including Peter Williams and Cato, so that they could join the state or Continental ranks.[38]

New Jersey law, like that of other states, allowed draftees to provide substitutes to serve in their place in the military when a militia conscription for Continental service occurred, and at least some men sent their slaves. Samuel Sutphen, a Somerset County slave soldier, substituted for his master, Caspar Berger, for several tours of duty in both the militia and the New Jersey Continental Line between 1776 and 1780. He was present at the battles of Princeton and Monmouth, fought in numerous engagements, including the battle of Long Island, and was wounded in a New York state skirmish with British troops following his return from the 1779 campaign against the Iroquois Indians. General Dickinson personally presented Sutphen with a musket for capturing a prisoner during an action at Van Nest's Mill during the Forage War, and he kept the gun for the rest of his life. Sadly, Sutphen's expectation of personal liberty at war's end in return for his sacrifice was denied, although he eventually purchased his freedom and then that of his wife. In his old age, Sutphen was denied a pension by the federal government, apparently because he served as a slave and substitute, rather than a free man, despite the testimony of numerous witnesses to his service. Eventually the New Jersey General Assembly did the right thing, awarding the old veteran a special stipend in 1836. Samuel Sutphen, a good man and a good soldier, died at the age of ninety-four, on May 8, 1841.[39]

An in-depth analysis of African-Americans serving in the ranks at the Battle of Monmouth—extrapolating from an August 28, 1778, return of black soldiers in a number of Continental army regiments listing 580 African Americans out of a total strength of 7,751—gives a probable total of around 880 black soldiers in American ranks at the battle.[40]

American Indians fought in Continental ranks as well, and Hessian Captain Ewald was particularly fascinated by them. Following the Barren Hill fight against Lafayette, he noted that several American prisoners, Oneidas who had joined Washington's army, were "Indians who were armed with bows and arrows, the first that we have seen. It is said to be the Stockbridge [Massachusetts] tribe that has joined the Americans. They were handsome and well built people, who had a rather deep yellow skin." During the Monmouth campaign, fifteen Mohicans from Stockbridge served in the Eighth Massachusetts Regiment and three more in the Fourth Massachusetts. A number of Marshpees of Barnstable, Massachusetts, many of them of mixed Indian and African American heritage, also served in Massachusetts regiments at Monmouth.[41]

As the year 1778 began, the Continental army's infantry regiments were still organized along the lines proposed in 1775. This structure posited an eight-company regiment with ninety officers and men in each company, a strength never achieved in the field. Recognizing reality, a new organizational structure proclaimed in May reduced the number of men per company, but added a new ninth company of light infantrymen or riflemen to each regiment. As in the British army, these additional companies were designed to be consolidated and used as separate elite units as situations demanded. The changes were only partly implemented before the 1778 campaign opened, however, and the army that marched across New Jersey that June, while better drilled than ever before, was still a force in organizational transition.[42]

How far the Continentals had come in their transition to professionalism would soon be tested. The tail end of Clinton's army, including a detachment of light infantry, some grenadiers, Loyalists, and Hessian jaegers who had been serving as a rear guard, abandoned Philadelphia on June 17 and crossed the Delaware to Cooper's Ferry, where they rejoined the main army and its wagons. The last man to leave the city was, according to one source, "Lieutenant Colonel the Honorable Cosmo Gordon" of the foot guards. Gordon apparently overslept while nursing a hangover and, on awakening, discovered American patrols were entering the city. He eluded capture and made his way to the docks, where he was ferried across the river by a Tory boatman. By June 18, there were no British troops on the Pennsylvania side of the Delaware, save some deserters hiding out in Philadelphia awaiting an opportunity to surrender to the Americans. That day, the last ships of the British fleet weighed anchor and began to slip down the Delaware to the sea, carrying not only soldiers, supplies, and Loyalists, but the members of the Carlisle Parliamentary Peace Commission that had carried terms to Congress offering most of what Americans had once wanted, save independence, to find it was no longer enough.[43]

Once securely in New Jersey, Clinton ordered General Knyphausen's Hessians to march six miles inland and seize Haddonfield as the army's first campsite in the state, while a British regiment that had landed at Billingsport earlier marched north to join the Germans at Haddonfield. The remainder of the army followed. They were not long on the road when it became evident that Clinton had taken on a tough task, one that would not get any easier as his men marched deeper into the state. From the first day on, the New Jersey militia and Maxwell's Continentals, using a style of warfare the Jersey general had mastered in 1777, harassed the column continually. The Americans pulled up the planking of bridges, filled in wells, and delivered a sporadic stream of musketry into the enemy line of march. Captain Ewald, whose rifle-armed jaegers took the advance along with Simcoe's men on the route across New Jersey that June, recalled that "the skirmishing continued without letup. Many men fell and lost their lives miserably because of the intense heat, and due to the sandy ground which we crossed through a pathless brushwood where no water was to be found on the entire march."[44]

Although Clinton's ultimate destination was New York City, he postponed a decision on the final stage of his route until he was on the march. The British commander believed that in addition to maintaining a constant harassment by militiamen and detached infantry forces, Washington would probably attempt to attack him with a larger force, perhaps his whole army, somewhere along the way, in hopes of disrupting the movement. Clinton had arranged his marching order to divide his command into two strong divisions, under Knyphausen and Cornwallis, to protect his twelve-mile-long baggage train of some fifteen hundred wagons, with half the army marching ahead of the wagons and half behind. This security measure, though necessary, affected his rate of march and made the long column more vulnerable to Maxwell's harassing operations. In a partial solution, once the army was on the move, he divided his force into separate columns, each capable of defending itself, with Knyphausen responsible for the baggage. As had Howe before him, Clinton issued strong orders to his men against "marauding," and went so far as to threaten soldiers caught away from their units and pillaging the populace with "execution on the spot." Even the notorious John Simcoe of Hancock's Bridge infamy, now a lieutenant colonel, advised his Queen's Rangers that "an abhorrence of plunder . . . distinguishes the truly brave from the cowardly ruffian," and ordered his officers to march in the rear of their companies to make sure that "no soldier quitted his rank on any pretence, but *particularly to drink* [italics in the original]. This practice would be the death of many a valuable soldier."[45]

On the morning of June 19, Clinton marched his Third, Fourth, and Fifth British brigades north out of Haddonfield in two columns. The first detachment arrived at Evesboro in an early evening rain that soaked men and baggage and ruined some ammunition supplies. The rain would continue for fourteen hours and then give way to suffocating heat, validating the old nostrum that if you don't like the weather in New Jersey, wait a day and it will completely change. The alternately drenched and parched soldiers were also attacked in force by the infamous Jersey mosquito, compounding their misery and leaving them "swollen past recognition." Clinton's second column moved up the King's Highway and across Pennsauken Creek under similar miserable conditions. The British marched through Evesboro, conducting a running fight with Captain John Ross of the Third New Jersey Regiment and a fifty-man detachment supplemented by militiamen, as they moved on to Moorestown, where they encamped around that village's Quaker Meeting House.[46]

Local militia Captain Jonathan Beesley was badly wounded and captured in the fighting around Evesboro. Although closely questioned as to the disposition of American troops, he steadfastly refused to disclose any information. When Beesley died of his wounds, Clinton ordered him buried "with all the honors of war" because "he was a brave man." Despite Clinton's gentlemanly behavior toward the late captain and his precampaign proclamation banning marauding under penalty of death, it appears that the British soldiers reverted to their previous habits on the march through New Jersey and "plundered the [local] inhabitants of their household goods, their grain, horses and cattle . . . at every opportunity." Major Richard Howell of the Second New Jersey Regiment reported that the local people were "villainously plundered." The opportunities were less than they had been in 1776, as many farmers drove their stock into hiding places like Deer Park Swamp near Moorestown to successfully hide them from the British.[47]

Another unfortunate American soldier wounded at Evesboro was militiaman John Fisher. As the British army passed through the area after the fight, Simcoe's men captured Fisher, who they quickly determined was a British deserter. A former drummer in the Twenty-eighth Regiment of Foot, he had absconded from his unit on April 11, 1777, and moved to Morristown, where he married and gained employment as a laborer. Although Fisher claimed that he had not deserted, but merely lost his bearings and

Clinton's army begins its journey across "the Jerseys" as portrayed by a nine-teenth-century artist. (*Library of Congress*)

had enlisted in the militia so he could get close enough to the British army to rejoin it, an impromptu court-martial did not buy his story. He was convicted of desertion and hanged alongside the road. Shortly afterward, British troops charged a house from which militiamen had fired on them, captured two, killed three, and then burned down the dwelling, along with two men inside it who refused to surrender.[48]

On June 20, as John Fisher dangled from a tree alongside the road to Moorestown, Clinton moved his army on toward Mount Holly in the predawn rain, halting there that afternoon. The precipitation ended but was followed by what at that point was the usual intense heat. Clinton camped through June 21 and waited for General Knyphausen's division, composed of two German brigades, the Hessian grenadiers, the British First and Second brigades, and some Loyalist units, as well as the baggage train, to move beyond Moorestown and catch up to him. Mount Holly's citizens had fled the town with all the property they could carry, but British soldiers burned the local ironworks and the homes of Colonel Israel Shreve of the Second New Jersey Regiment and local Committee of Safety Chairman Peter Tallman. Horrified, General Clinton offered a reward of twenty-five guineas for information as to the perpetrators, evidence that the general's warnings about "marauding" had fallen on deaf ears, as had those of his predecessor crossing New Jersey in the opposite direction two years before. Officers tried, apparently in vain, to enforce the general's orders, and on June 21, Lieutenant-Colonel Alured Clarke of the British Seventh Regiment of Foot issued an order condemning the "irregularity and excesses that have been committed with these few days." Clarke thought the events, which he did not detail, were "Disgraceful" and "humiliating" to his unit and instructed his officers to "prevent its happening again," threatening punishment "with the utmost Severity." It continued. British captain John Andre wrote that "a good deal of attention was paid to enforcing the Orders respecting plunder," but another captain recorded that even with "all the precautions taken, a good deal of plundering [was] going on." Although he protested Hessian innocence, blaming the bad behavior on the British, Major Carl von Bauermeister wrote that "there was much plundering, which disturbed General Clinton . . . It has made the country people all the more embittered rebels." In 1776, many British had blamed the Hessians for looting civilians. Pillaging the populace, while admitted, seems to have always been the fault of someone else.[49]

Bauermeister's protestations to the contrary, it appears that some Hessians did loot, although they had to dodge their sergeants and junior officers to do so. Despite persistent threats, the British lower-command echelons seemed less concerned, and at the end of the campaign, Clinton felt "obliged to say that the irregularity of the Army during the March reflected much disgrace on that discipline which ought to be the first object of an Officer's Attention." British grenadier Lieutenant William J. Hale was offended by his commander's reprimand "for disorder and plundering," which he attributed solely to "the followers of the Army." While chasing deserters near Recklesstown, however, Hessian lieutenant John von Krafft came upon a party of "English soldiers with stolen goods." American private Joseph Plumb Martin, part of a force of picked men shadowing the British, recalled the "dev-

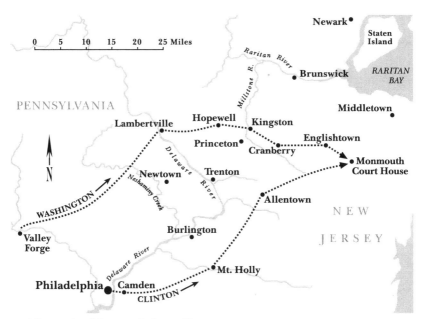

The road to Monmouth Court House.

astation" they left along their route, including "cattle killed and lying about the fields and pastures, some just in the position they were in when shot down, others with a small spot of skin taken off their hind quarters and a mess of steak taken out; household furniture hacked and broken to pieces; wells filled up and mechanic's and farmer's tools destroyed." To be fair, the filled in wells were probably the work of the New Jersey militia in an attempt to deny water to the British.[50]

The reunited British army, which now received word that Washington was on the move as well, marched through Slabtown to Black Horse (present-day Columbus) on June 22. The army was led by mounted jaegers, Simcoe's Rangers, and some light infantry intended to clear the way of harassing rebels, but also by engineers whose job it was to rebuild the bridges that had planking removed by the New Jersey militia and Maxwell's Continentals. At Black Horse Clinton divided his force once more, this time into two parallel columns that advanced on Bordentown, where he arrived on June 23. From Bordentown

Cornwallis's column marched toward Crosswicks, skirmishing with militia while crossing a creek at Watson's Ford, where several men were killed and wounded on both sides. Knyphausen's division passed through Gibbstown and reunited with Cornwallis at Crosswicks.[51]

The British crossed Crosswicks Creek at Walnford, after a sharp skirmish with local militia stiffened by Continentals from the New Jersey Brigade that cost Clinton's advance guard ten jaegers killed and wounded. The army divided again, and slowly pushed on. Cornwallis's division made only four miles because of the excessive heat, and went into camp at Eglinton Mansion in Allentown, while Knyphausen's men reached Imlaystown. At Allentown Clinton decided to push on to Sandy Hook, where he could board his army on ships for the final leg of the journey to New York, rather than take a route to the city through New Brunswick to Perth Amboy and Staten Island. The shorter route would not only save time, but remove the risk of crossing the Raritan River at New Brunswick with the huge unwieldy baggage train and, at the same time, lead him away from the American army, which had crossed the Delaware and was advancing on him. Clinton was in need of guides and approached his Loyalists for help. Lieutenant Colonel Simcoe was able to provide first one, then two more, Monmouth County natives, but none who knew the route to New Brunswick. Simcoe later claimed that his men's knowledge of the county was instrumental in convincing Clinton to march to Sandy Hook, but there is no other provenance for this.[52]

Keeping his army divided into two divisions, Clinton ordered Knyphausen to take the advance, followed by the baggage train and then Cornwallis. They all moved out toward Monmouth Court House, a village of less than a hundred souls, on the morning of June 25, struggling over sandy roads in increasing heat. Knyphausen halted four miles south of the town, with Cornwallis's division camping six miles further south at the Rising Sun Tavern. The tempo of American harassing attacks had increased, and a combined Continental and militia force under New Jersey Continental Major Joseph Bloomfield hung within a quarter mile of the British rear, closing with and firing on the enemy "several times during the night." Bloomfield's detachment "took 15 prisoners & had several skirmishes with the Jagers," with the major personally claiming three jaeger prisoners.[53]

The old court house at Monmouth, New Jersey. It is no longer standing. (*U.S. Army Historical Section*)

On the afternoon of the following day, June 26, the head of the British column reached Monmouth Court House. Knyphausen's division passed through town and camped on the road to Middletown, and Cornwallis halted west of the village along the Allentown Road. American attacks kept increasing in tempo. Captain Ewald, commanding a rearguard detachment, reported that he was "hard pressed" that day and lost "over 60 men out of 180 foot Jaegers and 30 horsemen, among which may well be some 20 men who dropped dead from the great heat and fatigue." His figures seem inordinately high, and Monmouth Battlefield Park historian Dr. Garry W. Stone believes that, although Ewald is quite accurate in most instances, he had a tendency to inflate losses on both sides to make his own role seem the more important. On arrival at Monmouth Court House, both commands pushed patrols out on the roads beyond town, and Clinton established headquarters in a house owned by Mrs. Elizabeth Covenhoven. Most of the inhabitants had fled, taking everything they could carry with them, before the British arrival, but that did not stop soldiers from looting what remained. A Hessian lieutenant recalled that "every place here [Monmouth Court House] was broken into and plundered by British soldiers." While the Hessians watched, "the English soldiers had . . . been breaking and destroying everything in the city-hall-house, even tearing down the little bell in the steeple." On June 27, the exhausted British army rested at Monmouth Court House.[54]

Washington, meanwhile, had been preparing to leave Valley Forge since early May, when it became evident that Clinton was preparing to evacuate Philadelphia and cross to New Jersey. His first move was to strengthen the Continental army presence in New Jersey by dispatching General Maxwell and the remaining two regiments of the New Jersey Brigade to join the First and Second New Jersey regiments already encamped at Mount Holly. Maxwell's men crossed the Delaware at Burlington on May 8. The brigade, recently reinforced by drafted militiamen, numbered about thirteen hundred soldiers, many of them, however, inexperienced and learning soldiering on the job. There was also a shortage of muskets for the New Jersey recruits, although they had been offered a bonus if they brought their own weapons to the army. The arms deficiency was remedied when the northern army sent the Jerseyans a shipment of guns, either new French Charlevilles or Land Pattern muskets captured from Burgoyne's army. The brigade's officers took the opportunity of a lull in action before the British left Philadelphia to drill the draftees, who continued to arrive in small groups through early June, by "introducing the Baron de Steubens Instructions." Maxwell heeded Washington's advice not to deploy his whole brigade at Bordentown, where there was danger of being cut off, and established headquarters at Mount Holly, with outposts at Haddonfield and Moorestown, among other locations. The advance posts were evacuated as the British crossed the river and marched north. Maxwell sent the brigade baggage to Trenton for safe storage and prepared to conduct a running fight. He would have help. The brigade was reinforced by New Jersey militiamen under General Philemon Dickinson, who would coordinate with the New Jersey Brigade commander in the weeks ahead.[55]

On June 18, George Washington received the responses he had elicited from his generals on their recommendations for a course of action when the British left Philadelphia. The consensus was that while precipitating a general engagement might prove dangerous (although Nathanael Greene said if battle came it should be accepted), the enemy should be pursued and harassed to the utmost across New Jersey. At eleven thirty that morning, Washington received a report from militia scout George Roberts that American troops had entered the now abandoned city, and that Delaware militia captain Allen McLane had already captured more than thirty British stragglers. The following day Washington issued a detailed movement plan. He ordered General Lee's new division to lead off the march north and cross the Delaware above Trenton, perhaps indicating his distrust of his second in command by providing detailed instructions on the rate and route of march, and requiring daily progress reports from Lee. Washington also stressed that march discipline be strictly enforced, to "protect the persons and property of the inhabitants from every kind of insult and abuse." Although Continentals had not been immune from plundering in the past, this time, unlike Clinton's order to the same effect, it appears Washington's order was obeyed. Lee was followed, in stages, by the divisions of generals Wayne, Lafayette, and Major General Baron Johann DeKalb, General Knox's artillery, and then General Alexander's division. While the main army moved out, Washington dispatched a Massachusetts regiment reinforced by Pennsylvania militia under the command of Major General Benedict Arnold, who was recovering from a leg wound received at Saratoga, to take control of Philadelphia. Another regiment was left behind to guard the army's rear area at Valley Forge. The Americans, who had absorbed Steuben's training well, moved more swiftly and efficiently than they had in prior campaigns, and their supplies were transported in a more than adequate wagon train organized by General Greene with the same efficiency. As the American army marched, Maxwell, feasting on "Turtle & Punch" with his officers and local patriot squires at Mount Holly, was interrupted by the news that everyone was on the march, rapidly alerted his outposts and prepared to resist the British.[56]

The British march across New Jersey, and Washington's advance toward contact with the more than twelve-mile-long enemy column, created a problematic situation for both commanders. Clinton was deep in Rebel territory, surrounded by hostile militia with the main enemy force bearing down on a collision course with his army, and had the example of Burgoyne's disaster at Saratoga to remind him that this situation could turn out very badly. New Jersey, perceived as a hotbed of Loyalism less than two years before, was now classified by one British officer as "an enemy's country, universally hostile, and where he [Clinton] could expect no assistance." There would be no welcome mat laid out for the British, even in the Woodward brothers' former stronghold of Loyalist sympathy, Upper Freehold Township. General Maxwell certainly considered the possibility that, with a little luck, Clinton could be "Burgoyned." On the other hand, should the American main army engage the enemy and be decisively defeated, the war could quickly turn sour in the other direction. The Saratoga example could certainly serve as an encouragement for the Americans to attempt a repeat performance and effectively end the war. Realistically, however, such an outcome was extremely unlikely, due to the fact that there was a lot less distance to be covered, the terrain was nowhere near as hostile or isolated, and the balance of forces more equal. All of those factors strongly militated against a likely repeat of the Burgoyne disaster.[57]

The main American army camped at Doylestown, Pennsylvania, on June 19–20, and moved on to Coryell's Ferry on June 21. Washington could not discern, at that point, what Clinton's exact route across New Jersey would be, but it was now apparent that the British were heading for New York City, although it seemed likely that either New Brunswick or Sandy Hook would be intermediate destinations. General Dickinson established militia outposts along both possible routes for intelligence gathering purposes, and the small American mounted force of dragoons under Colonel Stephen Moylan was sent to reinforce Dickinson. The following day Washington began to move his main army across the Delaware into New Jersey, reaching Hopewell on June 23.

While the Americans moved northeast on an axis intended to intersect with the British, Maxwell's Continentals and militiamen directly, if circumspectly, engaged the enemy. "Scotch Willie" did not take any chances, possibly missing an opportunity to do some real damage to the enemy as the British labored to move their artillery across a ravine near Mount Holly. Clinton later claimed to be surprised that Washington did not bring on a major battle at Mount Holly by opposing him on good defensive terrain near the town. Clinton's opinion may have been chagrin, or at least wishful thinking, as he was apparently ready to spring a Long Island-style outflanking maneuver on any American force that confronted him at Mount Holly. British commanders throughout the war seem to have been obsessed with both the disaster of Bunker Hill and the success of Long Island, hoping to avoid the first while reenacting the second. The fact that Long Island ended inconclusively and in the end proved of no lasting strategic value seems to have eluded them.[58]

As the pursuit continued, Washington continued to up the ante. On June 22, he assigned Colonel Daniel Morgan's riflemen to join Maxwell's mixed force of Continentals and militia then shadowing the British. This force, composed of rifle-armed companies detached from Virginia and Pennsylvania regiments, was increased by an order to the American line infantry brigades to each send Morgan "an active spirited officer" and their "25 best Marksmen." The regiments of the North Carolina brigade, which had put into effect the new organizational plan, were instructed to detail their light infantry companies in lieu of marksmen. These reinforcements raised Morgan's total strength to around eight hundred men. Although the "best marksmen" were not riflemen, but soldiers armed with less accurate smoothbore muskets, they had apparently at some point proved their ability to hit man-sized individual targets with them at reasonable ranges. Although they could not shoot as accurately with their muskets as Morgan's soldiers with their rifles, these marksmen would prove a more effective addition, considering his tactical task, than ordinary infantrymen.[59]

On the morning of June 24, while the bulk of his troops rested at Cranbury, preparing for action by cleaning their muskets and cooking two days' rations, Washington called a council of war at Hopewell. His generals' opinions on a future course of action were far from unanimous. Lee, seemingly oblivious to the effect Steuben's reforms had on the troops, maintained that the

American army (with which he actually had little familiarity since he had been a British prisoner for two years) was absolutely unable to stand up to Clinton's in any serious contest. Lee opined that Washington should limit himself to harassing the British along their way, an eighteenth-century concept known as providing an enemy with a "bridge of gold," or major combat-free passage out of one's territory. Lee's opinion reflected his overall strategic view of avoiding battle, withdrawing to the west and letting the French alliance win the conflict for the Americans. Generals Alexander and Knox concurred with Lee, at least in this instance, but generals Wayne, Greene, Lafayette, Steuben, and Brigadier General Chevalier Louis Lebègue DePresle Duportail espoused a diametrically opposed view. Lafayette, as impetuous as Lee was cautious, believed it would be "disgraceful and humiliating" for the American army to allow the British to withdraw to New York without making them fight, and Steuben, who was more cognizant of the state of combat readiness of the American forces than anyone, agreed. These officers lobbied for aggressive offensive action against the enemy columns, which Lafayette, for one, thought could produce a decisive war-winning battle.[60]

In the end, Washington took a middle course. The American commander ordered another force of picked men, this one more than fourteen hundred strong, selected from different regiments and under the command of Brigadier General Charles Scott, forward to harass the British left flank and rear guard as opportunity permitted. This practice of selecting picked men for what was, in essence, a light infantry task, followed the precedent Washington set with Maxwell's ad hoc unit from the previous year. It is reasonable to assume that since then, the Steuben drill had improved the ability of soldiers detailed from different regiments to function as a cohesive formation—they could work reasonably well together. Scott's force was stiffened by the addition of four artillery pieces from the Third Continental Artillery Regiment. Fiery young Lieutenant Colonel Alexander Hamilton, as eager for a fight as Lafayette, was not satisfied with his commander's middle ground, and is quoted as saying that Washington's decision "would have done honor to the most honorable body of mid-

Washington's Hopewell Council of War on June 24, 1778, as portrayed by sculptor James E. Kelly in one of four relief sculptures he created for the Battle of Monmouth monument erected in Freehold in 1884. (*Joseph Bilby*)

wives and to them only." Still, the new order moved more American forces to the front and increased the likelihood of a battle in the near future.[61]

Despite Lee's misgivings, Washington's force was indeed ready for that fight. American morale was soaring. Although the troops were still ragged and ill uniformed, they had the distinct pleasure of seeing the British withdrawing and their own army in pursuit. Seventeen-year-old Private Martin, selected for Scott's elite formation, marched through Princeton to the cheers of a crowd dispensing casks of free "toddy." Martin glowed in the admiration of the young women who flocked to watch "the noble exhibition of a thousand half starved and three quarters naked soldiers pass in review before them." Writing more than a half century later, he recalled that "they were *all* beautiful. New-Jersey and Pennsylvania ladies are, in my opinion, collectively handsome, the most so of any in the United States." Many would still agree.[62]

As his army reached Rocky Hill on June 25, Washington learned that the British had left Allentown and were on their way toward Monmouth Court House. He added a thousand more picked men and two artillery pieces under General Wayne to the advance, ordering Lafayette to bring that force forward, merge it with Scott's and assume command of all the American units in active contact with the enemy—which by this point was a sizeable detachment numbering almost five thousand men—and harass the enemy's left flank and rear with "every degree of annoyance," to cause them "the greatest impediment and loss in their march." Lafayette was given a good deal of discretion to conduct his mission, and was instructed to attack the British "as occasion may require by detachment," but also, "if a proper opening sh[oul]d be given, by operating against them with the whole force of your command." To date, however, British march discipline had been largely effective, and although harassment had been intense, there were few opportunities to strike a decisive blow on their line of march. Colonel Morgan reported that the British were "in so compact a body" that he could not inflict any significant damage on them."[63]

In the wake of Lafayette's assignment, Lee, who had originally disdained the command of the American advanced forces, consistent with his counsel against seriously engaging the enemy, complained to Washington that the job should have been his by right of seniority. Acceding to Lee's demand, Washington ordered him forward with a six-hundred-man detachment and orders to take command of all the men under Lafayette. On June 26, Lee arrived at Englishtown, within five miles of the British position at Monmouth Court House, where he superseded the young Frenchman and began concentrating his advance troops. Some historians state that placing Lee in charge of the army's forward elements was a fundamental campaign error by Washington, but others argue that considering Lee's rank, the American commander really had no choice once Lee decided the command should be his.[64]

Clinton had disposed his men around Monmouth Court House in a defensive posture, in a line about four miles long, with Dickinson's New Jersey militia hovering to his west, and Morgan's riflemen deployed to the east. The tiny American mounted force of thirty men under Moylan patrolled the roads around the British position, and more New Jersey militiamen were scattered around the country-side.

On June 27, while their army rested, the British held a curious court-martial in Monmouth Court House, considering the apparent lack of control their officers had been able to exercise on troops committing depredations. Two women, "followers of the army," Mary Colethrate and Elizabeth Clarke, had been arrested by Major John Antill of the New Jersey Volunteers for "plundering" the house of a farmer along the route. According to Antill, the farmer "begg'd for Protection, as some women were plundering &

Marquis de Lafayette was instructed by Washington to relinquish the troops under his command to General Lee. (1757–1834). (*Musée de Versailles*)

destroying his house, that upon going into the house, he found everything in the greatest Confusion, the feather Beds being cut open and the feathers strewed about, and many other things destroyed; that there were about twenty or thirty Women in the house," among whom Colethrate and Clarke were most prominent; Colethrate with an apron load of flour and Clarke rifling a closet. The farm wife claimed Clarke "beat and abused," her and that another woman stripped her children and took their clothes. As we have seen, looting was not particularly unusual among British forces in New Jersey, but perhaps Antill, a Jerseyman himself, albeit a Loyalist, felt a twinge of regret or a belief that the war would not be won by abusing the civilian population, and this motivated him to arrest the women.[65]

Both women claimed innocence. Colethrate said she had merely hopped off a baggage wagon to "Light her pipe" and that the item in her apron was merely "Biscuit" baked with army flour, while Clarke stated that she had just stopped by for a drink. She did not explain the "unfinished pair of shoes & some other

Articles" found in her apron by the soldier who took her to the provost marshal. Colethrate was found innocent, but Clarke was convicted and sentenced "to receive one hundred Lashes on her bare back with Cats of nine tails, and then to be drummed out of the Army, in the most public manner possible." There is no record as to when, where, or even if the sentence was carried out.[66]

The British army would soon have more to worry about than two undisciplined camp followers. At four o'clock on the morning of Sunday, June 28, General Clinton's army, led by General Knyphausen's division, began to pull out of Monmouth Court House on the road to Middletown and Sandy Hook. At 3:00 a.m., General Lee had ordered Colonel William Grayson to lead a detachment to probe the enemy position and perhaps exploit an opportunity to do some damage, without starting a major fight. Grayson's soldiers, who were camped behind Englishtown, marched into town, where they met Lee at 6:00 a.m. and briefly halted for instructions, and then moved out in relative morning cool toward Monmouth Court House, on into the heat of a day that would prove more intense than they could imagine.

four

"Food for powder, their most appropriate destination next to that of the gallows":

TACTICS, TRAINING, AND WEAPONS

THE BRITISH AND AMERICAN ARMIES MOVING across New Jersey into war-torn Monmouth County assuredly added to the wartime miseries already visited upon the local population. Unlike the Retaliators and Refugees who bushwhacked and pillaged each other in the county and other areas of New Jersey, however, these soldiers were professional fighting men, ostensibly under formal military discipline, and on the move, limiting the opportunity for potential pillaging. Although citizens living along the line of march, particularly of the British columns, would suffer much damage and loss of property, most soldiers would not roam far from their respective armies, both of which had narrow goals for the campaign that did not involve staying in the county. Those farmers on whose property the inevitable battle would take place, however, would witness concentrated mayhem not seen in New Jersey before or since. The Continentals were ready, even eager, to face the British in battle and fight it out—after studying under

Steuben, there was no longer any doubt on their part that they were the equal of their red-coated opponents.

The American army's lack of training and organization at the outset of the war is well known. Less recognized, ironically, considering the conventional historical wisdom, is that many of the British troops who came to America at the beginning of the conflict, and during its course, were recent recruits, not old soldiers, although as noted previously they usually had some rudimentary training at the unit level. Rapid expansion of the army to cover prewar responsibilities, and at the same time fight a colonial rebellion that turned into a worldwide conflict, often produced men at least as green as their American counterparts at the outset of their own military service. A British lieutenant in command of a grenadier unit at Princeton noted that his men came under heavy enemy fire at a range of forty yards, "which brought down 7 of my platoon at once, [and] the rest, being recruits, gave way." It could actually be reasonably argued that many American Revolutionaries, with militia training and combat experience in the French and Indian War, were more prepared for war than the average British recruit.[1]

In the popular imagination fostered by film and fable, perhaps best symbolized in artist Howard Pyle's 1898 painting of Bunker Hill, well-disciplined, bright scarlet-clad British soldiers march into battle in rigid lines with elbows touching, to be cut down by long-range fire from crafty American riflemen concealed behind trees and rocks. To be sure, Bunker Hill proved the frontal assault was not a wise tactic against American militiamen ensconced behind earthworks, but it provided a graphic lesson that influenced British tactics for the remainder of the Revolution. As such, it should not be taken as a model for subsequent military confrontations. In reality, the war looked quite different.

The line became the basic military formation in the eighteenth century, superseding the previously standard large block formations of pikemen and musketeers. The line took advantage of the musket's increasing rate of fire and also made it easier to perform outflanking maneuvers, and the introduction of the bayonet eliminated the need for the pike. Effective tactical use of the new, more flexible formations, however, required soldiers skilled in efficient battlefield movement, which necessitated intensive training. Aggressive offensive tactics, professionally conducted by an army that could move quickly and efficiently and deliver brisk artillery and musket fire, became a hallmark of success. The ideal of such a force is perhaps best illustrated by the army of Frederick the Great of Prussia, whose victories provided textbook examples of best tactical practices, including cadenced marching, rapid deployment from column into line and from line into echelon, coupled with a rapid fire (albeit unaimed) musketry of as many as seven rounds a minute per man.[2]

As firepower became a more important factor in European tactics, it became necessary to make sure a sufficient number of loaded muskets were available at all times to a maneuvering line of battle. The British army line was three ranks deep, and a variety of "firings" were developed to provide a more or less consistent rate of musketry along the line. Although all three ranks could fire simultaneously, with the front rank kneeling, the aftermath would provide an embarrassing silence, save for the sounds of desperate reloading, as the enemy closed in. Soldiers could, however, fire by file, by rank, or by section. The latter was generally thought the best method, and the British adopted it with Humphrey Bland's 1727 *Treatise of Military Discipline*, which advocated platoon firing, with designated platoons or subsectors of a regiment, singly or in various multiples, firing while other sections held fire in reserve. This system could be used to either maintain a consistent regimental base of fire over a period of time, or to deliver varying amounts of fire at any tactically critical moment. Platoon firing was theoretically useful in both defense and offense, although rigid discipline was necessary to maintain momentum in the offense after soldiers stopped to fire and reload. The British platoon system contrasted with the early eighteenth-century French concept of closing with an enemy before firing one massive volley and charging home with bayonets. Like many tactical theories over the years, platoon firing apparently never actually turned out the way it was planned, however. It was a complex system based on ad hoc tactical, rather than normal

administrative regimental subdivisions like the company. To
make matters worse, training was surprisingly infrequent.
Witnesses to an attempt at platoon firing at the Battle of
Dettingen in 1743 described it as an undisciplined "utter shambles." In the 1764 regulations, the platoon system was simplified
into one in which companies fired alternately, a significant
improvement.[3]

LIGHT INFANTRY
The concept of using light infantry as a screening force to provide
cover for the main battle line in advance or withdrawal was at
least as ancient as the Roman Empire, but had waxed and waned
over the centuries. The term has its origins in the fact that "light"
infantrymen were equipped with lighter and less bulky equipment
than "heavy" infantry in order to facilitate speed of movement
and the ability to engage and disengage the enemy rapidly, as circumstances demanded. In the decades just prior to the American
Revolution, the light infantry idea experienced one of its periodic
renaissances. The Austrians made good use of irregular moun-
taineers known as "Pandours, Croats, Tolpatches and Crabbates,
according to the district in which they were recruited." A British
historian noted that "within a circle of these ruffians the troops of
the line marched in dignified security."[4]

General Edward Braddock's disastrous 1755 wilderness defeat
at the hands of French and Indian irregular warriors inspired a
new look at light infantry tactics in the British army. Lord George
Howe, older brother of William, arrived in America in 1757 as an
advocate of tactics shaped to fit local terrain and enemy activity,
and patrolled with Major Robert Rogers's Rangers in the area
around Lake George. Although he was killed during the 1758
attack on Fort Carillon, Howe's influence persisted. An improvised light infantry battalion composed of "five hundred and fifty
marksmen . . . drawn from the different regiments" was raised for
the 1758 Siege of Louisbourg. The British Sixtieth (Royal
American), Eightieth, Eighty-fifth, and Ninetieth regiments, as
well as several Highland units, were designated as entirely light
infantry formations. Men in these regiments were expected to use

their muskets in individual aimed fire and move rapidly and aggressively toward the enemy, although according to one source, they were sent into battle "without proper training . . . or much else in the way of drill." The Royal Americans continued the light infantry tradition after the war, most notably under the skilled commander Colonel Henry Bouquet, who, leading a composite detachment including Highlanders of the Forty-second Regiment, defeated a force of Native Americans on their home ground at Bushy Run in 1763.[5]

In the wake of the French and Indian War, the British army lost institutional interest in the light infantry, reducing the number of men in designated units and even disbanding some, as the army leadership prepared for the next war in Europe, where it was thought light infantry were less useful than in colonial combat. Although light infantry companies were restored to all line regiments in 1770, men were not necessarily assigned to them because of their military skills. Even worse, according to military historian J.F.C. Fuller, the light companies were "looked upon as penal settlements, and were filled with the worst characters of the battalions." One officer characterized light infantrymen, known colloquially as "light Bobs" and "young and insolent puppies," whose "worthlessness was recommendation for a post of danger, in the way of becoming food for powder, their most appropriate destination next to that of the gallows." William Howe thought differently, and it was through his efforts that the light infantry began to regain respect. The new light companies were so poorly trained that in 1774 Howe, "by order of King George III," formed a camp at Salisbury "for the instruction of seven companies of light infantry in certain manoeuvres invented by General Howe." Perhaps inspired by the example of his late brother George, Howe was a leader in efforts to make the light infantry an effective force. Prior to the Long Island campaign of 1776, Howe consolidated his regimental light infantry companies into light infantry battalions, and did the same with his grenadiers, creating, in effect, two elite strike forces.[6]

Special training was essential to effective light infantry tactics, which depended on speed of movement, and Howe's manual, "principally calculated for a close or woody country," became the army standard, although it is really only a series of instructions on how to deploy a light infantry unit from its parent unit into a more open formation. Details on how to adapt to local terrain and move and shoot as individuals are left up to unit commanders conducting the training. The ability to perform rapid maneuvers and maintain fast and reasonably accurate musketry was not inherent, but an acquired skill. It can be safely assumed that the troops that Dr. Robert Honyman, an American physician visiting Boston in March 1775, saw prior to the onset of hostilities, were drilling according to Howe's precepts. Honyman left a detailed contemporary record of British army training that belies the popular mythology of British tactics being limited to an inflexible line and bears quoting in its entirety.[7]

> Some of the Regiments were extremely expert in their Exercise, & the manouvres & manner of fighting of the light infantry was exceedingly curious. Every regiment here has a company of light infantry, young active fellows; & they are trained in the regular manner, & likewise in a peculiar discipline of irregular & Bush fighting; they run out in parties on the wings of the regiment where they keep up a constant & irregular fire; they secure their retreat & defend their front while they are forming; in one part of their Exercise they ly on their backs & charge their pieces & fire lying on their bellies. They have powder horns & no cartouch boxes.[8]

Although Honyman was impressed by their drill, General Thomas Gage's light infantry and grenadiers proved "unable to cope" with American militiamen sniping at them during the retreat from Lexington. In the aftermath one correspondent wrote: "It is said that General Gage could hardly contain the Troops from going out—as to the loss of the Flanking Parties, I do not wonder at it—for it is not a short coat or half gaiters that makes a Light Infantry man, but as you know, Sir, a confidence in his Aim, & that Stratagem in a personal conflict, which is derived from Experience." In his twentieth-century thesis on light infantry, J.F.C. Fuller contended that "faulty training" was at the root of the disaster, and opined that had the British force been composed of "expert light infantry, under an able light infantry commander . . . the rebels would have been routed within a few minutes of opening fire, and the mile after mile of continuous 'sniping' would never have taken place." Gage followed the inglorious retreat with a "moral disaster" at Bunker Hill, where, as Fuller comments, he failed to use light infantry as skirmishers in front of his main line of battle, evidence to him that, even though he had formerly commanded a light infantry battalion in the French and Indian War, Gage was, to be kind, a "mediocre general."[9]

It could be argued that Fuller was too critical of Gage, however, since the man actually in charge of tactical operations at Bunker Hill was none other than the father of the late eighteenth-century light infantry movement, William Howe. Fuller provides an ex post facto excuse for the general, seemingly contradicting his early point by maintaining that Howe used his light infantry improperly because the "light infantry had been so neglected that they were found incompetent to fight in extended order," even though they had impressed Honyman. Despite excusing Howe's involvement, however, Fuller may have had a point, as one officer wounded at Bunker Hill wrote that light infantrymen fired into his own grenadier unit deployed to their front. Captain James Abercrombie noted that after he warned them to cease-firing, "they forbear firing for 8 or ten minuts then . . . killed two officers & 3 privates & shot me through the theigh." Abercrombie, who later died of his wound, concluded that, "Our men must be drilled before they are Carryed to action again." Howe does seem to have learned a lesson from the defeat, and did not repeat the frontal assault errors of Bunker Hill during his New York campaign in the summer of 1776. Effective maneuvering and the extensive use of better-trained light infantrymen as the spearhead of his offensive operations became the general's hallmark. One observer wrote that a light infantry company behaved "amazingly" in the New York fighting. The company commander had trained his men to "form to right or left or [s]quat or rise by a par-

Two contemporary illustrations by Amos Doolittle of the battle of Lexington and the British retreat. A British light infantry and grenadier force, above, scatters the American militia at Lexington. The firing appears to be by company. The British force retreating from Lexington and Concord, opposite, was harassed by American militia firing into the column.

ticular whistle . . . he being used to Woods fighting and having a quick Eye had his Company down in the moment of the Enemies present & up again at the advantegious moment for their fire . . . he drove the enemy before him." Unlike the Bunker Hill stereotype, the British light infantry usually deployed in an "open order" with at least an arm's length between soldiers, which could stretch out to distances ranging from five to fifty yards, depending on conditions. Even line troops, by 1780, were occasionally arrayed in formations with up to five feet of space between men.[10]

In addition to the light infantry battalions Howe created, the British fielded both ad hoc Loyalist and hired mercenary units that filled similar roles. Patrick Ferguson's company, armed with his unique breech-loading rifle, and infantry detachments of units like Simcoe's legion also performed in light infantry roles, as did the German jaegers under command of officers like Captain Ewald. The jaegers, who had a long tradition in Hessian service, were the most useful light infantry beyond the formal companies and battalions, as they provided potentially longer-range accuracy

In a situation like this, light infantry from the column was supposed to deploy and, with rapid movement and good marksmanship, clear the flanks. The fact that such effort were not very effective was later attributed to poor training on the part of General Gage's light infantry. (*Connecticut Historical Society*)

than troops armed with muskets. German marksmanship traditions were well established by the time of the American Revolution. The Landgrave of Hesse first fielded rifle-armed troops as early as 1631, and Bavarian light infantry units founded in 1674 mustered several riflemen in each company. From two companies arriving in America in August 1776, the number of jaegers in British service in all areas of North America expanded to five companies with a nominal strength of 1,067 men a year later, although actual field strength of these units was about 600 riflemen.[11]

American soldiers with combat experience in the French and Indian War, including George Washington, were familiar with the light infantry concept and its American applications, although Washington did not follow Howe's example of creating semipermanent light infantry formations, sticking instead to the "seasonal" organizations he had witnessed during the earlier conflict. The riflemen sent to the Siege of Boston from Pennsylvania, Maryland, and Virginia served in a light infantry role. The new

Continental regiments raised in 1777 were each supposed to have
a light infantry company, subject to deployment with other such
companies in ad hoc battalions when necessary, although compli-
ance with this order seems to have been erratic. Some of the light
infantry companies in the "Second Establishment" of Continental
units were rifle companies, while others were armed with smoothbore muskets. Daniel Morgan was detached with the army's rifle
companies to reinforce the northern army's fight against
Burgoyne in 1777, and thus became the first independent
American light infantry commander. As previously noted,
Washington created another temporary organization under
General Maxwell for the Philadelphia campaign. Maxwell's unit,
composed of men designated by their regimental commanders,
was disbanded and its soldiers returned to their parent organizations following the Battle of Germantown. In the summer of 1778,
all of the Continental units of picked men could be considered as
serving a light infantry function, although Morgan's mixed unit
of riflemen and musket "marksmen" were the army's official light
infantry unit which, unfortunately, never entered battle at
Monmouth Court House. Morgan was replaced by General
Wayne as light infantry commander in 1779. Wayne's "Light
Infantry Corps" was based upon consolidating the light infantry
companies of the line regiments, which had all been created by
this time. It served as a battalion for independent service during
the campaigning season, and was disbanded at the end of that
year. The battalion was remustered for the 1780 campaign season
under Major General Arthur St. Clair and then Lafayette.
Disbanded over the winter and instituted again in 1781 under
Lafayette, the Continental light infantry distinguished itself during the Yorktown campaign. Training presumably followed
British example, but with a Steuben twist.[12]

LINE INFANTRY

In addition to emphasizing the light infantry role in combat,
General Howe also ordered his line infantry to cease using the
standard three-rank formation and adopt a more open two-rank
formation to adapt to American conditions, although this practice

seems to have been in effect, at least in part, prior to his arrival in America on May 25, 1775. An order from "Head Quarters Boston" dated February 29, 1775, reads: "The Regts when formed by companies in Battn or when on ye Genl. Parade are always to have their files 18 inches distance from each other which they will take care to practice for the future, it being the order they are to ingaged the Eneminey." By August, one officer recorded that "the infantry of the Army without exception are ordered upon all occasions to form two deep, with the files at 18 inches interval till further orders." The resultant formation, which presented a much broader front than the usual three-rank close formation used in Europe (and inaccurately portrayed in Pyle's Bunker Hill), along with the aggressive light infantry tactics, came to be known as the "loose file and American scramble" battle formation, used along with the outflanking maneuvers so favored by British commanders after the Bunker Hill disaster. One historian maintains that "Howe then took the whole process a stage further by effectively training all his regular infantry as light troops." One surviving document, however, indicates that Howe's initial order to deploy in two ranks may not have been inspired by the idea of a more open and flexible formation. Instead, it may have been an attempt to cover a wider front per battalion with understrength units, which he used as an argument to convince Germain to send him replacements to bring his regiments up to authorized strength and increase each battalion to ten-line companies, although that step had already been taken, at least in theory.[13]

General Steuben's task in reforming American tactical training was to tighten up formations and make sure they moved with celerity and organization to a standard formula. Assuming that after three years of war, the soldiers already knew the basics of loading and firing their muskets, in the interest of expediency, Steuben began his training regimen in the spring of 1778 by skipping musketry drill and moving on to instruction in marching and maneuvering. Continental regiments received initial training from their own commanders using a variety of manuals, and the Prussian drillmaster would eventually produce one that would supplant all other publications. In the meantime, however, his cadre style of instruction, accelerated due to the need to create a universal system for the forthcoming campaign, quickly took hold. He soon had soldiers marching in "direct step, common time and quick time," fixing the problem that even a military naïf like John Adams perceived when the army marched through Philadelphia the year before, and then moving in unison in line and at oblique angles. Transferring these skills from the cadres to larger formations to eventually include the whole army was Steuben's goal, and he succeeded. There were two hours of drill every day in the waning months at Valley Forge, and when Washington's army took the field in June, it was as well prepared as it could be to stand up to the enemy on that enemy's own terms.[14]

UNIFORMS

British soldiers not only moved and shot better than their film stereotypes convey, but also had a different appearance in the field than popular portrayals indicate. By midwar, most British troops had adapted their clothing to the rough-and-ready combat conditions in America. Starting with light infantry units and spreading to the line companies, uniforms were heavily modified; coats were cut short, or dispensed with altogether in favor of waistcoats with sleeves sewed on; cocked hats were "unflapped" or converted to caps; and tight knee breeches and gaiters were replaced by more comfortable cotton duck "trouser-gaiters." Company officers dispensed with wigs and braid, and wore comfortable clothing similar to what they would wear while engaging in hunting or other outdoor sports at home. German jaegers wore green uniform coats as did Loyalist units like Simcoe's Queen's Rangers, "accoutered for concealment," and Simcoe himself noted that the gradual fading of the natural dye in his men's coats from green to brown over the campaign season provided an unintended camouflage asset.[15]

While British soldiers adapted their uniforms to American conditions, and sometimes suffered shortages due to long supply routes, the inadequate American supply system often failed to supply not only uniforms, but clothing of any sort, to the

Soldier of the Forty-second Foot "Black Watch" Regiment. This man is a member of the Grenadier Company, which would have fought at the hedgerow as part of Clinton's First Grenadier Battalion. The soldiers of the Forty-second's first battalion, who engaged Cilley's picked men late in the afternoon, would have looked very similar, the only uniform difference being the shoulder "wings" designating he is a member of one of the regiment's elite companies. (*Painting by Don Troiani www.historicalartprints.com*)

Continental army. Confusing state and Congressional responsibilities added to the problem. John U. Rees's detailed study of the New Jersey Brigade's clothing reveals that there was little, if any, uniformity of dress in the brigade by the Battle of Monmouth Court House. Although, as Rees points out, New Jersey's logistical situation was in some ways unique, since the state had no major ports of entry, and the British controlled both Philadelphia and New York for much of the time between 1776 and 1778, his conclusions can serve as a model for what much of the American army probably looked like at Monmouth. The "Second Establishment" New Jersey Brigade of four regiments was organized in the early part of 1777, but there is no evidence of uniform issue until May of that year, when the Third Regiment was issued blue coats with red facings, reminiscent of the "Jersey Blues" uniform of the French and Indian War. Inferential information from deserter descriptions suggests a mix of clothing, including blue and brown coats and linen hunting shirts, along with buckskin breeches, in the brigade's other regiments. Although there was no strict uniformity, all the men were reasonably well clothed by mid-1777, with most having uniform coats of some kind. Thus dressed, the Jerseyans fought in the Philadelphia campaign.[16]

Much of the Jersey Brigade's 1777 clothing issue was worn out by early 1778. In February and March, the unit received a few uniform coats and cloth to make a few more, but the Jerseymen were quite literally charity cases, as New Jersey civilians and church congregations collected blankets, coats, shirts, breeches, socks, and other articles of clothing to send to their troops at Valley Forge. Colonel Israel Shreve of the Second Regiment and Lieutenant Colonel David Brearley of the Fourth Regiment personally sought clothing and cloth for their men in Salem County. The nine-month service draftees that joined the brigade in late spring were even more diversely dressed than their Continental comrades in arms. Most apparently were issued an eclectic array of clothing, including civilian coats, linen hunting shirts, and wool breeches, by the state, but others supplied their own, probably civilian, garb in return for a "clothing bounty." Rees concludes that 25 percent of the nine-month "levies" wore their personal

A contemporary watercolor by a French officer of American soldiers at the time of the battle of Yorktown. From left to right, they represent a private of the 1st Rhode Island Regiment, a soldier of an unidentified infantry regiment, a rifleman in hunting shirt, and an artillery officer. (*Brown University Library*)

clothing to the war. In 1775, New Jersey's "Minute Men" were instructed to wear hunting shirts, and some may have been worn by former Minute Men among the levies. Although it is impossible to know for sure, the probability is that the long-service Continentals in the brigade were dressed in a similar manner, with a few leftover uniform coats, hunting shirts, and civilian clothing. Surviving evidence indicates that most of the rest of the army was similarly outfitted. The American army became better and more uniformly dressed by 1779, when uniform supplies from France arrived.[17]

WEAPONS

Muskets

The vast majority of Revolutionary War soldiers, no matter the army they served in, were armed with flintlock ignition smoothbore muskets. The smoothbore flintlock, or "firelock" musket, the most common small arm on the field at Monmouth, had a long and honored tenure, and was in service for a longer period of time than any other small arm system in military history. Although various models and styles of this gun—primarily of British and French, but also German and occasionally of other European or domestic American manufacture—were used by both sides at Monmouth Court House, they were all alike in that they used flint striking steel for ignition and were loaded from the muzzle, with the interiors of their barrels bored smooth, like a modern shotgun.

Although it could be loaded using a powder horn and attached measure, and separate spherical ball encased in a greased patch or wadded with tow or paper, the musket's ammunition usually came in the form of a paper cartridge containing powder charge and ball. The soldier tore open the base of the cartridge with his teeth, used some of the powder charge to prime the gun's priming "pan," poured the remainder down the barrel and then inserted the ball, still wrapped in cartridge paper, in the musket's muzzle and rammed it down with the ramrod, which was carried in a stock slot underneath the barrel. When the trigger was pulled, a piece of flint in the jaws of the hammer struck a steel "frizzen" and showered sparks into the priming powder in the pan, which, when ignited, flashed through a vent hole to explode the main charge in the barrel, firing the gun.

Almost universal acceptance as the best infantry weapon of its day did not save the musket from being disparaged by some military men, however. Its historical reputation for inherent inaccuracy rests, for many modern readers, on an oft-quoted 1814 passage by Revolutionary War veteran and British colonel George Hanger. Hanger served in the American War at one point as, improbably, the commander of a Hessian jaeger company, a rifle-armed unit, which no doubt contributed to his contempt for the musket.[18]

> A soldier's musket, if not exceedingly badly bored, and very crooked, as many are, will strike the figure of a man at 80 yards, it may even at 100 yards, but a soldier must be very unfortunate indeed who shall be wounded by a common musket at 150 yards, provided his antagonist aims at him; and as to firing at a man at 200 yards with a common musket, you may just as well fire at the moon, and have the same hopes of hitting your object.[19]

In fact, David Harding (whose four-volume study of the weapons of the British East India Company is a firearms history tour de force) found "no evidence to substantiate Hanger's assertion that either in the Royal or [British East India] Company's service 'many' muskets were 'exceedingly badly bored, and very crooked.'" Harding notes that of 7,500 muskets sent to Bengal in 1799, only 0.61 percent were found, on inspection, to have "crooked barrels," a percentage that is probably similar to that of the muskets of other major powers of the era.[20]

In fact, a well-bored firelock smoothbore musket, if properly loaded, aimed and fired by a trained individual, is capable of reasonable accuracy on man-sized targets up to eighty yards or so, and effective on large formations at ranges up to two hundred yards. Although this conclusion, on examination, does not materially disagree with Hanger's statement on individual target hit ratios, it recognizes the reality that large formations were routinely encountered in combat in the eighteenth century, and that effective musket range on the battlefield was therefore longer than a first reading of Hanger might suggest. In other words, the accuracy of the flintlock musket was adequate for the job it needed to do. That and other attributes made the musket the preferred military weapon of its time for good reason.

The flintlock was a vast improvement over the matchlock system it replaced even though both muskets were loaded with powder and ball from the muzzle. The matchlock was fired by means of a slow burning, potassium nitrate soaked cord or "match," held in the jaws of a piece of metal called a "serpentine," which, when lowered into the priming pan, fired the gun. When King William III landed in Britain from Holland in 1688 as successor to the deposed James II, he brought with him an aggregation of foreign troops and weapons. William's battles with James's Irish loyalists at the Boyne, Aughrim, and the Siege of Limerick were fought with a mix of arms. Flintlock muskets, however, outnumbered matchlock guns in the Anglo-Dutch Williamite army, and provided an initial tactical advantage over Irish Jacobites armed mostly with matchlocks. The few flintlocks in the Irish ranks were issued to "fusiliers" guarding the artillery, where waving a glowing match was deemed imprudent around large powder charges. To redress the arms imbalance, the Jacobites ordered 3,000 flintlock "fusils" from their French patrons.[21]

Not only was the matchlock a more dangerous system for both the shooter and those around him, it had a significantly slower rate of fire than the system that replaced it. A matchlock's burning match had to be constantly readjusted between shots and, to minimize the danger of inadvertent explosion, was removed from the musket during the loading process. An inert flint did not have to be removed from the gun, was good for a relatively large number of shots, and could be chipped, or "knapped," to fire a few more shots when it became dull through use.

Despite these improvements, the flintlock did have, by modern standards, a high percentage of misfires attributable to a number of possible causes. The British army came to think that an improperly "set" flint that did not strike the frizzen in the proper place, about one-third of the way down its length, was a major cause of misfires, leading to an 1809 General Order stressing the importance of securing the flint in the cock at the proper angle, but there is no evidence that such serious attention was paid to the problem in 1778. The overall musket misfire rate, whether as a result of poor installation of the flint in the jaws of the cock by the soldier, a defect in the flint itself, a wearing down of the flint's initially sharp edge, or other mishaps, including insufficient priming placed in the pan, weak mainsprings, clogged vent holes, or weather conditions, appears, according to extensive early nineteenth-century tests, to have been around 15 percent. Recocking the gun and pulling the trigger a second time often resolved the problem.[22]

Despite its drawbacks, the flintlock was a vast improvement over the matchlock. Imported European flintlocks predominated in British service until the reign of King George I. In 1715 George's government created the "Board of Ordnance," which established the "Ordnance system of manufacture." The system created standards of government acceptance for weapons and developed a network of domestic contractors who supplied the

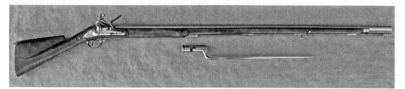

A modern handmade reproduction by Phil Ackerman of a .75 caliber First Model Long Land Pattern musket with socket bayonet. The bayonet securing lug atop the barrel also served as a crude sight. This musket has the original issue type wooden ramrod. Many were later replaced with iron or steel ramrods. (*Jeff Williams*)

government with musket parts, which were delivered to approved gun builders, who assembled them into finished muskets.[23]

Although the Board of Ordnance reduced British dependence on foreign firearms makers and raised the quality and quantity of domestic musket manufacturing, the guns produced in the board's early years demonstrated a lack of standardization, with both Dutch and French influences apparent. By the early 1730s, however, the distinguishing characteristics of what came to be known as the "King's Arm" or "Long Land Pattern" musket, including a forty-six-inch .75-caliber barrel, walnut stock, "banana"-shaped lock plate, and brass furnishings, were standardized.[24]

The design evolved and improved in succeeding years. Some changes, like ramrod pipe and trigger guard configuration, lock plate profile, and stock carving patterns, were largely minor and cosmetic. Others, including variations in the shape and strength of the cock, the addition of a "bridle" supporting the priming pan, and the replacement of the gun's wooden ramrod with a stout steel or iron one, were decided improvements on the musket's efficiency and durability. The metal ramrod adopted after 1750 was a particularly important innovation, as it not only eliminated the possibility of guns becoming useless through ramrod breakage, but also actually increased a soldier's rate of fire since the heavier rod drove a load home more rapidly. Many Long Land Pattern guns were modified and updated while being repaired. The most common upgrade was replacing a wooden rod with a steel one.[25]

A "Short Land Pattern" musket, initially conceived as a dragoon carbine, appeared in the early 1740s. The only difference between this gun and its Long Land counterpart was the newer model's shorter forty-two-inch barrel. Although the Short Land musket became the standard British infantry weapon in 1768, both Long and Short Land guns were produced simultaneously for many years after that, and both were issued to British troops and their Loyalist allies serving in America during the Revolutionary War. The shorter pattern predominated, but some Long Land Pattern guns were still being made in Britain as late as 1790. Many Long Land Pattern muskets in service in Loyalist units still had wooden ramrods midway through the Revolutionary War. Some of the newer British East India Company "India Pattern" muskets, shorter and with simpler hardware, apparently saw service in America as well.

A perennial question regarding the Land Pattern musket is how and where it gained the "Brown Bess" nickname commonly used today. There is some question as to whether or not the sobriquet was actually in use during the Revolution. A number of stories regarding its origins, none of them really satisfactory, have been advanced. It is generally agreed, however, that the term "Brown Bess" made its first appearance in print in 1785. It has been conjectured that the word "Brown" refers to either the barrel finish or the color of the gun's stock. In fact, "browning," as a British military barrel finish, was not introduced until New Land Pattern musket production, some seventeen years after the term Brown Bess appeared in print. There is also no evidence for the theory that the Long Land Pattern stock, left in its natural brown color, departed from an alleged previous practice of painting gunstocks black and gave rise to the name. Some have maintained that "Bess" is a reference to Queen Elizabeth I, but this seems improbable, since "Good Queen Bess" passed from the scene 182 years before the first mention of the words "Brown Bess."

Interestingly, a late eighteenth-century slang term for enlisting in the British army was to "hug Brown Bess," and the words were, for many, no doubt, endearing ones–but not for all. Some British soldiers were not that enthralled with the "King's Arm." Even after standards were improved, the system of using numerous contractors to produce guns had its weaknesses. In 1774, British commanders in the field complained about the "new Firelocks" issued to their units. The guns had "stocks swelled so much [from improperly seasoned wood], that the locks would not stand at half Cock . . . Feather Springs and Dog Screws which being soft, lost their hold," and "Breech Pins [breech plugs]" that "obstructed the Touch [vent] holes," among other things. Gunsmiths had to be dispatched from London to fix the problems in the field. One officer, who served in the Peninsular Campaign more than thirty years later, was quoted by historian Paddy Griffith as noting that his men's guns were "of bad quality." The officer added that "soldiers might be seen creeping about to get hold of the firelocks of the killed and wounded, to try if the locks were better than theirs and dashing the worst to the ground as if in a rage with it." Conversely, he believed that the French "fine, long, light firelocks, with a small bore [.69 caliber], are more efficient for skirmishing than our abominably clumsy machine." Another critic carped that "the Brown Bess was the very clumsiest and worst contrived of any firelock in the world." Not everyone shared that opinion. A mounted New Jersey militiaman reported that he picked up British muskets dropped by the enemy at Monmouth Court House, "as many as I could conveniently manage on my horse, with their bayonets fixed upon them," and "gave them to the [American] soldiers as they stood in rank. They threw away their French pieces, preferring the British." One rationale for the preference could be that the Americans had fired so many rounds that their French muskets had fouled, making it difficult to ram down ball and cartridge paper. The larger-bored British musket would still function well with the smaller French ammunition.[26]

What then, was the battle record of this allegedly clumsy, inaccurate piece of ordnance? It was, for the most part, as good as the men who carried the gun and those who led them. The combat honors of the series of Land Pattern British muskets are long, beginning with the War of the Austrian Succession, from 1740 to 1748. The tried and true musket won Britain the Indian jewel in the crown of empire and conquered Canada as well. That it failed to secure the American colonies was not its fault.

Kevin Marshall fires a reproduction .69 caliber Charleville musket in shooting tests conducted using original style ball and buck and ball cartridges. (*Joseph Bilby*)

Significant stocks of Long Land Pattern muskets, and colony-owned guns that were close copies of the standard British arm were in private possession and local government stocks at the outbreak of the Revolutionary War, and until French muskets began to flow into patriot hands, were the most common Continental army weapons. It is probable that any privately owned guns brought to the Jersey Brigade and other Continental units by militia draftees in the spring of 1778 were Long Land Pattern muskets or locally manufactured copies. American made guns were often dual-use paramilitary-style weapons, suitable for hunting as well as meeting militia requirements. Individual colonies also purchased muskets quite similar to the official military pattern from private contractors in England before the war. Early pattern French muskets captured during the series of wars for empire that ended in 1763 were also in private and colony possession in 1775. As the Revolution progressed, states like New Jersey rewarded British deserters who brought their weapons with them into American lines. Four deserters who made their way to Trenton in February 1778 were paid sixty dollars for "four stand of arms," a term that would include a cartridge box and bayonet for each. There is a strong possibility that those weapons may have been issued to the levies sent to reinforce the Jersey Brigade before the Monmouth campaign.[27]

American agents began to seek arms abroad at the outset of the Revolution, and the shadow corporation of Hortalez & Cie was used to covertly purchase arms from the French government beginning in the summer of 1776. By the end of that year, muskets and other arms and ammunition by the shipload were arriving in America. By the Battle of Monmouth, most Continental units had been completely rearmed with new French muskets, chiefly 1763 models. These guns were different from the British pattern in two significant ways. Their barrels were held to the guns' stocks by barrel bands that encircled both rather than pins, which ran through the stock and tenons affixed to the bottom of the barrel, and they were of .69 rather than .75 caliber. Although the French muskets are usually identified as Charleville pattern arms, that classification is not exactly correct, as there were two French national armories that produced and marked these guns, Charleville and Maubeuge. Many, but not all, French muskets in American service were marked "US" or "U States."[28]

Rifles

The rifle was a far more accurate arm, at least in theory, than the musket, and some were probably in use at Monmouth Court House—on both sides. Spiral grooves, or rifling, cut in a gun barrel's interior, stabilized a ball fired in it and made the arm more accurate for a longer distance. In order to engage the grooves, however, the undersized ball had to be encased in a tight-fitting greased patch while loading the gun from the muzzle, so that spin could be imparted to the ball on firing. American rifles did not use cartridges, and the powder charge was poured from a powder horn into a measure and then down the barrel. Measuring powder and ramming tightly patched balls slowed down the loading process so that the rifleman's rate of fire was half or less the speed of a man armed with a musket. Thus, although rifled arms were available in central Europe by the sixteenth century, smooth-bores—cheaper to manufacture and faster to reload—remained in favor for the majority of military tasks for several hundred years. Rifled arms definitely saw some military service in the ranks of seventeenth- and eighteenth-century European elite troops, however, including Austrian and German jaegers, and French

A Pennsylvania rifle of the 1780s, probably made in Berks County, Pennsylvania. The gun has a 42-inch octagonal barrel, curly maple stock, and fittings of brass. (*Courtesy Norm Flayderman*)

tirailleurs and chasseurs. King Christian IV of Denmark put rifles in the hands of his bodyguard detachment prior to 1622, some French cavalrymen were issued rifles in the 1670s, and Tsar Peter the Great introduced rifles for special-service troops in the Russian army in 1715. Rifles came to be considered important special purpose weapons by both sides in the Revolution. German jaegers and even some British light infantrymen and Loyalists, as well as American frontiersmen, were armed with rifles throughout the war.[29]

Some popular mythmakers credit the superior accuracy of the American rifle over the British smoothbore musket as a factor in the loss of the American colonies, but there is absolutely no evidence that this was the case. Although locally important on occasion, and useful for special purposes, the rifle, which was not equipped to mount a bayonet, was not a decisive weapon, and General George Washington converted many of his riflemen into musket-wielding light infantrymen late in the war. Washington's disenchantment with riflemen may have begun early, since an account of the 1775 Siege of Boston includes the observation that riflemen, many of whom came to the army with a frontier ethos, were an "undisciplined set of villains" and that "Mr. Washington is very sensible of this." Actually, many eighteenth-century Americans were ignorant of the rifle and its capabilities at the outbreak of the Revolution, as evidenced by John Adams's surprised comment on the accuracy of "a peculiar kind of musket, called a rifle," carried by Virginians, Marylanders, and Pennsylvanians joining the 1775 Siege of Boston. Although riflemen certainly contributed to the Revolutionary cause on a number of battlefields, most notably Kings Mountain (where Americans fought each other), their overall tactical importance has often been grossly exaggerated.[30]

Many larger-than-life tales of American riflemen can be traced to press propaganda designed to scare British soldiers scheduled to serve in America, as the stories were often reprinted in English newspapers. In the event, the British, although they may have been apprehensive at first, learned to deal with the rifle threat through spirited and rapid offensive movements. Captain William Dansey of the Thirty-third Foot's Light Infantry company noted that "they [American riflemen] are not so dreadful as I expected," after his regiment routed and captured a rifle-armed unit following a vigorous bayonet charge on Long Island in 1776.[31]

Most present-day antique arms collectors classify American-made colonial-era rifles as "Pennsylvania" rifles, in reference to the notable group of rifle makers located in that state, but rifles were made in a number of areas adjacent to the frontier in the eighteenth century, including Maryland, Virginia, and the Carolinas, often by craftsmen of German heritage. Although some rifles were apparently purchased by state governments during the war, most appear to have been the private property of the men who used them. The typical rifle of the era was between .50 and .60 caliber, with a barrel at least forty inches long, and a "patch box" inset or cut into the butt stock. The patch box, used to hold shooting patches and a beeswax and tallow lubricant, had a sliding wood cover in earlier guns, with later versions usually featuring hinged iron or brass covers. Most of these rifles lacked the ornate brass and silver ornamentation like that featured on rifles produced in the 1790s.[32]

Despite the apparent problems of American riflemen—often more attributable to lack of discipline than their weapons—the potential military usefulness of the rifle in special operations led to limited issue in the British army as early as the French and Indian wars. Rifles were shipped from Britain to Louisbourg as early as 1746, a dozen rifles were issued to General Braddock's 1755 expedition, and ten "Rifled Barrelled guns were delivered out to each regiment to be put in the hands of their best marksmen" in General James Abercromby's ill-fated 1758 expedition to capture Fort Carillon.[33]

The principal riflemen of the British army in America during the Revolution were the German jaegers, armed with rifles that were shorter barreled and of somewhat larger caliber than those of their American counterparts. All but one company of these soldiers were also armed with short swords rather than bayonets. Surviving guns attributed to the jaegers average around .65 caliber, and probably fired a patched .615-diameter ball, which is the British "carbine"-size projectile. As riflemen with the training and discipline of a regular military force, jaegers were, at least initially, arguably more effective soldiers than their more independent-minded American counterparts.[34]

There were also rifles in British light infantry ranks. In 1776, the Crown contracted one thousand rifles for service in America. One officer reported that "the Highlanders who have many marksmen & Deer Killers amongst them are particularly desirous of having 5 of these pieces [rifles] per company." At least some of the British Pattern 1776 rifles, and perhaps all of the barrels used to make them, were imported from Germany, and reflect German design ideas. The limited British rifle issue supplemented the far more numerous German jaegers. Although only several hundred jaegers were on duty with Clinton's army crossing New Jersey in the summer of 1778, De Witt Bailey, the most astute student of eighteenth-century rifle use in the British army, totaled up the numbers of German riflemen from various principalities on duty in all areas of North America during the entire course of the war, and added the known numbers of rifles issued to British regular troops, to arrive at a total of fifty-one hundred rifles in service at one time or another in royal ranks during the conflict. That does not include Loyalists who brought their own rifled arms to the fray, or American rifles acquired by the British from prisoners and deserters and available for reissue to British soldiers, Loyalists, or Indian allies.[35]

The Pattern 1776 British rifles began to reach the field late that summer and were issued throughout the army. They were German-style short-barreled guns of "carbine bore," the same caliber as surviving jaeger rifles. Muzzles were "coned" or taper bored, larger than bullet diameter to facilitate more rapid loading and possible loading with paper cartridges. Issue records remain vague, but it appears that Highland regiments, as requested, received five rifles per company. Rifles were apparently also issued to a dismounted company of the Sixteenth Light Dragoons, which arrived in America in September 1776. There is also evidence that some light infantrymen in General Grey's force at Paoli were armed with rifles, as well as one company of Simcoe's Queen's Rangers. It is highly probable that some Pattern 1776 rifles were on the field at Monmouth in the ranks of Clinton's light infantry and the Forty-second Foot.[36]

Undoubtedly, the most exotic firearm that saw possible, even probable, if limited service at Monmouth Court House was the Ferguson breech-loading rifle, the invention of British officer Patrick Ferguson. Brilliant, brave, arrogant, and foolhardy, Ferguson was born in Edinburgh, Scotland, on June 4, 1744. His parents, James and Anne Murray Ferguson, were members of the minor gentry who socialized with Scottish Enlightenment figures like philosopher David Hume and novelist Tobias Smollet. Young "Pattie's" military career began in 1759, when his father purchased him a cornet's commission in the North British Dragoons (later the Scots Greys). Britain was then engaged in the Seven Years' War, and Ferguson served with his regiment in Germany until 1761, when he was invalided home with an ulcerated leg. After a stint in the West Indies and another convalescence, he returned to active duty in 1774, when the military talents he displayed at General Howe's light infantry training camp caught the eye of the British general.

It is likely that Ferguson's interest in training and leading light troops was responsible for his desire to develop a breech-loading rifle, which, combining accuracy and rapidity of fire, would be an asset to soldiers fighting independently and engaged in diverse duties. Breech-loading firearms were not a new phenomenon in the late eighteenth century, but most early versions suffered from excessive gas escape at the breech on firing. Frenchman Isaac de la Chaumette designed one of the best of these guns in 1700, and received an English patent on it in 1721. To operate the Chaumette, which used a vertical screw breech plug limiting gas escape, the operator swiveled its trigger guard in one direction to open the breech for loading, and in the other direction to close it prior to firing. Once loaded, the gun's pan was primed, and it was cocked and fired in the same manner as a muzzle-loading flint-lock. Several prominent British gun makers built Chaumette-style breech-loading rifles, including one for King George I.[37]

The Chaumette action was advocated for trial use in cavalry carbines by French marshal Maurice de Saxe, who also advocated aimed fire by light infantrymen to pave the way for an assault, but there is no evidence that the French army ever adopted the weapon; nor did the British military, although a Chaumette wall gun was used to fire an eight-ounce ball eight hundred yards in Dublin in 1761. The Chaumette's major drawback as a military arm was that its action screw threads began to fill with burned powder fouling after a small number of shots, making it difficult to operate and reducing its rate of fire. This defect was not impor-tant in hunting guns, but rendered the action unsatisfactory for military applications. In 1762, the British Board of Ordnance test-ed rifles based on two variants of the Chaumette "screwplug sys-tem" and purchased samples of other variants in succeeding years. Although none were accepted for service, the board was hardly unaware of the existence or functioning of breech-loading rifles, including their advantages and disadvantages, prior to Ferguson's invention.[38]

Ferguson's solution to the fouling problem was to cut trans-verse channels across the screw threads, reducing accumulation, and thus improving the overall rate of fire, although there is so lit-tle difference from the original Chaumette design that one mod-ern scholar noted that "it is extremely difficult to see what inno-vations Ferguson was patenting." In the spring of 1776, he demon-strated his breechloader for a number of important government officials and army officers, including Lord Viscount Townshend and Lord Amherst. In "a heavy rain and a high wind," Ferguson loaded and shot his rifle for five straight minutes, maintaining an aimed fire rate of four rounds a minute, and, at one span, six

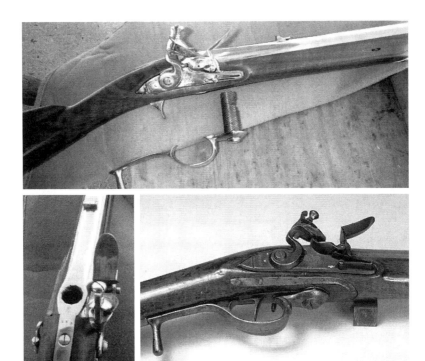

Top, reproduction Ferguson breechloading rifle, with trigger guard screw breech completely out. When firing, the breech was lowered but remained in the gun. Bottom left, reproduction Ferguson breechloading rifle showing breech hole where bullet and powder charge were loaded. (*Joseph Bilby, Courtesy Bill Winslow*) Bottom right, very rare original Ferguson rifle at Morristown National Military Park. Note repair to stock. The few surviving Fergusons commonly have a similar repair, leading to the conclusion that they were fairly fragile in this area. (*National Park Service*)

rounds in a minute. His performance was notable, and included hitting a bull's eye of unreported size at one hundred yards from the prone position. A subsequent demonstration at Windsor Castle, at which he told the king he could fire seven shots a minute, gained his invention even more favorable publicity.[39]

While the Ferguson rifle's normal rate of fire was not significantly higher than the British army-issue smoothbore musket, which a well-trained man could fire three times a minute, it was much more accurate than the musket. It was also faster to load than the usual muzzle-loading rifle, which needed a patched ball to properly engage the rifling. A Ferguson shooter merely dropped a naked ball into the open breech, followed it with a powder charge, and then swiveled the breech closed and primed the gun's pan. More significantly, the Ferguson was easier for a prone soldier to load. The Board of Ordnance, impressed by Ferguson and his gun, instructed gun makers already making 1776 Pattern muzzle-loading rifles to produce a hundred Ferguson breechloaders as well. William Grice, Benjamin Willetts, Mathias Barker, and Galton & Son each subsequently manufactured twenty-five Fergusons, all made to fire the .615 ball.[40]

Captain Ferguson was authorized to raise a one-hundred-man company of green-clad light infantry "formed for the purpose of making experiment of some Rifle barrel pieces of a new Construction" for American service. These soldiers were not selected due to any civilian marksmanship background (minimal to nonexistent in Britain among the common folk), but drawn from a detachment of raw recruits and noncommissioned officers of the Sixth and Fourteenth regiments of foot stationed at Chatham Barracks. Ferguson assumed command of the company on March 6, 1777, and conducted a brief but intensive training regimen in tactics and shooting. The company was supplied with green uniform coats, powder flasks, slings, high-quality rifle powder, and bullet molds before taking ship for America at the end of the month, where, as previously noted, Ferguson and his riflemen first saw action during the later stages of the New Jersey Forage War, skirmishing at Bonhamtown and Short Hills, and as part of the rear guard when the British evacuated New Jersey in June 1777.[41]

During the road up to Brandywine, Ferguson and his company, along with other light infantry troops, conducted reconnaissance missions and then engaged local militia and Maxwell's American light infantry. On the morning of September 11, 1777, the overconfident British advance guard was badly shot up in a Maxwell ambush, but recovered and continued to press forward in a confused running gunfight up to Brandywine Creek. In a letter recapping his experience that day, Ferguson stressed the advantage his men had of being able to fall on the ground and reload from that position with their breechloaders. They could, he recalled, "keep up a rattling fire from the ground," which proved advantageous. Of course, as Dr. Honyman's observations reveal, regular light infantrymen were trained to fire from the prone position as well, although their rate of fire would have necessarily been slower with muzzleloaders.[42]

Badly wounded in his right elbow joint during the battle, Ferguson gamely refused amputation and painfully convalesced in British-occupied Philadelphia for the next eight months, undergoing several operations without anesthetic to remove bone fragments from his now permanently disabled arm and teaching himself to write left-handed. Following Brandywine, Ferguson's men were reassigned, with their rifles, to the light infantry companies of their original regiments to fight alongside light infantrymen armed with muskets and Pattern 1776 muzzleloaders. Although one account has the breechloaders turned in and stored for the rest of the war, recent research indicates that was not the case, as a memorandum penned in New York on July 24, 1778, mentions that any Ferguson rifles, bayonets, and powder flasks still in service be turned in for repairs. A Ferguson trigger guard was uncovered in an archaeological dig at a British campsite near New York City in 1986, showing probable use for at least some period of time after Clinton's 1778 arrival in the city.[43]

Although disabled, Captain Ferguson, whose original orders stated that he should return to his regiment at the close of the Philadelphia campaign, remained with the main British army, and was probably with Clinton when he marched across New Jersey. It is exceedingly likely that some of his breechloaders were still in service that summer in the light infantry battalions, although not in the hands of men under his command. After the British army reached New York, Ferguson was promoted and assigned to lead a composite force of Loyalists and regulars. In October 1778 he raided Little Egg Harbor, New Jersey, burning privateer ships, salt works, and the village of Chestnut Neck on the Mullica River, and conducting a successful surprise attack on Colonel Casimir Pulaski's Legion. Ferguson's star was on the rise once more, and the following year he commanded an "American Volunteer" corps of 175 soldiers drawn from New York and New Jersey Loyalist battalions, and deployed in the south after the capture of Charleston. There is no evidence however, that any of his breech-loading rifles, if they were still accessible, were used to arm either the Egg Harbor raiders or the American Volunteers. The Ferguson rifle apparently fired its first and last shots in combat in New Jersey in 1777 and 1778.[44]

As the British field army under General Cornwallis moved north through the Carolinas, Ferguson, commanding an increasingly ragged force of Tory militia and volunteers, served as its left wing. Rashly, as was his wont, Ferguson penetrated deeper into the American interior than he should have, and when the "over mountain men" responded to his bluster by mobilizing and moving across the Blue Ridge to join the patriot militia of the Carolinas, he fell back to Kings Mountain, where, on the afternoon of October 7, 1780, he met his end as the Americans overran his position in an hour-long firefight. Ferguson died in a hail of gunfire along with his mistress, Virginia Sal, as they attempted to escape. The victors took two pistols off his body. There was not a breech-loading rifle to be found on the field.

Some modern authors, taken with the romance of the Ferguson story, and accepting the facts of his rifle's superiority at face value, believe that the gun, if manufactured in large numbers, would have been a war winner for the British. One writer has explained British failure to recognize what to him should have been obvious policy as due to "the political incompetency of Lord North's administration and the military incompetency of the War Office." According to this theory, "a large number of these weapons in the hands of trained men would have won the Revolution for the British in its first few months." Of course, this viewpoint ignores the political, social, and military complexity of the war, as well as the limits of eighteenth-century production capabilities, reducing the conflict to a cartoon-like shootout, but also fails to recognize technical problems apparent in the Ferguson design.[45]

Just how effective was the Ferguson in actual and potential use? The National Park Service actually test fired an original specimen in its collection in a Washington laboratory many years ago.

Three shots fired at a range of thirty yards from a bench rest provided a less than spectacular result, with the gun turning in a four-inch group. A 2003 test with a reproduction Ferguson made by Narragansett Arms, conducted by one of the authors, proved more successful, with one shooter firing a two-inch group offhand at twenty-five yards, and three different shooters consistently hitting cans and gallon jugs at fifty yards' range, using a charge of forty grains of GOEX FFFg black powder. Interestingly, enough powder remained on top of the breech after loading to quickly flick some down into the priming pan, which may have helped Ferguson achieve his rapidity of fire. After a half-dozen rounds, accumulated powder fouling made it necessary to push the ball forward with finger pressure on loading, which would reduce the rifle's long-term rate of fire. True to the design's promise, no gas escape was noted.[46]

The facts then, suggest that the Ferguson rifle, despite its seeming potential, failed to materialize as an effective firearm in extended field service. The chief problem seems to have been the weakness of the stock around the action, caused by the necessity to remove wood to fit the breech section and lock. Surviving rifles show evidence of "extensive damage and in one case contemporary repair" in this area. In addition, although Ferguson claimed great things for his handful of riflemen on the road to Brandywine, the truth is that their activities had absolutely no effect on the outcome of the battle. In his book *British Military Flintlock Rifles, 1740–1840*, small arms scholar De Witt Bailey effectively demolishes the myth of the Ferguson rifle as a potential war winner.[47]

CAVALRY AND OFFICER WEAPONS

Mounted forces played a limited role in the American Revolution, although the Sixteenth Light Dragoons had a part in the opening stages of the fight at Monmouth Court House, and sabers and pistols were both used in that action. Handguns were largely limited to cavalrymen and privately purchased by higher-ranking mounted officers, who carried them in pairs in saddle holsters. On the British side, only two mounted regiments, the Sixteenth and

Seventeenth Light Dragoons, served in America, with many of their men in a dismounted role. Loyalist units like Simcoe's legion were deliberately organized with mounted and dismounted components, and hastily mounted Loyalist units organized toward the end of the war in the south were armed with a variety of weapons. American cavalry, although originally planned as a brigade organization, never met expectations, and only about thirty American dragoons were with Washington's army in the summer of 1778. American mounted men were supplemented by militia "light horse" in performing reconnaissance duties, although in this case the light horsemen would be better described as mounted infantry.

Dismounted British dragoons were issued short muskets or Pattern 1776 rifles, but mounted men were usually equipped with sabers and a brace of pistols, although they could also be issued a carbine. The issue handgun pattern remained virtually unchanged during the era. These flintlock pistols were usually .66 caliber to take a carbine ball, and had ten–inch smoothbore barrels, although some were bored to .56 caliber and fired a .517-diameter ball. All ammunition was loaded into paper cartridges. Handguns issued to American horse soldiers would have primarily been captured British issue or French imports, although some pistols were locally manufactured. Cavalry handguns were only effective at point blank range and practically impossible to reload on horseback during an action, so the saber became the main weapon of the mounted soldier. While making a reconnaissance of the British positions near Monmouth Court House just prior to the Battle of Monmouth, Baron von Steuben was pursued by some Queen's Rangers cavalrymen. Before hastily leaving the area, he fired both his pistols at them. There is no reason to believe he hit anybody, and it is one of the few documented instances of handgun use, aside from an ineffectual barrage of dragoon fire at Wayne's infantry a little later in the day.[48]

Company grade officers often carried an "espontoon" (also spelled as "spontoon") a spear-like weapon that was also useful for keeping battle lines straight when held parallel to the ground.

Many officers serving in America, however, whether Continental or British, carried fusees or "fusils," the latter term no longer simply a synonym for flintlock, but a term used to describe a light musket, usually of carbine bore. Officers' fusils were usually privately purchased and better-quality arms than the standard issue musket. For American service, many British sergeants, previously armed with halberds, a relatively useless weapon carried more as a sign of rank than as a serious combat arm, were issued government-purchased carbines and fusils. Some officers even carried standard infantry muskets, and this seems to have been the rule with company-grade American officers at the time of the Philadelphia campaign. A 1777 regulation required the states to provide "Muskets & Bayonets" to all "subalterns." Joseph Bloomfield, an officer in the New Jersey Brigade, carried a fusil or musket. In one fight with British raiders in Woodbridge on March 30, 1777, he reported that he "Fired eight

A line officer of the 3rd New Jersey Infantry in 1778. He is carrying a "spontoon," or "espontoon" which was both a badge of rank and a deadly close-quarters weapon. (*Peter Culos*)

Rounds myself being the first time I was ever in an action or saw the Enemy in the Field." At Brandywine, he wrote: "I was wounded, having a Ball with the Wad [probably cartridge paper] shot through my left forearm . . . a stranger dressed my wound with some tow from my Catorich [cartridge] box, & wrapped my Arm in my handkerchief." Tow was a coarse bundled fiber used for cleaning firearms and occasionally as wadding, and the fact that

Bloomfield was wearing a cartridge box indicates he was still carrying a musket or fusil. British Lieutenant-Colonel Cosmo
Gordon of the Third Foot Guards had "his bayonet shot off from
his fusee" during fighting at Monmouth. In January 1778,
Washington instructed brigades to issue "Aspontoons" to junior
officers, although supplies of the weapon were to prove insufficient, and as late as 1779, lieutenants and ensigns were still largely equipped with firearms. It may be assumed that company officers carried a mix of fusils, muskets, and espontoons at
Monmouth.[49]

AMMUNITION AND MARKSMANSHIP

The heart of the flintlock was, of course, its ignition, which, as
noted, could be problematic. Even when sharp and properly "set,"
a flint had to be firmly secured in the jaws of the hammer or
"cock" to avoid being knocked askew on firing. This task was
accomplished by wrapping the flint in material that was gripped
firmly by small teeth set in the jaws. Although leather was widely
used, the preferred wrapping was sheet lead. If there was no
inherent defect in the flint, it could last for numerous shots. The
figure of twenty shots is often cited, but an early nineteenth-century test revealed that the average life of a good flint was thirty-
three shots, with some lasting as long as seventy-five shots. There
are reports of British soldiers in the Revolution complaining
about the lifespan of their flints, with one colonel asserting the
"badness of the pebble stone" his men were issued caused them
to wear out or break after as little as six shots, in contrast to
American flints that lasted much longer. He went on to demand
that the government issue the black flints used by English gentle-
men in their sporting arms. The problem with the British flints
appears to have been due to the area from which the raw material
to make them was quarried. Through the 1790s, most British
flints came from contractors in Kent, and the stone used "was too
near the surface of the earth, and was too soft and easily crum-
bled." The Board of Ordnance did not begin purchasing the black
flints from Brandon in Suffolk so highly prized by eighteenth-century sportsmen until after the war. Those black flints, still available through muzzle-loading supply houses, are considered

among the best available by modern American flintlock shooters. It should be noted that the superior "American" flints the colonel referred to may well have been imported French ones.[50]

The basic and preferred ammunition form for muskets was the stiff paper cartridge, which contained powder for priming and main charge as well as the projectile, and served as wadding to encase the undersized ball in the barrel, assuring it would not roll out, and also acting as a stabilizing sabot on firing. Powder for British cartridges came from various contractors and was supposed to meet a declared standard—a sample two drams of powder had to "raise a weight of 24 lbs to 3 1/2 inches" when exploded under it. Consistency and quality of the powder supplied to the army during the war was apparently a significant problem, which led to the government purchase of its own powder mills. Cartridges were made up by the Ordnance Bureau and also on a regional and regimental basis. The Royal Artillery Field Train was usually responsible for making cartridges for use by an army on the move like Clinton's in 1778, although the actual work seems to have been performed by infantry details under artillery supervision, or entirely within a regiment. The completed cartridges had to pass through a gauge insuring they would easily fit the standard musket bore.[51]

The first gunpowder mill in America was established at Milton, Massachusetts, in 1675. Powder making in America in the next century was always hampered by an insufficient supply of saltpeter, or potassium nitrate, a necessary component along with sulfur and charcoal. During the war every state but Delaware established powder mills, and about 700,000 pounds of imported saltpeter was used in the domestic production of powder. About a third of the gunpowder used during the Revolution was domestically produced, and the remainder was imported. Cartridges used in American service were provided by contractors or made up by the troops themselves, who often cast their bullets from molten lead, as well as loading them into cartridges.[52]

Cartridges could contain one or multiple projectiles. By the time of the American Revolution, it was common practice to load smaller buckshot, usually around .31 or .32 caliber, along with a musket ball, in the cartridges used in .69- and .75-caliber muskets, to create a load known as "buck and ball." New Hampshire militiamen of 1776 were required to have "a pouch containing a cartridge-box that will hold fifteen rounds of cartridges at least, [and] a hundred buckshot." In June 1776, George Washington recommended that his men "load for the first fire, with one musket ball and four or eight buckshot according to the strength of their pieces." An October 1777 order specified that "buckshot are to be put into all cartridges which shall hereafter be made." The number of buckshot per cartridge used during the Revolution varied. In the 1775 American attack on Quebec, Captain Henry Dearborn carried a musket "charged with a ball and Ten Buckshott." Buckshot recovered from the walls of Nassau Hall in Princeton, where British soldiers were besieged during the January 3, 1777, battle there, are on display in the museum collection of the Historical Society of Princeton, and fired buckshot have been recovered during archaeological work at the site of the Monmouth Court House battle. Lieutenant-Colonel Sir John Wrottesley, commanding the "first company of the first battalion of [Foot] Guards," was grazed by a buckshot in close-range fighting in a woodlot at Monmouth.[53]

Most writers have assumed that adding buckshot to cartridges was a uniquely American practice. Recent research proves this not to be the case, however. British forces, at least in America, were using buck and ball cartridges at least as early as 1756, when a record of ordnance supplies at Fort William Henry on the shores of Lake George included fifty pounds of buckshot. On the 1758 expedition against Fort Duquesne, the men of each regiment were instructed to "provide themselves with buckshot," which was available from the artillery train, and in April 1758, a ton of buckshot was shipped to Albany. In May 1776, British troops in Boston had 600,000 buck and ball cartridges, with four buckshot loaded in each, available for use, and 1,344 pounds of buckshot were sent to Rhode Island in 1778. Other types of multiple projectile loads were not unknown as well. At least one British sentry served on guard duty with his musket loaded with a ball cut into eight pieces. In 1755, Colonel (later General) James Wolfe advised his officers to have their men load "two or three bullets into their pieces."[54]

The round balls loaded in cartridges in addition to buckshot, a practice which, although apparently common, was not universal, varied in diameter, but were usually well undersized in relation to the bore of the gun in which they were to be fired. British Long and Short Land Pattern muskets were a nominal .75 caliber, and the round balls fired in them were a nominal .690 to .693 in. diameter. A micrometer measurement by the author of five "Brown Bess" balls dating from the early nineteenth century revealed an average diameter of .690. The French muskets used by the Americans were a nominal .69 caliber and were loaded with round balls .650 in diameter. Cavalry carbines, pistols, and Pattern 1760 light infantry carbines were of nominal .66 bore and used a .615 or smaller ball, as did the Pattern 1776 rifles and the Ferguson breechloader. Archaeological digs conducted on Monmouth Battlefield State Park by Dan Sivilich's team uncovered round balls in .690 and .650 diameter, as well as buckshot, evidence that both Land Pattern and Charleville pattern guns were in general use.[55]

Traditional popular imagination has the soldier of the Revolutionary War era loading his musket with a charge of powder from a powder horn, which seems unlikely considering the stress placed on the use of paper cartridges, as well as the more rapid reloading possible with the prepared cartridge. In fact, powder horns were in use by both sides. American militiamen, unsurprisingly, frequently carried their spare powder in horns, loading powder and ball separately, but often with some prepared cartridges for rapid reloading when called for. Use of the horn was standard with rifle-armed American troops, since each rifle had a particular load with which it performed most accurately, and using a powder horn and custom measure would best enable that accuracy. When loading from horn and measure, undersize musket balls were usually supplemented with wadding of some sort, most often tow, to ensure better individual accuracy, and that they would not roll out of the muzzle after they were loaded. British light infantrymen were often supplied with powder horns and bul-

Powder horn of Daniel Denise of Smock's Light Horse, a unit of the Monmouth County militia. Denise served numerous duty stints with the militia and was present at Monmouth Court House. The butt end is carved with his initials "D. A. D." and the date "1775." (*Joseph Bilby, Joseph Bilby Collection*)

let pouches in addition to their cartridge boxes, but there seems no consensus as to why. There may be several reasons. When priming a musket from a cartridge, it was impossible to use the exact amount of powder every time, and also possible to spill a significant amount. This would affect the main charge rammed down the barrel and cause potential inaccuracy, or at least point of impact change on the target. Using a horn to prime the pan after loading the cartridge would allow for a more consistent load, more in keeping with maintaining light infantry individual marksmanship capabilities. In 1758, an American ranger captain made just this argument to John Campbell, 4th Earl of Loudoun, adding that the priming powder be of a finer grain than that used in the cartridge for better ignition. In addition, the powder horn, when filled with musket powder and used in conjunction with a measure providing consistent charges, and a ball encased in a greased patch or paper or tow, would very likely produce superior accuracy, even in a musket. To whatever end, Dr. Honyman made note that the light infantry men he observed training in Boston before the outbreak of hostilities were wearing, and presumably using, their powder horns. One of the authors has extensive experience firing a carbine-bored flintlock smoothbore, which, when loaded with a measured charge and patched ball, provides rifle-like accuracy up to fifty yards. Priming, however, seems to have been the usual use, if any, of the powder horn during American service, and in 1784 light infantrymen were provided with a small priming horn, and the ball bag and large horn retired from service.[56]

Most soldiers of the Revolution on either side carried their ammunition in cartridge boxes to protect it from weather and rough handling. The boxes were usually leather-covered wooden blocks drilled with holes to hold individual cartridges. They varied in size, construction, and capacity, ranging from nine to more than thirty cartridges. Some British soldiers carried two cartridge boxes, a "belly box" holding from nine to eighteen rounds usually carried on a belt at the front of the body, as well as a larger "battalion box," with as many as thirty-nine additional cartridges slung on a strap over the shoulder. The battalion box also carried extra flints and tools for disassembling and cleaning the musket. By the time of Monmouth Court House, the standard British issue was a thirty-six-round-capacity battalion box. American boxes were similar, although often of cruder manufacture. A surviving Connecticut militia box carried during the New York campaign of 1776 has a nineteen-round capacity.[57]

Although an American calculation indicated that a ball fired from a smoothbore musket retained "sufficient force to pass through a pine board 1 in. thick" at 500 yards, the British board of 1846 concluded that "as a general rule, musketry fire should not be made at a distance exceeding 150 yards and certainly not exceeding 200 yards, as at and beyond that range it would be a mere waste of ammunition to do so." A British government test conducted in 1841 found that a smoothbore musket had a maximum range, with dramatically elevated muzzle, of 700 yards, and scored a 75 percent hit ratio on a six-foot high by four-foot wide target at 150 yards. The gun failed to hit even larger targets at ranges up to 250 yards. Another test in 1846 produced similar results, concluding that the maximum range of a smoothbore with a muzzle elevation of five degrees to be "about 650 yards, the point blank range being 75 yards." After establishing range parameters, the 1846 ordnance testers fired a smoothbore at "a target 11 ft. 6 in. high by 6 ft. wide." Ten shots fired at a range of 250 yards missed the target entirely, while five hit it at a range of

150 yards. At 200 yards, the board found that it was necessary to aim five and a half feet above a target to come anywhere near it. As is evident, the test results reiterate that Colonel Hanger's anecdotal conclusion as to individual musket accuracy, unlike his assessment of construction quality, was not too far off the mark.[58]

The mere ownership of a rifle, however, was not a guarantee of combat accuracy. Stories like that of Timothy Murphy picking off a British commander several hundred yards away at Saratoga are countered by incidents such as the one at Weitzell's Mill, North Carolina, in 1781, where twenty-five "select" American riflemen fired over thirty shots at a mounted British officer at relatively close range, and missed him with every one.[59]

In combat, smoke, confusion, noise, exhaustion, fear, and the unpleasant sensation of being fired at—as well as firing—all conspired to drop the hit ratio of musket and even rifle fire much lower than in any controlled tests. One authority of the day opined that one needed to fire a man's weight in musket balls at him to hit him. A critic of American marksmanship declared that only one bullet out of 300 fired hit a British soldier during the retreat from Lexington and Concord. Estimates vary somewhat, but most conclude that the chances of a fired musket ball hitting an enemy soldier during the Napoleonic wars were between 2 and 5 percent. At the Battle of Vittoria in the Peninsular Campaign, it was estimated that 3,675,000 musket balls were fired to inflict 8,000 casualties. Ironically, with the blizzards of bullets spewed out by today's automatic weapons, the modern ratio is actually quite worse.[60]

The Land Pattern British guns, their American-made copies, and the French and other foreign muskets used in the Revolution were all typical infantry arms of the day, with all the advantages and disadvantages that this implies. Rapid-fire musketry in ranks was the eighteenth-century equivalent of automatic weapons area fire in a later era. Individual aimed fire, however, even in a smoothbore gun, would have considerably greater accuracy potential. Most historians have simply accepted the premise articulated by Mark Boatner III that "American marksmanship during the Revolution was very bad and British marksmanship was almost nonexistent." This, as we shall see, was not necessarily the case.[61]

Aimed projectile fire was always a desirable skill for light troops, and in the 1740s Frenchman marshal Maurice de Saxe began to emphasize aimed fire over unaimed volleys. Contrary to popular belief, individual aimed fire with muskets was valued early on in the British army, especially on service in America. Precedents for marksmanship training were firmly established during the French and Indian War, with basic loading and firing techniques, as well as the distribution of technical information to the "other ranks" stressed by progressive unit commanders. In 1759, one officer bragged to a friend that the men of his regiment were "without exception the very best marksmen in the English Amy," as individuals and as groups firing at ranges up to 200 yards. In 1756, Lord Loudoun ordered officers to have their men "fire at Marks," and "be taught to load and fire, lyeing on the Ground and kneeling." After the Braddock disaster, British soldiers in America were ordered to "tree all," or find a tree to use for cover while returning individual fire after being ambushed.[62]

Although British marksmanship training lapsed during peacetime, with a penurious government restricting ammunition supplies, the emphasis returned in the months prior to the onset of hostilities of 1775. Dr. Honyman, previously cited, also left a detailed description of British army small arms training that belies popular mythology and is worth quoting in its entirety.

> I saw a Regiment & the Body of marines, each by itself, firing at marks. A target being set up before each company, the soldiers of the regiment stept out singly, took aim & fired, & the firing was kept up in this manner by the whole regiment till they had all fired ten rounds. The marines fired by Platoons, by companies & sometimes by files, & made some general discharges, taking aim all the while at Targets the same as the Regiment.[63]

Marksmanship continued to be stressed in British orders as the war progressed. In Philadelphia in February 1778, the army that would fight at Monmouth Court House was instructed to "exercise When Ever the Weather will Permitt & to Practice Ball Firing." Twelve rounds per man were allotted for target practice.[64]

The oft-quoted recollection of an American soldier who was captured at Fort Washington in 1776, that British soldiers, Highlanders in this case, "took no aim" when firing at Americans at ranges from twenty to fifty yards, does not square with what we know about British marksmanship training, especially in Scottish regiments, whose soldiers were even issued some of the limited quantity of rifles available because of their supposed inherent light infantry skills and shooting ability in civilian life. It is quite possible that the American, recalling the incident many years later, confused his captors with Hessians, who may well have been using the German technique of delivering fire, which stressed rapidity over aiming, since Hessians also participated in the attack on Fort Washington.[65]

Although credit for superior small arms accuracy in American ranks during the Revolution has been largely attributed by historians to American riflemen from Pennsylvania and Virginia and other states, close reading of the available sources reveals a body of evidence suggesting that marksmanship with smoothbore muskets was indeed valued in the Continental army. As the Forage War got underway in early 1777, Washington wrote: "Our Scouts and the Enemy's Foraging Parties, have frequent Skirmishes, in which they always sustain the greatest loss in killed and wounded, owing to our superior skill in Fire Arms." Although there were riflemen in the ranks of the Continental army, the general was, in fact, referring to New Jersey militiamen and Continentals armed with smoothbore muskets, who were hardly frontier marksmen.[66]

When Washington created Maxwell's Light Infantry Corps prior to the Philadelphia campaign to replace Daniel Morgan's riflemen, who had moved north to join the forces deploying against Burgoyne, his selection criteria was "one hundred of the best marksmen from each of seven brigades." There was nary a rifle among these men. Likewise, when the American commander requested additional "sharpshooters" from the ranks of his Continental units for his ad hoc battalions of picked men, as the campaign of 1778 unfolded, he was referring to those armed with muskets. In the months following the Battle of Monmouth, a board of review considering General Steuben's revised regulations made only one change to the German's work—replacing the traditional command "Present!" with "Take Sight!" as the order immediately preceding "Fire!"—a modification personally approved by Washington.[67]

Despite the marksmanship training, troops in the Revolution, no doubt on both sides, demonstrated the perennial tendency to fire high when in action. Sometimes this high fire did have some physical effect on the enemy, at least according to John Simcoe. Simcoe recalled noticing early on in the war that "a number of firelocks were, in action, rendered useless by being carried on the shoulders, from casual musket-balls [hitting them], which could not be the case were the arms carried in the position of the advance."[68]

Part of the research for this book involved a series of tests of a flintlock musket and rifle, using aimed live fire. Although reproduction arms, they were faithful copies of weapons of the era. The musket was a .69-caliber Charleville made in Italy and imported by the Navy Arms company a number of years ago, and the rifle was a .50-caliber early Pennsylvania–style gun manufactured by Tennessee Valley Arms. In order to make the experiment as realistic as possible, we used original-style paper cartridges made by Arthur Green, who had two ancestors in the battle—one on each side. The cartridges included ball ammo with a .65-caliber ball as per the originals, and "buck and ball" rounds with four buckshot resting on top of the .65-caliber ball. As noted previously, varying numbers of buckshot were often used in cartridges of the era, and that number, although deviating from the standard nineteenth-century American load of a ball and three buckshot, was thought representative. The cartridge also held eighty grains of GOEX brand FFg granulation black powder, approximately ten grains of which were used as priming. Original charges were heavier, but powder quality in the eighteenth century was erratic and usually not as powerful as black powder made to modern specifications. The rifle was loaded with a .49-caliber ball encased in a greased cloth patch in front of ninety grains of GOEX FFg loaded from a horn with a

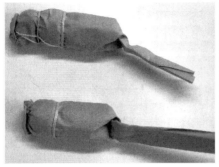 

Left, cartridges used in shooting experiment, tied to original specifications. Buck and ball (top) and ball (bottom). Right, five hits with "buck and ball" cartridge containing a .65 caliber ball and four .31 caliber buckshot at 25 yards range. (*Joseph Bilby*)

powder measure, and was primed from a small priming horn filled with GOEX FFFFg, a finer-grained priming powder.

Although the battle itself took place in record-breaking heat in June 1778, our tests were conducted on a Monmouth County, New Jersey, rifle range in January 2010. Heat can affect the velocity of ammunition and thus somewhat affect results on a target, but the advantage of firing over frozen ground with a light covering of snow is that misses and ricochets can be readily detected by an observer. In our experiment, the test shooter was muzzle-loading hunter and shooter Kevin Marshall, who had three ancestors at the battle on the patriot side, with Steven Garratano and coauthor Joseph Bilby, both with long experience using muzzle-loading rifles and muskets, acting as observers. The targets were standard police silhouettes, spaced in a group of three at a "loose file" distance of eighteen inches apart.[69]

The first test involved firing five shots at the center silhouette with musket and ball cartridge at a distance of fifty yards using a dead center hold. Two shots hit approximately dead center several inches apart, and a third nicked the silhouette. One round hit the ground in front of the target and ricocheted into the backstop between what would have been the silhouette's legs, and another hit the backstop several feet above the target. Repeating the exercise with buck and ball resulted in no hits on the target aimed at, or the one to its right, with either ball or buckshot, and but one buckshot hit in the silhouette to the left. Other buckshot and balls hit all around the targets, from ten yards in front to above, on either side and between the silhouettes into the backstop. A subsequent five-shot test with the musket and ball cartridge at one hundred yards on a similar target setup resulted in a first round center hit, with the other four balls hitting left or right and mostly above the targets. A buck and ball round fired at that distance scattered ricocheting projectiles from forty yards down to the one-hundred-yard backstop, but did not hit a silhouette. Conversely, a shot at twenty-five yards resulted in a pattern with all four buckshot and the musket ball in the torso area of the target. As expected, the rifle, although slower to load, produced much better results, with five hits out of five shots on the target at fifty yards, and one dead center hit for one shot at one hundred yards.

Although testing was admittedly limited, the results confirmed, unsurprisingly, that the musket was at its best, accuracy wise, as a short-range weapon, but that individual aimed fire hits were distinctly possible at fifty yards, and even on occasion at one hundred yards when firing a single ball cartridge. Adding the buckshot, however, virtually destroyed that individual accuracy beyond twenty-five yards. On the other hand, the dispersion of both ball and buckshot at fifty and even one hundred yards was potentially damaging, not only to the soldiers in the front rank of an advancing formation, but to those men following behind in the second rank and supporting lines some distance beyond. At twenty-five to fifty yards, the distance at which some of the Monmouth fighting around the hedgerow line took place, the smoothbore musket, loaded with either ball or buck and ball, was surely a devastating weapon.

BAYONETS

In addition to the well-delivered line volley, or a steady barrage of relatively accurate aimed fire from the light infantry, the ideal of many British officers was to end an action quickly with a bayonet charge. By the early eighteenth century, the bayonet had evolved from a weapon with a "plug" handle, which was inserted into the musket's muzzle, to the "socket" bayonet, with a triangular blade attached to a hollow, slotted offset handle extension. The extension, or "socket," slipped over the muzzle, and the slot engaged a lug on the barrel, which held it in place and, in the case of the Land Pattern musket, doubled as a crude front sight. The socket design allowed the musket to be loaded and fired while the bayonet was fixed. The British found the bayonet charge particularly effective early in the war, when Americans would often break and flee from a determined and rapid "cold steel" assault on Long Island and in the Philadelphia campaign. Bayonets were also useful for surprise night attacks, like those at Hancock's Bridge and Paoli. Even when he was not advocating the bayonet alone, General "No Flint" Grey ordered his troops to "Rush upon the Enemy with their Bayonets; immediately after having thrown in their fire . . . thoroughly convinced of the Great Advantage they have over the Enemy in this manner of Fighting." Although he raised an ad hoc unit of musket-armed sharpshooters by selecting "sober, active, robust men from each regiment" in the army with which he moved south into New York in 1777, General Burgoyne still believed "the onset of Bayonets in the hands of the Valiant is irresistible," and criticized his men who were still "preferring [firing] to the Bayonotte." Unfortunately for him, in the forests of northern New York, firepower trumped cold steel. The single rifle bullet that killed Brigadier General Simon Fraser and left his reconnaissance in force confused and leaderless on October 7, 1777, sealed the fate of Burgoyne's army.[70]

Early in the war, the Americans, particularly in militia units often armed with locally made and/or privately owned civilian and military dual-use firearms, had few bayonets, putting them at a decided disadvantage. As French muskets became generally available, however, the Continental regiments were issued bayonets with the imported guns and learned how to use them well. Anthony Wayne gained revenge for Paoli by leading his light infantry in a successful night bayonet attack on Stony Point, New York, on July 16, 1779. Bayonets were even becoming common in the militia by 1778, and New Jersey militiamen bayoneted British baggage horses in sporadic attacks on Knyphausen's column on June 28. The Americans had gained so much cold steel expertise by Yorktown, that even Washington was encouraging his men to "place their principal reliance on the bayonet."[71]

Although the bayonet could cause terrible wounds, and was used to great effect at the Hancock's Bridge massacre and the fights at Paoli and Stony Point, all surprise night attacks, actual bayonet fights were rare. During the Napoleonic Wars, a British surgeon observed that regiments "charging with fixed bayonets, *never* meet and struggle hand to hand and foot to foot; and this for the best possible reason, that one side turns and runs away as soon as the other comes close enough to do mischief." Opinions of officers who were also historians had not changed by the American Civil War, when Colonel Henry B. Carrington of the Eighteenth United States Infantry, a scholar as well as a soldier, wrote "'crossing bayonets' is never done by any considerable force. Few well-authenticated cases are found in history." Still, the ability to make that bayonet charge and cause the enemy to flee before closing with them was a valuable military asset. Although there were no decisive American bayonet charges at Monmouth, the Continental infantrymen at that stage of the war were finally capable of mounting one.[72]

ARTILLERY

Well-served American artillery played a significant role in the course of battle and outcome at Monmouth Court House, making the final American line virtually impregnable. The battle proved not only the making of the American infantry under Steuben's tutelage, but also validated the structure and training imposed on the artillery branch by General Henry Knox, a Boston bookseller and amateur soldier, whose grasp of the most technical combat arm of the service completed the professionalization of Washington's army.

By the time of the American Revolution, artillery, the first weapons system to use gunpowder to toss a projectile at a hostile force or fortification, had been on the military scene for more than four hundred years in one form or another. Artillery pieces had been largely static weapons, difficult to move and with very slow rates of fire, mostly useful in sieges and manned by civilian contractors, until King Gustavus Adolphus created mobile field artillery for his army in the early seventeenth century. In succeeding years the French professionalized the skills of gunnery, establishing schools to teach the craft.

British field artillery made its debut in America in the 1740s, and British guns in various militia armories, along with seizures of ships and forts, provided the initial ordnance for the American artillery in 1775. Additions were made in succeeding years by local casting and the acquisition of French guns. In 1776, there were five hundred American artillerymen in service, but they were outnumbered four-to-one by those brought to America by General Howe.

Seventeenth-century artillery pieces bore a confusing set of names, including, among many others, "minion" and "culverin." In the eighteenth century, the terminology was simplified. Artillery theorist John Muller established a mathematical basis for artillery dimensions and calibers, in which field artillery cannon barrel lengths usually were established as a ratio to their bore diameters in increasing multiples, and cannons were identified by the weight of the solid shot they fired, such as, "six pounder." Howitzers were designed to fire explosive shells at a higher trajectory and mortars at a still higher trajectory; both had less range than cannons, but could drop their explosive shells atop and behind fortification walls. The barrels of both of these guns were much shorter than those of cannons, and they were identified by the diameter of their bores, as in "eight inch mortar." All types of guns were manufactured in both iron and "brass," the latter usually an alloy of copper and tin, sometimes with a bit of lead mixed in and more properly termed "bronze." They also ranged considerably in size from very light field pieces that could be manhandled around the battlefield to heavy siege guns. The usual armament for an army in the field would include light cannons and some howitzers. Mortars, regardless of size, were usually reserved for siege work.[73]

Eighteenth-century muzzle-loading artillery ammunition included solid shot, which were spherical iron cannon balls used for long-range accuracy against all targets, including large forma-

Reproduction French "four pounder" light field piece in common use in the American army, on display at Monmouth Battlefield State Park. (*Joseph Bilby*)

tions of troops and counterbattery fire against enemy artillery; and exploding shells, or "bombs," which were hollow cast-iron projectiles with an explosive charge fired in howitzers and mortars, and appropriate for long-range antipersonnel use—a shell with a sputtering fuse rolling through the ranks would unnerve the stoutest of troops before it burst. At closer range, scatter shot, which included case or canister, a metal container filled with musket balls or scrap metal as well as grape shot, larger iron balls stacked around and held to a central wooden rod by heavy cord that came apart on firing, was preferred. Incendiary shells were also used, primarily against ships or fortifications. The most common field artillery ammunition used at Monmouth Court House appears to have been solid, case, and grape shot, although General Clinton did employ some howitzers, which would have fired shells. Artillery ammunition was usually "fixed," with the projectile strapped to a wooden sabot, and a powder bag attached to the rear of the sabot, which allowed rapid reloading by trained and experienced crews.[74]

American and British artillery at Monmouth Court House included cannons in three-, four-, six-, and twelve-pounder sizes, along with some howitzers. Monmouth would witness a gun duel that some thought the biggest artillery fight of the war to date. It would also produce the most enduring heroine of the conflict, and perhaps American history, "Molly Pitcher." By the morning of June 28, 1778, "Molly's" date with destiny was mere hours away.

five

"For many years after, the graves were indicated by the luxuriance of the vegetation":

THE BATTLE OF MONMOUTH COURT HOUSE

LATE IN THE AFTERNOON OF JUNE 27, 1778, General Washington met with General Lee, now in command of the entire division-size American advance force, along with Lee's subordinate officers, Generals Lafayette, Maxwell, and Scott. Washington advised Lee that he should consider an attack on the British army encamped near Monmouth Court House if an opportunity presented itself. The American commander appeared unhappy, however, that Lee appeared to have no knowledge of the enemy's dispositions or the terrain over which he would have to advance to launch such an attack. In a later meeting he held with Generals Maxwell, Lafayette, and Wayne, Lee conceded he was still not quite sure exactly where the British were or how they were deployed, and consequently did not believe in proposing any firm plans for the following day at all, save advancing in the general direction of the enemy and reacting to developments.[1]

Alexander Hamilton would subsequently testify that later that evening Washington, who had concluded that the enemy might move out of Monmouth Court House under cover of darkness, or even launch a preemptive surprise night attack on the Americans (there was the example of Paoli), directed him to notify Lee by letter to advance a reconnaissance force as soon as possible to monitor British activity and attack the enemy if they started to move, in order to hold them until the rest of the army could arrive to exploit any favorable situation that developed. Although this correspondence has never been found, and it should be noted that Hamilton was a proponent of aggressive action, more so than Washington, circumstantial evidence suggests Lee may have believed he was implementing this or a similar order on the morning of June 28, when he instructed Dickinson and Morgan by letter to advance on Clinton's position, and ordered Colonel William Grayson's detachment, then camped behind Englishtown, to march on Monmouth Court House. Lee advised Grayson that Morgan would support his right and Dickinson his left, and that Lee himself would follow with the rest of the division. Lee's parting instructions to Grayson in Englishtown were indeed to observe and keep the general informed of enemy movements, in line with Washington's wishes. New Jersey Adjutant General William Stryker, the battle's first comprehensive historian, posits that Grayson's mission is evidence of Lee's deliberate disobedience of orders, since the force did not deploy until morning. Grayson, as noted, had no idea of where he was going, however, and had to wait for a guide, who turned out to be none other than the Monmouth County patriot political and military boss, General David Forman.[2]

Grayson's detachment was composed of the Fourth, Eighth, and Twelfth Virginia regiments, and Grayson's and Colonel John Patton's Additional Continental regiments, with a total strength of just over 600 men. (Many of the Continental regiments, understrength to begin with, had been further depleted by detaching soldiers for the picked men units.) The detachment was supported by two artillery pieces under the command of Captain Thomas Wells of the Tenth Company, Third Continental Light Artillery.

With incomplete intelligence as to British positions, beyond the militia report that part of the enemy army had begun to move toward Middletown several hours earlier, Grayson advanced cautiously toward Monmouth Court House. He was to be followed by other composite detachments under Colonel Richard Butler and Colonel Henry Jackson, Brigadier General William Woodford's brigade and the rest of Brigadier General James Varnum's Brigade, although Varnum himself was not present and the brigade was commanded by Colonel John Durkee. Varnum's Brigade was supported by two artillery pieces under Captain David Cook of the Eleventh Company, Third Continental Artillery. Both Cook's and Wells's guns were under the overall supervision of Lieutenant Colonel Eleazer Oswald of the Second Continental Artillery. Anthony Wayne's 1,000-man detachment with four artillery pieces, and then Scott's men with four more guns followed Varnum's Brigade. "Scotch Willie" Maxwell brought up the rear with his Jerseymen, supplemented by two artillery pieces. Washington had determined that since almost 40 percent of Maxwell's men were new recruits from the militia draft, some of them not even equipped with cartridge boxes, one of the picked men ad hoc light infantry units would be "fitter to make a charge," and Maxwell conceded the seniority of position owed to him to the commander's wishes.

There remains confusion to this day on the exact number of soldiers under Lee's command, with several conflicting claims. Lee himself stated his division mustered some 4,100 men; his adjutant came up with a total of 4,190, and Wayne, who added Maxwell, the artillerymen, and a small detachment of cavalry to the total, estimated the entire force at 5,000. One historian has noted that 700 men were left behind in Englishtown to guard baggage, including knapsacks and coats shed due to the intense heat, which was already evident early in the morning. Theoretically, Morgan's 600 riflemen and light infantry and Dickinson's 800 militiamen were under Lee's control, giving him a potential of 6,000 men with which to face Clinton's rear guard. In fact, due to circumstances and his own errors, the force under Lee's immediate command and control when he actually engaged the enemy was significantly smaller—one estimate has it at 2,100.[3]

Monmouth Court House, also known as Freehold, the town toward which the Americans were advancing, was the major settlement of Freehold Township, incorporated in 1693. The county seat of Monmouth County was a patriot stronghold where the fearsome David Forman and his associates held sway in normal times, when the whole British army was not in town. Needless to say, these were not normal times, and the local politicians and militia had fled on the approach of Clinton's massive column, shipping out Loyalist prisoners, several under sentence of death, to Morristown several days before the enemy arrived. Most of the town's buildings, which included two taverns, one store, one church, a courthouse, a tanyard, and a scattering of private residences, were left empty and open to pillage by British soldiers and camp followers. Some citizens remained, however, and seventy-four-year-old widow Elizabeth Covenhoven, whose home General Clinton appropriated as his headquarters, may have escaped having her personal property looted (one account says it was), but "was obliged to sleep on a cellar door in the milk room for two nights." Despite Clinton's assurances of protection, all of her cattle were killed and eaten by British soldiers, or perhaps Hessians, as the German troops were finally given permission to "take cattle wherever they should find any and kill and slaughter if for the use of the regiment." At least one postbattle account describes the American army, which had outrun its rations, as "equally rapacious." No one, however, has accused the Continentals and militia of burning and looting houses.[4]

The terrain between Englishtown and Monmouth Court House was a mix of farmland and woodlots, with creek beds bordered by marshy wetlands or "morasses" wending through it. Although the land has never been extensively built over, and is preserved within the confines of a state park today, intensive agricultural use, as well as a nineteenth-century railroad bed, have changed its configuration noticeably over the years. In the century following the battle, trees were cut down, brush cleared, and marshes drained to increase effective farm acreage. By 1834, area farming was described as "fast improving under the present mode of culture," which involved the use of marl as fertilizer. In 1850, Benson J. Lossing described the area around what was called the "west morass," actually Spotswood Middle Brook and its attendant wetlands, as formerly a "deep quagmire and thickly covered with bushes," but "now mostly fine meadow land, coursed by a clear streamlet." An 1872 account refers to the battlefield as "good meadow land with a fine stream of water running through it." By 1898, William Stryker, a meticulous military scholar, wrote that "the topography of the ground has undergone and is now undergoing such changes that it is often quite difficult to ascertain the various points referred to by participants in the battle. Scarcely a single definite name is given in history to any of the various localities." It should be noted that the middle and west "morasses," one of which was described by Private Martin as a "muddy, sloughy brook," were not impassable to infantry, but merely difficult to cross; at least one soldier lost his shoes in the muck. They were, however, virtually impossible for artillery to navigate through, and while the southern segment of the "east morass" was similar to the creeks to the west, its northern portion appears to have been a true swamp.[5]

General Dickinson's militiamen, including the Somerset County "Light Horse" under Captain John Stryker, supplemented by a detachment from the Fourth Continental Light Dragoons under Lieutenant Colonel Anthony W. White, were covering that terrain, and beyond, all along the road to Middletown, early on June 28. The militiamen were in much closer contact with the enemy than any troops under Lee's direct command, and some actually launched limited attacks on the British baggage train. There is some evidence that the militia had more success in capturing, or at least disrupting some portions of the British column than they had previously, as Captain Joshua Huddy's company broke into Knyphausen's division and bayoneted some horses and drivers. At 4:30 a.m., Dickinson advised both Lee and Washington by messenger that the British advance division and the army's baggage was on the road to Middletown, and by 7:00 a.m., the rest of Lee's division was assembling to follow Grayson down the road toward Monmouth Court House. There seems to have been some initial confusion as to the order of march, however, and the entire column, including Lee himself, did not actually begin to advance until an hour or perhaps an hour and a half later. These delays, combined with Lee's lack of personal knowledge, not only of the terrain to his front, but also of his troops and their commanders, since he had been absent from the army for almost two years, did not bode well for the outcome of the forthcoming engagement.[6]

Sometime after Grayson's men had left Englishtown, one of Lee's staff officers, Captain Evan Edwards, advised the colonel that the New Jersey militia had lost contact with the British and told him to increase the pace of his advance, contradicting the original orders to use caution. At the time Edwards delivered the message, Grayson had already crossed the bridge over Spotswood Middle Brook. But he had two more creek bed wetlands, the middle and east morasses, more accurately described as the division ditch between the Ker and Rhea farms and the headwaters of Spotswood Middle Brook, to his front. He picked up his pace and was marching up a hill when his only reconnaissance element, six American dragoons, rode back to report that Dickinson's militia had not only regained contact with the enemy, but had moved from observing to actually skirmishing with them. By this point mounted staff officers, aides, and couriers were crisscrossing the fields west of Monmouth Court House, going to and from the advancing Continentals, Dickinson's militia, and back to Generals Washington and Lee. Events began to develop rapidly, and the information these riders brought often conflicted with reality, with the British being reported well on the road to Middletown, or still concentrated in Monmouth Court House. In actuality, both interpretations could be considered correct, as Knyphausen with half the army and the baggage was on the way to Middletown, but Cornwallis had moved into the position Knyphausen had left, and a strong rear guard of more than two thousand men was still deployed in the vicinity of the Court House. Washington interpreted the information as an indication that Clinton was going to slip away to Sandy Hook undamaged unless he was aggressively pursued. He dispatched one of his aides, Lieutenant Colonel Richard K. Meade, to Lee with instructions to engage the enemy, presumably the rear guard, "as soon as possible," and ordered the main army, then several miles away from Englishtown, to march forward to reinforce Lee's division.

Washington understandably wished to engage the enemy "as soon as possible" for several reasons. The main British army crossing New Jersey was more vulnerable than it had been since Howe had arrived at New York two years before. Clinton's campaign objective was not to fight a major battle against the American army, but to bring his own force, with its long baggage train intact, safely to New York, where it would be available for redeployment in accord with the new strategic realities brought on by the French intervention, as quickly as possible. The pursuing Americans were in a position to choose a time and a place to initiate any action and largely control the extent of that action, which Washington hoped to be minimal, yet useful to the American cause should it occur. If Clinton made his way safely to the high ground around Middletown and then to Sandy Hook beyond, where his army could board ships protected by the guns of the Royal Navy to complete its change of base, the chance to strike a blow of some sort to gain a propaganda advantage would be lost. Monmouth Court House was the last best chance to initiate a limited fight for limited ends, which was what Washington sought, on ground in any way favorable to the Americans. As Nathanael Greene told his chief, "people expect something from us."[7]

The experience of several years of combat and the training conducted by General Steuben at Valley Forge had forged a Continental army better prepared than ever before, in both morale and tactical skill, to confront the enemy. These factors allowed Washington to calibrate any risks he might take in attacking a portion of the British army to force a fight. If he was correct in his assumptions, the Continentals would, at the very least, stand up to the British effectively and, with some luck, might inflict damage on them with minimal risk of forcing a major action. Although even in the best case scenario it was unlikely that Clinton, with his entire force, or even a significant portion of it, could be "Burgoyned" (printed fliers left along the British line of march deridingly suggested such a fate, and Washington certainly did not have such a prospect in mind), the longer he delayed in "the Jerseys" the worse his overall outcome would be in terms of casualties, desertions, and a potentially embarrassing, albeit limited, combat action involving part of his army. Whether or not Lee understood all of this, or was capable of implementing the policy Washington had in mind with officers and men he was unfamiliar with is unclear, but seems doubtful.

During the entire march across New Jersey, the state's militiamen, aided by Maxwell's Continentals and later by Morgan's detachment of light infantry and riflemen, had harassed the British, who had pushed back in turn, but only in a limited manner, since their primary mission was to reach New York. It would seem appropriate, then, that a militia unit would fire the opening shots of the Battle of Monmouth. When a party of Hunterdon County mounted militiamen escorting General Steuben and several staff officers, including John Laurens, appeared close to the British lines on a reconnaissance mission around 7:00 a.m., Lieutenant-Colonel Simcoe, whose Queen's Rangers were detailed to guard British army headquarters, was ordered to attack them. Simcoe's men had more reason than usual to press the attack, since Clinton, according to a report Laurens later received from a British deserter, had recognized that a high-ranking officer was with the party. Simcoe led twenty mounted hussars trailed by forty grenadier infantrymen from his legion in a rapid attack on Dickinson's men. The mounted Loyalists dispersed the patrol, and pursued Steuben down a trail through a woodlot until they were checked by dismounted militiamen firing from behind a fence line. Simcoe then dispatched the hussars on an encircling movement and launched a frontal infantry assault on the militia with his grenadiers. It was a close-run affair, but Steuben and his party successfully eluded the hussars, and Simcoe was caught up short when the fleeing militiamen rallied as reinforcements appeared on the scene, and he saw even more Americans, Grayson's Continentals, marching toward him in the distance. Simcoe, exercising a sensible discretion, withdrew his force, including five wounded men, one of them mortally injured. Slightly wounded himself, Simcoe carried off Steuben's hat as a war trophy. In his memoir, he would characteristically brag that he had routed Dickinson's entire command of eight hundred to one thousand New Jersey militiamen, who were, in fact, spread out over a large area west and north of Monmouth Court House that morning. It was around 8:00 a.m. as the Queen's Rangers hustled back to Monmouth Court House and the cover of the British rear guard.[8]

Lee caught up with Grayson shortly after the militia fight, which Grayson had observed, and, with the rest of the division halted and strung out behind them, the two officers held an impromptu conference with General Dickinson atop a knoll just beyond the Rhea farm division ditch. Lee still had no idea exactly where the enemy was and soon got into a squabble with Dickinson, who had arrived seeking support for the militiamen engaged with Simcoe. The militia commander reported that the British had turned and engaged his men, and maintained that if Lee advanced his entire command across the Spotswood Middle Brook bridge, it would be vulnerable to a British attack with no easy way to withdraw if things turned out badly. In fact, the militia skirmish did not signal any significant enemy change of plans, and was merely another of the flank-clearing operations that the Queen's Rangers, dragoons, jaegers, and light infantry had been performing since the British left Philadelphia. As Lee debated the matter with Dickinson, more information, much of it contradictory, arrived. In the end, Lee decided to push his main force across Spotswood Middle Brook to join Grayson and advance on the enemy. He ordered Jackson's force to the front and removed Wayne from his immediate command to take charge of the reinforced advance. The hatless and exhausted Steuben, convinced from his own observations that the enemy was well on the road to Middletown, decided there would be no battle that day and rode back to Englishtown, where he took a much-needed nap.[9]

While Lee's division was moving toward Monmouth Court House in fits and starts, Knyphausen continued to labor up the road to Middletown with a long column that included the army's baggage, most of the Hessians and Loyalists, and the British First and Second brigades, with flank security supplied by the Seventeenth Light Dragoons. Dickinson's militiamen continued to snipe at the enemy along the whole route, in groups as small as a dozen and as large as fifty, and on one occasion penetrated the column, but the efficient German general continued his march, steadily leaving the little town behind him. Clinton himself had remained in town to supervise the overall withdrawal and handle any unforeseen events, and was initially confident that no serious threat was about to materialize. At around 8:00 a.m., the British commander had ordered Cornwallis to follow Knyphausen up the road with his own ten-thousand-man division, composed of some of the best troops in the army, including the Third, Fourth, and Fifth Infantry brigades, the First and Second Grenadier battalions, the German Grenadiers, the British Guards Brigade, and the Second Light Infantry Battalion. Cornwallis also provided the army's rearguard detachment composed of Simcoe's men, the Sixteenth Light Dragoons, and the First Light Infantry Battalion, which Clinton had deployed on the east side of the headwaters of Spotswood Middle Brook.

Once his main force began to cross over the Spotswood Middle Brook bridge at about 11:00 a.m., Lee started to shuffle his formations as he redeployed them in anticipation of combat with the British rear guard, which he could see in the distance. Due to American lack of knowledge of the terrain, continued conflicting intelligence on British dispositions, complicated by the fact that Lee had little personal knowledge of his officers and men, progress was slow and careful, and the Americans stuck to the woods as closely as they could, both for concealment and as relief from the increasingly debilitating heat. Significantly, one important segment of the American forward force, Daniel Morgan's riflemen and light infantry, was absent from the field. Morgan, who often had his own ideas of how a given mission should be conducted, had been operating on the British southern flank, complementing Dickinson and Maxwell, who had been harassing the British to the north, during the march to Monmouth Court House. On assuming command of the advance, Lee had ordered

The British approach march across the fields during the 1978 reenactment of the battle. (*National Guard Militia Museum of New Jersey*)

Morgan to attack the enemy as they moved out of Monmouth Court House, but also allowed him considerable tactical leeway by advising him not to put his men in a position where they might be trapped by an enemy counterattack. Morgan halted three miles south of the developing battle and remained there, apparently confused by Lee's latest instructions that morning and/or the date on them, which was incorrect, and awaited further orders.[10]

While Morgan stayed in place, Lee sifted through the reports he was receiving and became convinced, correctly as it turned out, that the British were indeed leaving Monmouth Court House for Middletown and points north. He began to push his troops forward, hoping to encircle and trap their rear guard. Lee assigned Anthony Wayne to command an advance force consisting of Grayson's, Jackson's, and Butler's detachments along with four artillery pieces from the Second Continental Artillery. After temporarily misidentifying an American militia detachment as part of the British rear guard, Wayne's men began to push toward Monmouth Court House in a tactical formation, swinging south and then moving toward the outskirts of the battered village. Some of Wayne's Pennsylvanians entered the town around eleven thirty, and finding the British gone, halted to rest in the debilitating heat, by that time above ninety degrees Fahrenheit. Lee, developing a battle plan according to what he could see or thought he could see, subsequently ordered Wayne to stage a holding attack on the enemy rear guard, then north of town. He then ordered the Marquis de Lafayette, who was leading Wayne's former command, to march northeast in hopes of cutting off the rear guard from Cornwallis's division and encircling and capturing the entire force. Although Lee could now see the deployed British rear guard, he could not, unfortunately for him, see Cornwallis's division on the road only a short distance beyond. He apparently thought he was only confronting a total of about six hundred British troops, and developed an ad hoc plan to bag the whole lot.[11]

After redistributing ammunition during a midday meal break to some of Jackson's men who came to the fight from police duty in Philadelphia with but a dozen rounds in their cartridge boxes, Wayne began to implement his role in Lee's scenario by advancing Butler's and Jackson's men, screened by militia light horsemen, through an apple orchard toward the British. As the militia began to trot across an open field beyond the orchard, however, they were charged by the Sixteenth Light Dragoons and dispersed. The British horse soldiers kept coming until they spied the American infantry emerging from the trees forty yards to their front, then pulled up short, fired their pistols, and rapidly retreated as the Continentals delivered a volley. The dragoons rode back through their own dismounted skirmishers and some light infantry, throwing them into temporary disorder. Lee, apparently thinking this minor success put him on the verge of a larger one, ordered Wayne to push Butler and Jackson up the Middletown Road. The Continentals advanced until they made contact with the First Light Infantry Battalion supported by a pair of three-pounder artillery pieces. As the cannons opened fire, Butler and Jackson retreated into a nearby woodlot. By this time, Lee had succeeded in moving more troops forward, but was beginning to lose control of the overall situation. At one point, he apparently almost ordered an attack on Jackson and Butler in the belief that

British Grenadiers on the march during the 1978 reenactment of the battle. In 1778 they would have presented a more streamlined appearance, in uniform as well as body bulk. (*National Guard Militia Museum of New Jersey*)

they were the enemy. His attempt to capture the British rear guard, tenuous at best, ran into additional difficulties as Morgan failed to move, and the advance of Colonel Durkee's force was temporarily blocked by the swampy area surrounding the headwaters of Spotswood Middle Brook.

Lee's chances of success depended not only on perfect timing for his own attack, but on Clinton and Cornwallis reacting poorly to it. As the fighting unfolded, it became clear that neither eventuality would occur. The American advance ground to a halt across the battlefield and the British commander, subscribing to the old, if somewhat hackneyed, axiom that the best defense is a good offense, quickly decided to launch an aggressive counterattack. Clinton, who rode rapidly from the head of his column back toward Monmouth Court House as the action began, not only engaged Wayne with the rear guard, but ordered Cornwallis to return his entire command to Monmouth Court House to join the developing battle. The first to appear were the British and Hessian grenadiers, who had been held fairly close as a backup to the rear guard. Advised that it appeared the Continental army was advancing in strength, the British commander established headquarters on a nearby hill, from where he had a good view of the developing battle. Clinton ordered the returning German

American line of battle opens fire on the British at the Bicentennial reenactment of the battle. The front rank is kneeling, which would not have been the case in the two line formations actually used by both sides in the actual battle, but was probably adopted for safety reasons in 1978. (*National Guard Militia Museum of New Jersey*)

grenadiers (who had a reputation of moving slowly) to secure the Middletown road, and quickly began to feed Cornwallis's British grenadiers into the fight. Wayne could see the enemy moving in the distance, and was immediately apprehensive that his command was in danger. His units were soon in combat, repulsing probes by the emboldened British rear guard, and he launched limited attacks of his own in an attempt to gauge the strength of his opposition. Durkee's men finally joined him and began to suffer casualties almost immediately from British artillery fire.[12]

Lee, meanwhile, had joined Lafayette's detachment to the north. Unfortunately, although he reached a position he thought advantageous, in the vicinity of Forman's Mill Pond (present-day Lake Topanemus), his view of the field continued to prevent him from clearly seeing Cornwallis's division, which was now marching rapidly south to the assistance of the rear guard. Clinton, whose view of the field was much better, did not directly engage Lafayette immediately, but kept his reinforcements moving south to increase the pressure on Wayne, secure in the knowledge that Cornwallis could deal with any American presence on his right. Suddenly apprehensive about the security of his whole force, Lee tried to accelerate Lafayette's attack and issued a flurry of orders, which Lieutenant-Colonel Laurens later recalled as erupting "with a rapidity and indecision calculated to ruin us." It was all too little too late, for Cornwallis's men were rapidly approaching the American right flank. And the Continentals began to leave.[13]

While there would be dispute over exactly when and where the overall American retreat began, testimony during the subsequent Lee court-martial suggests it may have been initiated by some of Lieutenant-Colonel Oswald's artillery, initially deployed to support Butler and Jackson, which had become isolated in the open, and locked in a counterbattery duel with British guns when Wayne's infantry withdrew into the woods. By late morning, Oswald had two men and two horses killed, and had run out of solid shot, with his reserve supply of ammunition stuck on the far side of the bridge over Spotswood Middle Brook. The artilleryman decided he could do no further good where he was and that the developing situation could cost him his exposed guns, so he hitched up and headed for the rear. There is agreement that the first infantry unit to move was Scott's. As Oswald pulled out, Scott apprehended that Cornwallis's grenadiers, whom he could now see moving toward his open right flank in the distance, spelled big trouble. He approached Maxwell, whose New Jersey Brigade had formed up to his left, and suggested to the Jerseyman that they realign themselves to face the threat. While Scott turned, Maxwell marched his brigade in a counterclockwise arc around him to end up on his right flank in support. As Cornwallis's men steadily advanced, other jittery American commanders, including Jackson, Butler, and Grayson, as well as Durkee, who had finally joined Wayne's advance force, became even more confused as to what the plan of battle was, if any. Seeing the dust cloud raised by Maxwell's marching Jerseyans unhinged their confidence, and prompted more units to march to the rear. Scott apparently misinterpreted one American unit's move forward at an angle for a withdrawal, and, jittery already, began to retreat. At that point Lafayette, pushing on along toward the Middletown road with a mere three regiments and some artillery support, began to realize that he was quite alone. He had his artillery deliver a rapid covering fire while he pulled his infantry out to join what had become a general retreat. Around twelve thirty, Lee, following a thoroughly confusing conversation with Maxwell, in which neither man seemed to know what the other was saying, and seeing his division dissolve around him, formally ordered a general withdrawal, although the order was hardly necessary. With perhaps six thousand British soldiers now bearing down on his fragmented command, and more coming down the Middletown road, Lee realized that the situation as he had apprehended it earlier had dramatically changed; he was no longer the hunter, but the hunted.[14]

The retreat was never a rout. Most of Lee's rank and file were probably puzzled by the apparent turn of events. The Continentals had come to the field prepared to fight. Private Martin recalled that the Rhode Island captain in charge of his company of picked men had announced that, "You have been wishing for some days past to come up with the British, you have been wanting to fight—now you shall have fighting enough before night." Martin added that "the men did not need much haranguing to raise their courage," noting that even invalids tried to join the advance that morning. The retreat was the inevitable result of Lee's haphazard battle preparation and lack of terrain knowledge, combined with Clinton's aggressive desire to bring on an action to protect what he perceived was a serious attempt to seize his valuable baggage. It should also be noted that Clinton, having spent a day and night at Monmouth Court House, was more familiar with the roads and the lay of the land in the vicinity than Lee. The Americans fell back at a steady rate, mostly along the Englishtown road and across the fields on either side of it, except for Scott, who retreated along the Amboy road, and Butler, across the fields of the Craig farm, heading northwest. Although the first to pull out, Oswald twice redeployed his guns to face the enemy and then established a defensive position on the Ker farm, where he consolidated the artillery and cobbled together a ten-gun battery to cover the division's retreat.[15]

In the middle of a situation that could very easily have spiraled into chaos, but, in a sign of the maturation of the lower ranks of the American army, did not, Anthony Wayne received a query from Morgan, still sitting at Richmond's Mills, where his eight hundred men were in a position to attack toward Clinton's left flank. Morgan wanted to know if there were any orders for him to join the developing battle. Wayne, rather than seizing an opportunity to affect the flow of the fight by taking it on his own to tell Morgan to advance, or at least close up on his own force, or even passing on the message to Lee, with whom he had ceased speaking, instead sarcastically replied that since the army's advance units had retreated, Morgan should "govern himself accordingly." That was all Morgan, who displayed a singular lack of initiative that day, needed to justify his torpor, and he stayed put. Later, once the main battle had been joined, Morgan received instructions from Washington, who advised his fellow Virginian, by then inarguably too far away to offer ready support, to continue in his observation role and "by no means come to an Engagement with your whole Body unless you are tempted by some very evident advantage." Neither Washington nor Lee ultimately castigated Morgan for his lack of aggressive behavior. Wayne, not unexpectedly, blamed the retrograde movement entirely on Lee, and wrote his wife after the battle that "our Genl [Lee] thought Proper [to Retreat] in place of Advancing."[16]

It was, of course, far more complicated than Wayne claimed to perceive, and there was confusion on the British side as well, at least among some junior officers. Lieutenant William J. Hale of the Second Grenadier Battalion thought Lee had actually baited a clever trap to suck the British in. Turning his spyglass on some troops that seemed to be heading for his rear, Hale "saw from their variegated cloths they did not belong to our army," and feared encirclement. The British officer's perceptions to the contrary, however, a slow but steady swarm of American soldiers was moving toward their own rear as rapidly as the increasingly hot day allowed.[17]

As they moved to directly confront Lee's men, the British paused briefly to consolidate, and Clinton dispatched his light infantry and the Queen's Rangers, absent the wounded Simcoe, to move around the American left flank in the classic British Long Island maneuver. Lee, increasingly desperate to find a secure place to take a stand as the shaky line that Scott and Maxwell had established began to drift to the rear yet again, ordered another pullback. In doing so, he eventually and wisely sought the advice of local farmer and Monmouth County militia captain Peter Wikoff. Wikoff told Lee that he believed that either Combs Hill or a ridge east of the Tennent Meeting House—a Presbyterian church built more than twenty years before the war and named for its two most famous ministers, William Tennent Jr. and John Tennent—were the best defensive positions in the area. Lee, perceiving that Combs Hill, while it dominated the battlefield (and still does), could not be easily occupied since his men would have to crash through a thick wet hay meadow and marshy terrain that would bog down his artillery in the attempt, ordered Wikoff to begin guiding troops to a position near the Tennent Meeting House.[18]

As Wikoff rode west, the leading units of the eight thousand-man main American army, personally led by Washington, were marching east to reinforce Lee's beleaguered division. The Continentals were in light marching order, having dropped their knapsacks, and even their coats, prior to the march to mitigate the effect of the intense heat. Washington, riding ahead of the army, was advised by Colonel Hamilton that Lee had made contact with the British rear guard, but after the American commander rode somewhat past the Tennent Meeting House, he received word that Lee was rapidly retreating. The initial source of this information was a fifer from one of Lee's units. Washington questioned the young musician, had him placed under guard to prevent the story from spreading panic, and then dispatched aides to find Lee and discover the true situation. One of these staff officers, Lieutenant Colonel Richard Harrison, encountered Colonel Matthias Ogden, commander of the First New Jersey Regiment, who had deployed his men as a rear guard while other troops retreated across Spotswood Middle Brook. Ogden had withdrawn his own unit without ever encountering the enemy, and he was left alone as the tide of American troops swept westward. Explaining that he had no idea what caused the retreat, the exasperated Ogden said to Harrison, "By God! they are flying from a shadow." Another Washington aide, Lieutenant Colonel John Fitzgerald, finally reached Lee, who was at the disintegrating front—now rear—of his division. As the Sixteenth Light Dragoons, now screening not "a shadow," but a large advancing elite infantry force, began to close on the American line, Fitzgerald rode to the rear.[19]

Initially reluctant to pursue Lee once satisfied his baggage was safe, Clinton, seeing the increasingly rapid American retreat from what had been a tentative advance, decided to escalate the aggressive but limited counterattack he had launched into a general engagement. The British commander had his best men, the guards, grenadiers, and light infantry, as well as half of his dragoons—an arm in which the Americans were almost totally deficient—on the field, which made it seem worthwhile to push the issue. And push they did. As they drew closer to the Americans, the British infantry deployed from column formation into two battle lines, the first composed of, from left to right, elite troops of the First and Second Grenadier battalions and the Foot Guards Brigade, with the Third and Fourth brigades behind them in support. They came on hard and fast. Lieutenant Hale of the Second Grenadiers recalled that cross-country pursuit of Lee after Cornwallis's return to Monmouth Court House was "a march may I never again experience," along "sand [roads] which scorched through our shoes with intolerable heat; the sun beating on our heads with a force scarcely to be conceived in Europe." Men dropped with exhaustion along the way, and "two [soldiers] became raving mad, and the whole road, strewed with miserable wretches wishing for death, exhibited the most shocking scene I ever saw." It was equally bad in American ranks; Private Martin recalled that by 11:00 a.m., the air was like that in a "heated oven" and was "almost impossible to breathe."[20]

Washington, who had continued to ride forward toward the advancing enemy, encountered Captain Wikoff, who was leading the Second New Jersey Regiment back toward the line he hoped to establish along Perrine Ridge near the Tennent Church. When Wikoff explained his mission to the American commander, Washington ordered him to guide the Jerseymen to a woodlot

Three romanticized nineteenth century illustrations of the famous encounter between Washington and Lee at Monmouth. Lee who appeared to be confused about the battlefield conditions had ordered his soldiers to retreat. Washington rushed to Lee's position to question Lee's orders and stabilize the American situation, an action that may have saved the American army from defeat. (*Library of Congress*)

near the ridge where they could rest and assume a reserve position. He then proceeded on to his controversial meeting with Charles Lee, which took place on a hill east of today's Wemrock Road, then a lane leading to the Rhea mansion. There are a number of accounts of this confrontation, most of which were, to be kind, apparently considerably elaborated after the fact. General Scott, for example, claimed Washington swore at his chief subordinate "till the leaves shook on the trees." According to Lafayette, Washington called Lee a "damned poltroon." Neither of these officers was present at the incident, however, and Scott was a full three-quarters of a mile away. Private Martin, who was actually far to the north with Scott's detachment, admitted he was not near enough to hear, but claimed he witnessed the confrontation at a distance, and recalled that other soldiers told him that Washington's words were "d——n him," although Martin conceded that such a public display of anger would be "very unlike [Washington]." Private James Jordan, a nine-month draftee in the Second New Jersey Regiment who claimed to be a witness, gave a more nuanced account of Washington's words, recalling that the commanding general merely asked Lee, "What is this you have been about to day?" Lieutenant Colonel Tench Tilghman, Washington's military secretary, remembered Washington asking Lee what the situation was and why he was retreating, and that Lee appeared confused. Adjutant General John Brooks, who was there, remembered that Washington asked Lee why the army was retreating, and Lee responded that he had had poor intelligence and that his orders had not been obeyed. If this is correct, then Lee condemned himself as a commander, as intelligence of enemy activity and positions before ordering an advance were his responsibility, and once that advance was initiated, subsequent loss of command and control was his fault as well. Washington's response, described by Brooks as "warm," was that Lee should not have pressed for command of the advance force if he did not intend to use it to attack the enemy, to which Lee responded that he had been willing to obey Washington's orders, but that the situation had prevented him from doing so and that, by the way, an attack on the enemy that might result in a major action was not in the interest of the army or the country. The last statement—and Brooks, recalling from memory, was not sure of every detail— would sustain Lee's overall, if uninformed and incorrect, belief that the army was unable to stand up to the British. It was correct, however, in assuming that Washington had not intended to bring on a major battle. Another witness, Dr. Charles McHenry, recalled that Lee seemed confused and that his answers were hesitant. Unsatisfied with Lee's rationale, whatever it might have been, Washington moved on toward the front to assume direct command of the battle, but did not, contrary to popular opinion, formally relieve Lee on the spot.[21]

On the way forward, Washington also encountered Lafayette, Colonel Walter Stewart, and Lieutenant Colonel Nathaniel Ramsay, who were withdrawing, but advised him of their units' role in the fight thus far. Quickly assessing the situation as increasingly desperate, the American commander ordered Stewart and Ramsay to hold up the enemy advance, and fight a delaying action east of the bridge over Spotswood Middle Brook until he could establish a defensive line to the rear. In the event, two lines were established, one on a hill slightly south of Stewart's and Ramsay's position in a woodlot, extending it southward, and another, the "hedgerow" line, still further to the rear and closer to Spotswood Middle Brook.[22]

The hedgerow line began in a woodlot on the east side of the brook. The dominant feature of the position was the "hedgerow" itself, which gave it its name and probably served as a pasture demarcation line, and behind which Colonel Henry B. Livingston of New York halted and began to rally his battalion of picked men. Sometimes the hedgerow is described as a fence, but it was actually neither. According to Samuel S. Forman, a child living nearby at the time of the battle who claimed to have "heard the report of the cannon on that eventful occasion," responded to a question from the *Monmouth Democrat* newspaper while attending commemoration ceremonies in 1854, "the [hedgerow] fence was partly rails and partly young lopped trees."[23]

Washington ordered Lee to take charge of the hedgerow line, further confusing the situation. Lee sent a local civilian as a messenger to Colonel Jackson, ordering him to advance and form up his command behind a rail fence to the front of the hedgerow and hold off the Sixteenth Light Dragoons, who were closing in on the American rear. Jackson disputed an order from a civilian, and half his unit continued to the rear, but he stayed behind with the other half. Lee, seeing some of Jackson's men retreating, ordered another detachment, under Lieutenant Colonel Jeremiah Olney, to turn

Sculptor James E. Kelly's interpretation of Washington's arrival on the battlefield. (*Joseph Bilby*)

around and face the enemy, reinforcing Jackson, and it did. Olney's men were joined by some mounted militiamen and two of Oswald's artillery pieces. Colonel Ogden's First New Jersey Regiment anchored the far left flank, and was ordered to act as a rear guard to the rear guard should a further retreat become necessary.

Washington now ordered Livingston to move his detachment forward from the hedgerow to the advanced position on the hill south of Stewart and Ramsay, where Oswald had placed some of his artillery. Livingston apparently misunderstood the order and initially deployed his men in a way that masked two of Oswald's guns, then moved again, exposing the artillery's left flank. The remains of Jackson's detachment moved in to cover the open flank, but after firing at the enemy—rapidly advancing grenadiers—for a few minutes, the whole force fell back toward the hedgerow as the dragoons threatened the American right. At about this time Ogden, nervous about his open flank to the north, where British troops out of his line of sight (Quartermaster General Erskine, leading General Grey's Third Brigade, which Clinton had ordered to march around the American left flank and join the light infantry and Queen's Rangers) were actually mov-

"Grenadiers never heed forming!" A nineteenth century artist's rendition of the charge of the grenadiers on the hedgerow. (*Courtesy Dr. David Martin*)

ing, marched his men to the rear without orders. Although the defenders of the hill had joined the defenders of the hedgerow, both flanks of the new position were vulnerable.

Meanwhile Stewart and Ramsay, deployed about two hundred yards east of present-day Wemrock Road and stretching across today's Route 522, engaged the enemy as well. The location of this fight, also known as the "point of woods," was uncertain for many years, but has recently been confirmed by archaeological research. As the British Foot Guards Brigade closed on the woods, Anthony Wayne, in direct tactical control of the defense, ordered the Maryland, Pennsylvania, and Virginia troops to fire, and the Continentals dropped as many as forty men killed and wounded, including Lieutenant-Colonel Henry Trelawney of the foot guards. The Guards, apparently with help from some of the grenadiers marching to their left, rallied and made a bayonet charge into the woods in response. The Americans stood and fought initially, but the formations of both sides became broken and mingled among the trees, and the British, who outnumbered the Continentals, pushed them out onto open terrain, where elements of the Sixteenth Light Dragoons rode some Americans

Sculptor James E. Kelly's portrayal of the stand made by Lieutenant-colonel Ramsay of Maryland against the Sixteenth Light Dragoons as his men retreated from the point of woods. (*Joseph Bilby*)

down as they ran for their lives toward the bridge and across the marshy muck surrounding Spotswood Middle Brook. Ramsay, a thirty-eight-year-old attorney turned soldier commanding the Third Maryland Regiment, attempted to organize a rear guard but was dismounted, wounded, and captured in hand-to-hand combat as his men retreated, taking General Wayne with them. The British pursuit slowed due to heat exhaustion, as they "had several Men Dye on the spot with Thirst & Extreme Fatigue & still a greater Proportion not able to defend themselves."[24]

On the British left, following the collapse of the hill line, the dragoons and grenadier battalions had pursued the retreating Americans toward the hedgerow, where General Clinton, excited by what appeared now to be the prospect of a clear victory, pushed his men on. The general was in the thick of the fight, "galloping like a Newmarket jockey at the head of a wing of Grenadiers," and yelling, "Charge Grenadiers, never heed forming!" The Second Grenadiers and part of the First Grenadiers responded with a chaotic mob rush into a blizzard of American bullets and two of Oswald's guns firing canister shot at close range, a maelstrom which one British officer described as "the heaviest fire I have yet felt," but swarmed over the hedgerow in a fight that lasted about five minutes. Lieutenant Colonels Hamilton and Laurens, trying to manage the battle for their commanders, both had their horses killed. Before the hedgerow line collapsed, however, Oswald's guns pulled out under cover of Livingston's battalion and headed for the bridge over Spotswood Middle Brook, their only escape route. The American infantry at the hedgerow successfully disengaged and managed to conduct a disciplined withdrawal across the brook and bridge, with Colonel Olney, leading Varnum's brigade of New Englanders, covering the retreat. General Lee, still in command of the overall defense, was, true to his word to Washington upon being assigned to organize the rear guard, the last man over the bridge. He was followed by the British Second Grenadiers. By this time American artillery had deployed in force on Perrine Ridge, however, and blasted the pursuing enemy with grapeshot and canister, killing Lieutenant-Colonel Henry Monckton of the Second Grenadiers, whose men were unable to retrieve his body as they hastily retreated to the east of Spotswood Middle Brook. It has been speculated that Monckton fell victim earlier to one of Oswald's parting blasts, but new archaeological evidence reveals that some grenadiers indeed crossed the bridge only to be driven back by American artillery. That fact, and the fact that his men failed to recover his body, strongly suggest that Monckton died on the American side of the brook in the aftermath of the hedgerow fight.[25]

Once the hedgerow line was established, Lee had actually conducted a good rearguard action. His troops fought well while under aggressive attack by some of the best units in the British army, in heat so debilitating that men were literally dropping dead from it on both sides. The Continentals maintained unit cohesion for the most part, and infantry and artillery managed to get across Spotswood Middle Brook and its narrow bridge, a move that Dickinson had feared would lead to disaster, without losing a single color or gun, and suffering relatively light casualties. Steuben's instruction on efficient battlefield maneuvering paid off once more, allowing the American units to perform a retrograde move-

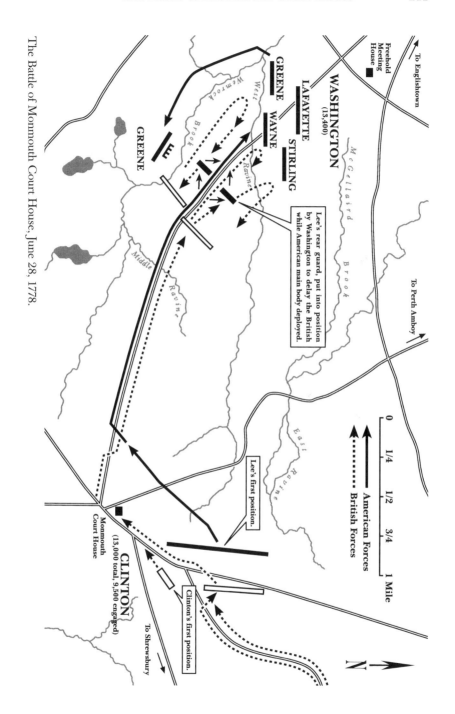

The Battle of Monmouth Court House, June 28, 1778.

Lee's rear guard, put into position by Washington to delay the British while American main body deployed.

WASHINGTON
(13,400)

GREENE
LAFAYETTE

GREENE

WAYNE

STIRLING

Freehold
Meeting
House

To Englishtown

To Perth Amboy

McGellaird Brook

Wemrock Brook

West Brook

West Ravine

Middle Ravine

East Ravine

Lee's first position.

Monmouth
Court House

CLINTON
(13,000 total, 9,500 engaged)

Clinton's first position.

To Shrewsbury

0   1/4   1/2   3/4   1 Mile

American Forces
British Forces

N

ment in the face of the enemy that might have produced panic in the same army the year before. It was yet another remarkable demonstration of how far the Continentals had come.

The delaying actions east of Spotswood Middle Brook proved critical to the outcome of the battle, as they allowed Washington to complete his second line of defense along Perrine Ridge, with fresh troops who continued to arrive on the battlefield and enough artillery to make that line impregnable. While following Captain Wikoff's advice, Washington also took advantage of information provided by Lieutenant Colonel David Rhea of the Second New Jersey Infantry to improve his tactical dispositions. Rhea, who knew the local terrain intimately—some of the fighting was across the nearby farms of his nephews, and Rhea had been born in the area—suggested that a swamp to the east of the ridge along Spotswood Middle Brook would prevent the enemy from turning the position on the American left, and that the woods behind Perrine Ridge would be a safe haven for reserves, and would provide them with shade to mitigate the intense heat. General Alexander (Lord Stirling), in command of Washington's left wing, deployed to the north along the ridge, while Nathanael Greene extended Alexander's line to the south, and later sidled to the right to make room for Wayne, who anchored the American center with five regiments. Greene, who had been ordered to watch the road to the south of the main American position to prevent a British flanking attack from that direction, also made a personal reconnaissance to and beyond Combs Hill to take the lay of the land.[26]

With the ridge secured before the hedgerow line gave way, Lee's rearguard troops marched through the new line to the rear. The units most actively engaged in the morning fighting moved, along with General Lee himself, toward Englishtown for reorganization and rest. Meanwhile, three infantry brigades and the First and Second New Jersey regiments were placed in a reserve position under Lafayette in the woods behind Perrine Ridge and beyond the Tennent Meeting House, as Washington began to build a defense in depth. Washington then ordered Steuben, who had awakened from his nap, to accompany him as he rode to the

View from Combs' Hill. Sutphin farm house, near the orchard where the New England "picked men" fought the Highlanders, is in the far distance, beyond the second tree line. The NJ Department of Parks and Forestry are gradually returning the landscape to what it was in 1778. (*Joseph Bilby*)

sound of the guns, and after assisting in establishing the Perrine Ridge line, to take command at Englishtown. The enthusiastic German, his fighting blood up, reorganized Lee's men and merged them with the army reserve, then turned command over to Maxwell and returned to the front. Lee, who did not object to Steuben's and then Maxwell's assuming command of part of his division, wandered forward again, apparently in an effort to continue the conversation with Washington regarding his initial retreat, but the still unhappy commander was too busy organizing the defense to listen to him. General Lee's command time at the Battle of Monmouth, and in the war, was over.[27]

Meanwhile, Scott's detachment of picked men from Lee's original left wing had withdrawn further north across the Craig Farm and toward the new American position on Perrine Ridge. The detachment was pursued by the Forty-second Foot, the famed "Black Watch" Highlanders, which was the advance unit of the British Third Brigade. Two of Scott's battalions continued to withdraw beyond the ridge toward Englishtown, but two others, under Colonels Joseph Cilley and Richard Parker, halted when the Scots ended their pursuit as they came up against American artillery fire from Perrine Ridge. The Second Battalion of the Forty-second fell back into a nearby orchard on the Sutphin farm, which provided some cover, and Quartermaster General Erskine, who had made off with a dining room set from Newark two years before, continued to move on to the right with the Forty-second's First Battalion and the rest of the Third Brigade, including a couple of three-pounder guns, to try to link up with the light infantry and Queen's Rangers. Erskine lost a few men to enemy fire and heatstroke in his drive, but was otherwise prepared to continue the attack. After a long hot march, skirmishing with militia and with men dropping dead or exhausted from the heat all along the way, however, the British force was halted by difficult terrain and exhaustion. Erskine concluded that he could not turn the American flank and withdrew a short distance to rest his men. Had he persisted and made it a bit further, he would have run into a solid reserve line of Continentals under Lafayette anchoring the American flank. There would be no Long Island on this day.[28]

With the infantry fight totally stalled by early afternoon through stiff American resistance along a well-manned front with secure flanks, Clinton brought up a number of artillery pieces, including twelve- and six-pounder guns and five-and-a-half-inch howitzers, to engage Knox's batteries sited along Perrine Ridge in a two-hour-long artillery duel, one of the longest such engagements of the war. The results of what one British general described as "the most terrible cannonade . . . he ever heard," and which American Lieutenant Colonel Henry Dearborn called "the finest music I ever heard," were inconclusive, as the range was extreme. No guns were dismounted and casualties were limited on both sides, but the duel supplied a future American heroine, "Molly Pitcher." "Molly," whose real name was apparently Mary Hays, was described in a recollection by Private Martin as "a woman whose husband belonged to the artillery," and helped serve a gun alongside her spouse on the Perrine Ridge line behind and north of Martin's position.[29]

Clinton's line also came under artillery fire from Combs Hill. While the British were unsuccessfully attempting to hook around the American left flank, in their turn the Americans had success-

There have been numerous artistic portrayals of "Molly Pitcher" over the more than 225 years since she helped man an artillery piece at Monmouth Court House. The latest, and most realistic, is the work of noted American military artist Don Troiani. (*Painting by Don Troiani www.historicalartprints. com*)

fully hooked around the British left. Colonel Rhea had advised Washington that he could guide troops to the top of Combs Hill, and after the reconnaissance conducted by General Greene, led General Woodford's Third Virginia Brigade to the crest. Combs Hill had been rejected by Lee as a defensive position earlier in the battle because he could not get his artillery across the marshy wetlands between it and his position near the hedgerow, but that same swampy land along Spotswood South Brook (present-day Wemrock Brook) now protected Greene's men from attack. The Americans moved artillery pieces up to join Woodford's men and the guns, personally sighted and under the direct command of Knox's French adjutant, Thomas-Antoine, chevalier de Maudit du Plessis, chimed in during the artillery duel. The American cannons on Combs Hill were positioned to deliver a raking enfilade fire on any infantry attack on Perrine Ridge, and could also discomfit the British gun line somewhat, although the distance was great.[30]

By late afternoon Clinton, realizing that he was not going to accomplish a Long Island or a Brandywine, that his artillery bombardment was having little effect and was running short of ammunition, but secure in the knowledge that at least his baggage was safe on the road to Middletown, decided to disengage and ordered a general withdrawal to consolidate his forces closer to Monmouth Court House. As the British began to fall back, leaving a number of dead, dehydrated, and seriously wounded men behind, Washington decided to encourage their leaving, and gain what advantage he could by launching a series of limited local attacks. The first was an assault on the position of the Forty-second Foot in the Sutphin farm orchard by Colonel Cilley's battalion. Cilley's 350 picked men, who would spearhead the attack, were drawn from five New England brigades, and Cilley himself was a New Hampshire man. The colonel recalled that he was ordered to "see what I could do with the enemy's right wing . . . in an orchard to our front." His battalion, which a detailed study of the orchard fight estimated brought 325 men to the action, was opposed in the ensuing standup fight by the Second Battalion of the Forty-second Highlanders, which had an estimated strength of 320 men at the outset of the battle and 275 present in the orchard by late afternoon.[31]

Cilley's battalion, which had been deployed as a skirmish line behind a fence at the bottom of Perrine Ridge in front of the main American artillery and infantry line, advanced on the Forty-second supported by Colonel Parker's 250 picked men, and some artillery. Cilley was able to use the terrain as cover to approach within two hundred yards of the orchard before beginning his assault. Although the battalion was one of Washington's recent ad hoc picked men formations, composed of officers and men from twenty different regiments, its movement was rapid and disciplined, once more providing unspoken testimony to Steuben's skills. On spotting Cilley's men, the Scots formed a line of battle along a fence bordering the orchard, but when they were taken under fire by an American six-pounder artillery piece pushed forward in fulfillment of Knox's tactical view of artillery directly supporting infantry attacks, quickly abandoned the fence line and fell back in a hail of grape and canister shot. Although he advanced the bulk of his battalion in line formation, Cilley also broke out a skirmish force, which pursued the enemy in a loose light infantry formation. The skirmishers were armed with muskets. Surprisingly, the archaeological evidence suggests that some of the Americans may have carried rifles, although it seems more likely that the approximately .60-caliber balls found in the orchard were from Pattern 1776 rifles in Highlander ranks.[32]

Under pressure, the Scots fell back through the orchard into a field beyond and up a slight rise, where they were safe from the Continental artillery, fired a volley at their pursuers and marched off further to the rear, where they took another position supported by two three-pounder artillery pieces. Cilley pursued, his men advancing through artillery fire and musketry to deliver a volley right into the enemy's faces at short range. After a few exchanges of small arms fire, the Highlanders withdrew again across the Spotswood Brook headwaters. Cilley did not follow. This fighting is probably the best-documented incident of the battle, since archaeological work has supplemented, and, more importantly, clarified the written record. Still, it is difficult to determine the actual casualties suffered by either side in the fight, other than that they were not heavy. There is no surviving direct report from Cilley, although General Alexander lists the battalion's loss as "trifling." The best estimate is that the Scots suffered no more than three or four fatalities in the action, although the regiment as a whole lost twenty-two men killed at Monmouth, more than in any other battle it participated in during the war. Private Martin may have accounted for one of them. Detailed as a battalion skirmisher, he "singled out a man and took my aim directly between his shoulders" at about twenty-five yards distance as the Forty-second fell back out of the orchard, but the smoke prevented him from seeing the results of his shot. This often overlooked skirmish provides concrete evidence of the cohesiveness, discipline, and tactical ability of the Continental army in June 1778.[33]

As the tempo of the orchard contest increased, Washington began to push back on his right as well, ordering Wayne, who, as was his wont, was looking for action, to launch a limited attack of

An artist's view of Anthony Wayne's attack on the retreating British at the end of the battle. The Tennent parsonage farm is in the background. (*Library of Congress*)

his own on the First Grenadiers, who were preparing to retreat on Clinton's orders. The grenadiers successfully disengaged and fell back beyond the hedgerow as the Thirty-third Foot advanced to cover their withdrawal. Wayne pursued the British with three small regiments, the Third Pennsylvania, and Malcolm's and Spencer's "Additional Regiments," and caught up with them at the present location of Wemrock Road. The grenadiers, trained to respond aggressively in both advance and rearguard actions, launched a counterattack that drove Wayne's men back to the hedgerow and into the fields of the Tennent parsonage farm beyond. As the British surged forward, however, they were caught in enfilade by the guns on Combs Hill and abandoned their pursuit, which, since they were withdrawing anyway, was necessarily limited in duration. One solid shot was credited with breaking the muskets of an entire rank of advancing grenadiers. While that story, which endured for many years, is likely apocryphal, it graphically illustrates the havoc that could be caused by enfilading artillery fire. Both Cilley's and Wayne's attacks were

Photo of the badly deteriorated Tennent parsonage farmhouse, mute witness to some of the heaviest fighting at Monmouth, in the 1850s. It was torn down shortly afterward. (*Kevin Marshall*)

minimally risky to Washington. Even if one or both forces were smashed, his army would remain intact.[34]

An alternate, albeit unlikely, theory regarding the death of Lieutenant-Colonel Monckton of the grenadiers has him killed in this encounter rather than the earlier one, with his body left between the lines as his men retreated. Early New Jersey historians James Barber and Henry Howe claimed that local resident Samuel Forman advised them that Monckton was killed toward the end of the fighting and the spot was marked, in 1844, by "an oak stump in the ploughed field about eight rods [forty-four yards] NE of the parsonage." Whenever and wherever he expired, Monckton's burial site was the Tennent churchyard, "within six feet of the west end of the church," where, some sixty-six years after the battle, there was "no monument . . . but his name, rudely cut on the building, marks the spot." A few years later a rude wooden slab was erected by a "Scotch schoolmaster, William Wilson," a few feet away from the building wall and reading, "HIC JACET [here lies] Col. Monkton KILLED 28 June

1778." That marker, still standing, although a little the worse for wear, at the time of the battle's centennial in 1878 was, in its turn, eventually replaced by a more modern stone marker. A sword said to be Monckton's, as well as a flag attributed to the Second Grenadier Battalion, were also taken by the Americans, specifically Captain William Wilson of the First Pennsylvania Regiment. Grenadier battalions, being ad hoc organizations of companies from various regiments, were not entitled to regimental colors, but the flag may have been one the battalion had made up on its own. There is no unit designation on the flag, now, along with the sword, in the collections of the Monmouth County Historical Association.[35]

In response to Clinton's withdrawal, Washington ordered an advance of his entire force all along the Perrine Ridge line toward Monmouth Court House, and instructed Woodford's Virginians on Combs Hill to attack the enemy's left flank. As the British fell back, however, heat exhaustion and, in the case of Woodford's men, the complication of difficult terrain, slowed the advance to a crawl and, shortly afterward, an effective halt. By the time the men of Lee's reorganized division arrived on the field from Englishtown under the command of Steuben, it was after 6:00 p.m. and Washington officially halted the advance, ordering his men to sleep on their arms on the battlefield, and be prepared to renew the fight in the morning. Washington himself slept out under the stars, Lafayette alongside him, near the Sutphin farmhouse.[36]

There would be no renewal of the fight. During the night, while the Americans slept on the field, Clinton—satisfied that he could use the fact that he had saved his baggage, now safely at Nut Swamp, just south of Middletown, with Knyphausen, to excuse his failure to achieve the decisive victory he had in mind at the early stages of the battle—began to move out of Monmouth Court House. The British march up the Middletown road was conducted in a thoroughly professional manner, and with so little noise that Washington did not realize the enemy was gone until morning, although some have suggested that the American commander, usually well informed by his militia scouts, knew they were going, and having decided that since the Continentals had fought well and he had fulfilled his immediate ends that day, in a sense extended them Lee's "bridge of gold." Clinton rested his force at Middletown, moving on to Sandy Hook on June 30, where he rendezvoused with Admiral Richard Howe's fleet. Today Sandy Hook is a peninsula, but in 1778 it was an island, separated from the mainland by a narrow sixty-yard tidal-cut channel, with the Loyalist raider camp, "Refugeetown," situated at its northern tip. The British constructed a pontoon-style bridge of barges to march over to the island, and subsequently boarded ships in an efficient evacuation operation that began on July 1 and was completed on July 5. The Third, Fourth, and Fifth brigades took ship for Long Island, the First and Second brigades for Staten Island, and the foot guards, Hessians, and dragoons for Manhattan Island.

Although Colonel Cilley was hopeful that "we shall Burgoyne him [Clinton] in a few weeks," Washington did not aggressively pursue the retreating enemy in the days after the battle. It was the correct decision. Clinton was clearly on his way out of New Jersey and the battle at Monmouth Court House, albeit tactically incon-clusive, ended with a British retreat and the Americans in control of the field, the enemy's dead and many of his wounded. It could, at the very least, be claimed as a victory for propaganda purposes. Clinton had secured an excellent defensive position at Middletown, and his force would be buttressed by the guns of British warships at Sandy Hook, so any renewal of the fighting would be on his terms. There was no need to endanger hard-won success in a pursuit that was not likely to bring decisive, or even useful, results. On June 29, Morgan, Maxwell, and the New Jersey militia were assigned to harass the enemy rear and pick up stragglers and deserters, while the rest of the American army rest-ed and began to clean up the battlefield. The road to Middletown and beyond was certainly viewed as a tough one by Captain Ewald and his jaegers, who were covering Knyphausen. Ewald and his men were cut off several times and he recalled that before, during, and after the battle the column was "attacked on all sides" by militia, and that "large groups of Americans (including

Huddy's company) penetrated several times between the intervals of the *Jaeger* platoons up to the wagons, killing men and horses." Loyalist Lieutenant-Colonel Thomas Rogers stated in a postwar loss claim that "at the Battle of Monmouth Lieutenant McAnally not being able to secure the Baggage Horses & as aforesaid they were taken up by the Enemy by which your Memorialist sustained a Loss of upwards of Three Hundred Pounds." Ewald lost men killed, wounded, and captured to the militia through July 2.[37]

The exact human toll of the fighting at Monmouth Court House is difficult to determine. Casualty reports were inconsistent and often framed to meet the propaganda goals of either side, or, for that matter, individual purposes. Andrew Bell, a secretary to Clinton, who estimated the American force at a hyperbolic 25,000 men, reported in his diary that: "Tis generally thought the rebels have lost 2,500, as General Clinton was master of the field [which of course he was not] and had an opportunity of observing. 'Tis said Lee is killed, and a French General."[38]

On July 1, Colonel Laurens reported 356 American casualties, including 69 men killed in action, 161 wounded, and 132 missing. Some of the latter simply collapsed from the heat and later rejoined their units, but others, an estimated 37, died from the severe heat in various locations around the battlefield. Some may have simply deserted and some may have been prisoners, as Andrew Bell reported that the British captured 60 men.[39]

British losses are more problematic. On July 6, the *New York Gazette and Weekly Mercury*, a Loyalist newspaper, reported a total of 358 British casualties, including 124 dead, 170 wounded, and 56 missing, the vast majority of whom were probably dead, prisoners or deserters. Lieutenant Hale of the heavily engaged Second Grenadier Battalion listed total casualties in that unit as "98 with 11 officers killed and wounded," including four fatalities in his own company. Another junior officer recalled that "our loss altogether was upwards of four hundred men killed, wounded and who died from the sun and want of water." Major

Bauermeister noted that the British casualties totaled 286, including 112 killed, 62 died of sunstroke, and 174 wounded. An
American after-action report summarizing the interments of various burial details, as well as accounting for British dead buried by
local residents, came up with a total of 217, and added 29
Americans, but some doubt has been cast on the accuracy of that
number by the discovery of an alternate total from one burial
party officer. Washington wrote his brother that his army buried
245 enemy dead left on the field and took 100 prisoners. A number of other accounts come close to those numbers. Deserters, not
listed in official British returns of losses, began leaving the ranks
as soon as the army began to leave Philadelphia. Major
Bauermeister admitted to at least 200 deserters from Hessian
ranks during the campaign, and one American account cites a
total of 600 deserters, 440 of them Germans, returned to
Philadelphia by July 6. Some modern historians question the casualty totals of both armies, since the ratio of killed to wounded
seems higher than it should be. Estimates range as high as 1,134
British and 500 Americans killed, wounded, and missing in the
battle itself. None of these accounts include casualties incurred on
the march before and after the battle. On June 27, Captain Ewald
noted that "the army had lost over two hundred men on yester-
day's march," and that both men and horses were being killed by
constant militia attacks on Knyphausen's column all the way to
Sandy Hook. Ewald, who did not fight at Monmouth, estimated,
from the information he received, that the combined casualties of
both armies totaled around 1,100 men. As has been noted, however, the accuracy of his casualty totals has been challenged.[40]

One thing is not debatable—the British left all of their dead and
most of their wounded, save those with minor injuries, on the
field or at Monmouth Court House. Four officers and forty
wounded enlisted men were left at a makeshift hospital in the
town of Monmouth Court House, and many more lay scattered
across the field. Lieutenant John Shreve, who brought up the New
Jersey Brigade baggage the day after the battle, noted that he
"halted at a Presbyterian Meeting House [Tennent Meeting
House] and barn, both filled with wounded men of the American

and English; the surgeons of both armies (the enemy had left several) after twenty-four hours of dressing the wounded, had not got through." Shreve took in the battlefield, with its rapidly decomposing dead lying amid the detritus of their arms and equipment, and found it a "shocking sight," as did surgeon Samuel Adams of the Third Continental Artillery.[41]

Dr. William Read, who came upon the immediate postbattle scene, recalled "regimental surgeons officiating, and administering to some wounded soldiers, and hearing the groans and cries of some men who crawled, or been brought off into the rear." The following day he rode down to the edge of the morass surrounding Spotswood Middle Brook and across it, noting "several dead soldiers in the bog, mired to the waist, and probably shot [and] an officer lying a few yards from the morass, nearly cut in two by a cannon shot." Reaching the scene where the grenadiers had been badly shot up during the initial assault on the hedgerow line, they saw "fifty or sixty British grenadiers—some dead, some alive, calling for 'help!' 'water!' uttering the most dreadful and severe imprecations on 'the rebels.'" Although a Rebel himself, Read and his servant carried water to these men and dressed their wounds with the shirts of the dead, then enlisted "some country people and Negroes coming to the field of carnage, to place twenty-one wounded British soldiers in straw filled wagons and move them to Monmouth Court House." Read continued to tend these men in the court house building, amputating limbs when necessary and sleeping on the Judge's bench. He was later awarded a surgeon's commission.[42]

It had been a hard fight for officers as well as enlisted men, with a significant number killed and wounded on both sides. Colonel Otho Williams, whose account of the course of the battle is otherwise somewhat confused and inaccurate, remarks perceptively that "it is very remarkable that more officers fell on both sides in this action in proportion to the number of privates than at any other time since the commencement of the present dispute." Among the dead were a couple of Loyalist civilians. Surveying the field after the fight, Colonel Shreve found it "most pleasing" that among the dead were "two Guides Sam Leonard and Thomas Thomson. Both lived in this Neighbourhood, and both killed in the first of the Action, Leonard was Laying Down, took with a Cannon Ball in the Left Sholder come out in his Belly." Many of the wounded of both sides, both officers and enlisted men, remained in the area until they recovered or died or, in the case of the British, were sent to prison camps, paroled, or exchanged. American casualties were often tended to in local homes. In at least one of these cases, a Captain Nealey, who recovered in "the dwelling of a Mr. Cook," ended up marrying into the family. Some wounded British soldiers were apparently nursed by local residents as well, including Janet Rhea Davis, Colonel Rhea's sister, who refused to leave her home during the battle, hiding with her seven children in the cellar until the fighting was over.[43]

The dead—probably, in the end, more than three hundred of them—would never leave the land west of Monmouth Court House. Although Colonel Monckton was carried to the Tennent Meeting House for burial, most of the British who were killed on June 28, according to Dr. Samuel Forman, when interviewed many years later, received less formal interment. Forman recalled that they "lay in heaps like sheaves on a harvest-field," and were "dragged . . . by the heels to shallow pits dug for the purpose, and slightly covered them with earth; he saw thirteen buried in one hole." One Continental soldier assigned to a burial detail wrote that on the morning of June 29, "our next business was to gather the dead together in order to bury them which we did going about in wagons, loading them up bringing them together and burying about twelve or fourteen." Most of the American fatalities were treated similarly. Forman went on to say that "for many years after, the graves were indicated by the luxuriance of the vegetation," but apparently remained otherwise unmarked. Other dead soldiers, especially those who had dropped from heat prostration in woods and along streams "where they had crawled for shade and water," were buried where they fell, their "countenances . . . so blackened as to render it impossible to recognize individuals." Another mass grave was established in town, where a number of wounded British soldiers died in improvised hospitals and were "promiscuously thrown into a pit on the site of the present [1844] house of Dr. Throckmorton, and slightly covered with earth." In 1898, that site was more closely defined as at "the southeast corner of what is now Main and Throckmorton Streets in Freehold." One "lonely grave" of a militiaman allegedly killed in an attack on Knyphausen's baggage train north of town in the early morning hours of June 28 received better treatment, and remains alongside a "public road" to the present day.[44]

A graphic hint of the postbattle scene at Monmouth may be inferred from the words of other Jerseymen in another war almost a century later; members of the Fifteenth New Jersey Volunteer Infantry describing a burial detail at Gettysburg on July 4, 1863. Lieutenant Ellis Hamilton wrote home that he was "sickened by dead men lying there all bloated up and with faces as black as ink, and pools of blood all around the ground." Sergeant Dayton Flint was shocked by bodies "so disfigured that it was impossible for their comrades to recognize them," and Sergeant Lucian Voorhees, whose burial detail interred two Yankees and eight Confederates, prayed that "such a stench as hovered over that battlefield may God never again give occasion for." At Gettysburg and other Civil War battlefields, the hastily interred Union dead were eventually gathered together in newly created national cemeteries, with their graves identified if at all possible. Such was not the case at Monmouth.[45]

On July 1, the American army began to march away from the horrors of the battlefield at Monmouth Court House. The Continentals headed north out of Monmouth County, through Spotswood to New Brunswick, where they camped through July 4 and celebrated their new nation's second birthday by drawing up the army in two lines. The assembled soldiers, with "Green-Boughs" in their hats, fired a salute from thirteen artillery pieces, followed by a triple *feu de joie* of blank musketry rippling from the "right of the first line to the left and the from the left of the rear line to the right" and a chorus of "huzzas." From there General Maxwell's Jerseymen, who had rejoined the army along with Morgan's force after the British reached Sandy Hook, eventually moved to Elizabethtown, to keep a watch on British activity on

Staten Island and provide a trained defensive force to reinforce the militia in case of any British or Loyalist incursions into eastern New Jersey. The rest of the army continued its march north, through Scotch Plains and Paramus to Haverstraw and then White Plains, New York, where Washington established a head-quarters that would monitor the activities of the British in New York City.[46]

The battle was not over for Charles Lee, however, and he would literally get his day in court as the army marched. Nursing a bruised ego from what he perceived was Washington's disrespect that visited a "cruel injustice" on him and was in need of "repara-tion," Lee wrote his commander a complaining letter. Washington, at his best when managing prickly personalities, was willing to meet on the matter, but two even angrier letters fol-lowed. Lee was just warming up, and went on what Thomas Fleming has characterized as "a literary rampage" of public and private self-justification correspondence. In one of his letters to Washington, Lee demanded a court-martial to clear his name. Washington, by this time fed up with his principal subordinate's self-indulgent whining, granted the wish and appointed General Alexander, the putative Lord Stirling, as president of the court. Alexander had charges drawn up accusing Lee of disobedience of orders for not attacking the enemy, misbehavior in the face of the enemy by conducting a chaotic and unnecessary retreat and dis-respect to the commanding general in his postbattle correspon-dence. The court, which convened in New Brunswick on the morning of July 4, heard from a parade of commanders and staff officers who had participated in the battle, and provides a unique primary source view of the fight through their eyes shortly after it occurred. The testimony of Generals Scott and Wayne, first to take the stand, was decidedly hostile to Lee. Both men main-tained that it was their understanding from previous conferences with Washington that his orders were to attack the enemy at all costs, even if it meant bringing on a general action, and that Lee had admitted that he had no battle plan as he advanced his force that Sunday morning in June. Lieutenant Colonel Richard K. Meade supported the generals' opinions that Washington wanted Lee to start a fight before the enemy left Monmouth Court House, and that Lee was dilatory and indecisive. All of the officers stuck to their version of events under questioning from Judge Advocate General John Laurance and cross-examination from Lee himself.[47]

The court moved north with the army, reconvening at Paramus on July 13. During the interim, Lee, characteristically, vented publicly on what he thought an unfair hearing, even though he had demanded it himself. In a letter to the *New Jersey Gazette,* the general ranted about the proceedings being an "atrocious attack" on him and declaring that his actions at Monmouth Court House had, in fact, saved the army and been responsible for a great victory gained through wearing down the British by making them march all over the landscape. The letter was dismissed by Anthony Wayne as a bit of "insanity."[48]

Unsurprisingly, perhaps, with testimony from John Laurens, Alexander Hamilton's best friend in the army and one of Washington's trusted staff officers, the new session did not begin auspiciously for General Lee. Laurens, whose father Henry was president of the Continental Congress, testified that Lee appeared to have no idea of what he was doing at Monmouth. (Laurens's father had suggested in a letter to his son that Lee's retreat was a deliberate action intended to assist the British.) The general sharply cross-examined Laurens but his question, "Were you ever in an action before?," provided a vivid example of the old axiom that a lawyer should not ask a question to which he does not already know the answer. Laurens, who had proved his courage in combat on several occasions,corrected Lee by saying that the situation on the morning of June 28 as he found it was not an "action," but a retreat. The exchange provides further evidence that Lee was totally out of touch with the troops and subordinate leaders he commanded, due to his long hiatus from the army. Hamilton followed his friend and testified that he came upon Lee leading a disordered retreat. Adding to the damaging testimony, the two disrespectful letters that Lee had penned to Washington while in his immediate postbattle tantrum were introduced in evidence by Judge Advocate General Laurance. The second letter, particularly, in its expression of wishing to have the "opportunity of shewing to America the sufficiency of her respective servants," revealed that Lee's fundamental belief that he was more fit to command than Washington was still operative.[49]

The court-martial displaced north once more, to Peekskill, New York, where, on July 19, Lee made an attempt to counter the damaging testimony so far by calling his aide, nineteen-year-old Major John Francis Mercer, in his defense. Mercer, one of the few Lee loyalists in the army, testified that Lee did indeed have a plan on June 28, and that it was Scott and Wayne, the latter assuming an authority he did not have, who retreated without any orders and were responsible for undoing it. Mercer responded affirmatively to leading questions posed by Lee, including that the general had been distraught at the conduct of his subordinates who had disobeyed his orders. The major went on to paint Hamilton as a poseur who had actually recognized Lee's cool command on the field and then dissembled in his subsequent testimony. Although Mercer and Lee's other aides portrayed him as alert and on top of the situation, militia captain Peter Wikoff, who, unlike the Continental officers, had no personal axe to grind, presented a Lee more in line with the Laurens and Hamilton portrayal, who "begged me to conduct his troops under cover of some wood for he could not make them stand in a plain or open field so well as in the woods." If Lee meant by this he wanted to get his men out of the direct sun on that day, it is understandable, but if he meant that they would not stand and fight without cover, it was yet another indication of the general's obliviousness to the army's transformation.[50]

As testimony concluded, Laurance authorized Lee to submit a justification of his actions in writing. The general stressed that the terrain at Monmouth was difficult, his intelligence was conflicted and that Wayne, assuming a command responsibility never granted him, initiated the retreat. To Lee, Wayne's disobedience, coupled with Clinton's aggressive response to the American advance, was responsible for the disorganized withdrawal, which, he maintained, would have ended on the same defensive terrain chosen by Washington. He concluded that instead of opprobrium, he should have received praise for his actions at Monmouth. The court did not agree. On August 12, Lee was convicted on all three counts and suspended from command for a year, a sentence confirmed by Congress in December. Never one to think himself lucky and get on with life with perhaps a semi-independent command in the future, Lee, his arrogance scarcely diminished, proceeded to Philadelphia and lobbied Congress to reverse the decision. During the process, he continued to insult everyone who provided the slightest bit of contradiction to his own view of the Monmouth narrative, came close to duels with both Steuben and Wayne, and actually participated in a duel with Laurens, who wounded him. Returning to his estate in Virginia to recover, on hearing that Congress was considering dismissing him from the army permanently, Lee sent the legislative body an insulting letter that assured that outcome and then moved to Philadelphia, where he died in 1782. Charles Lee was a man of many genuine talents, and while he was careless in initiating the fight at Monmouth Court House, the idea promoted by Wayne and others that Washington wanted to bring on a major engagement there is false. Lee recovered from his initial setback, and it could be argued that his final act supervising the defense of the hedgerow line was one of the most significant tactical accomplishments of the battle, even though it was needed to remedy his earlier mistakes. Were those mistakes greater than Wayne's allowing himself to be surprised at Paoli, or even Washington's failure to make a thorough reconnaissance at Brandywine? Perhaps not, but Lee is, unfortunately, more remembered for his abrasive personality, massive ego, total lack of diplomatic ability, and lack of faith in the military ability of the soldiers under his command, and the fault for that lies strictly with him. Thomas Fleming's conclusion was that Lee was "not a great general. His total failure at Monmouth to reconnoiter the terrain; his indecision and hesitation, which allowed Clinton to outmaneuver him; his failure to inspire either confidence or cooperation in his subordinates—all these mark him as a "third rate leader of men," is perhaps too harsh, but considering Lee's personal behavior throughout his career, perfectly understandable.[51]

What is inarguable about the events of that day in June 1778 is the significance of the Battle of Monmouth Court House to the outcome of the American War for Independence. Monmouth was the longest action of the war, measured from the initial early morning militia contact through the evening disengagement. It was also the last major battle in the north, although the June 1780 fighting at Springfield, New Jersey, which occurred when Continentals and militia resisted a British incursion based on the continued folly of invading the state and destroying property in hopes it would rally the population to the Crown, was a fairly substantial action. In the wake of the combat at Monmouth Court House, the Americans who fought there realized they had accomplished something memorable, and that the course of the war had been inalterably changed. Major Joseph Bloomfield wrote in his diary that the Continentals "drove the proud King's-Guards & haughty British-Grenadiers, & gained Immortal-honor, to the Shame and infamy of General Lee." Despite public claims to the contrary, some of the enemy tended to agree. Clinton's private secretary, who at one point claimed that his boss won the battle, also conceded that "the Rebels stood much better than ever they did." Captain Ewald admitted that, far from being chastised, "the Americans showed much boldness and resolution on all sides during their attacks" on the baggage train during and after the battle.[52]

Monmouth provided solid evidence that the Americans had indeed finally created a regular army out of a force that had taken its first solid steps toward that goal during the 1777 New Jersey Forage War. The professionalization of that army, which had grown into a long-service force able to integrate recruits seamlessly into its structure, was armed with new French muskets and drilled in what one historian has aptly characterized as a system of "uniformity of evolutions [while] simultaneously simplifying them" through the efforts of Steuben, inspired a confidence that allowed the Americans to stand up to the best Britain had to offer. One American infantry officer bragged with reason, "I don't think

Genl. Clinton will get no Laurels by this expedition—they cant say we sculked in the Bushes & fought like Indians—our Troops met them in the Open field." Knox's artillery had matured as well, into a force that its commander could credit with having a "full proportion of the Glory of the day." In addition, the Monmouth campaign provided an opportunity for the Continentals to perfect their cooperative tactics with the local militia that had their origins in the Forage War. A tough professional standing force, working with an aggressive militia and effective local political organization, spelled doom to British hopes for returning New Jersey, a state that had seemed a significant source of sympathizers less than two years before, to the loyal fold.[53]

Clinton, as is the wont of generals and other executives down to the present day, put the best possible public face on his role in the campaign and the battle, even when he had to dissemble to do so. On July 5, he wrote Lord George Germain a report intended for publication, asserting that he had, in fact, pulled off an almost perfect operation from the day he left Philadelphia until his arrival in New York. Clinton claimed that at Monmouth he was facing "an army far superior in numbers" to his own and downplayed his counterattack against Lee as simply a temporary diversion to protect his baggage which, when that "end was gained" and with his men "overpowered with fatigue," he decided to "press . . . no farther," and broke off the action on his own terms to move on. In a private letter to the Duke of Newcastle, however, Clinton was more candid. Granting that Washington's interception of his army was "well timed," he admitted that he fought the battle with two things in mind, protecting his baggage train, but also, "in the hopes of meeting his whole army in a critical situation passing the defiles which I know separated him from his avant garde." Clinton had, in fact, decided to fight a decisive battle once the action began, which accounts for his enthusiasm as he led the charge on the hedgerow line, looking, as a junior officer disparagingly wrote, like a "Newmarket jockey." A correspondent of Lord Amherst criticized the general by writing that Clinton "did not content himself with repulsing the attack but followed the enemys advanced body three or four miles—many instances of bravery were shown, perhaps too many by S Henry in person." Still strangely unwilling to concede the quality of the Continental troops (a belief he shared with Charles Lee), however, Clinton wrote Newcastle that "nothing but the intolerable heat prevented [success]; the Thermometer at 94 in the shade, is not a climate for troops to act with Vigour in at noon day." Although unsurprisingly crediting himself with unusual tactical talent and strategic foresight at Monmouth, Clinton apparently got the message from that day of hard fighting, and hoped that having survived it, he "shall therefore be permitted to go home." In this prescient moment in the days after the battle, he wrote, "America . . . possibly might have been recovered, as it is I fear she will be lost."[54]

Sir Henry had good reason to fear. In the end, Steuben's infantry and Knox's artillery had proved themselves the equal of their enemy. The fact that they had the opportunity to do so was, in large part, due to the French, whose intervention in the war sparked the British orders to evacuate Philadelphia. The retreat across New Jersey gave rise to not only a military coming of age for the American army, which had previously only defeated British forces in a war of outposts, relatively small unit affairs like Trenton and Princeton, or in the unique situation presented by Burgoyne's plunge into the wilderness of northern New York, but signaled the erosion of the political support that Britain had always hoped would greet its armies. As Stephen Conway notes: "British strategy proceeded from the assumption that thousands of loyal Americans were just waiting for a British lead to come forward and help put down the rebellion." When General Howe entered New Jersey in 1776, many of the state's citizens indeed flocked to sign loyalty oaths to the Crown, attempted to restore royal government, and even joined the British army. When General Clinton marched across New Jersey less than two years later, however, he didn't even bother to bring loyalty oath forms with him, and concentrated on getting safely beyond the state's borders as fast as he could. At Monmouth, the British and American armies faced each other on the road between the two most significant cities in America, New York and Philadelphia. Both sides fought to a standstill and, although the British succeeded in getting their baggage and army intact to New York, they were, in a larger sense, defeated. The British strategic retrenchment that occasioned the Battle of Monmouth had gone a long way toward not only securing New Jersey for the patriot cause, but of securing American independence. New England had already been conceded by the Crown, and now the Middle Colonies would follow. Loyal governance could not be restored at the point of a bayonet, and Clinton, his force reduced by a new strategic reality, never sallied out of New York to give serious battle to Washington's army for the rest of the war.[55]

There would, of course, be more war elsewhere. John Ferling, who posits a series of turning points in the conflict, albeit oddly missing Monmouth, cites the Southern campaign of 1780–81 as the "final" one. As Ferling notes, the Southern Strategy initially achieved "spectacular results," at least at first glance. The British captured Savannah and Charleston, defeated American armies in the field, and gave hope to Lord George Germain, who was assured that the campaign's apparent success heralded a "speedy and happy termination of the American war." In reality, however, the best Germain could hope for at that stage of the conflict was a rump southern Loyalist state that could confront an independent United States to the north. As with other British will-o'-the-wisp quests for a Loyalist surge solution to their American problems harking back to the invasion of New Jersey in 1776, things fell apart. A combination of active partisan militia activity culminating in the destruction of Patrick Ferguson's force at Kings Mountain, bolstered by the backing of solid Steuben-trained Continental reinforcements under the capable leadership of Nathanael Greene and Daniel Morgan, steadily eroded British strength until Washington, with critical French assistance on land and sea, bottled up Cornwallis at Yorktown for the final British disaster.[56]

A more sophisticated counterinsurgency plan initiated in 1776 might have made a difference, and perhaps sustained and expanded efforts like the Woodward boys' Upper Freehold counterrevolution. As Clinton's rear guard marched up to Middletown, however, the war was, in reality, as General Clinton dimly perceived, over, save some startling development, which did not prove to be in the offing. Unfortunately, it took several more years and a copious amount of bloodshed for everyone to realize it, including the brutal internecine combatants in Monmouth County itself. The strategic implications of the French intervention, which led to the Battle of Monmouth, however, together with the tactical skills of the now veteran army of George Washington, which made its defining stand west of Monmouth Court House, made British victory over the Americans and a restoration of the status quo antebellum an extremely unlikely outcome.

"Molly Pitcher" became the most iconic figure of the battle of Monmouth Court House. This nineteenth century painting is in the park visitor center. (*Joseph Bilby*)

"The mystic chords of memory":

THE BATTLE IN LEGEND AND

MEMORY

THE BATTLE OF MONMOUTH SURELY PROVED to be the making of the Continental army, an engagement in which George Washington's soldiers demonstrated that their hard-won combat experience, coupled with the rigorous training they had received during the winter encampment at Valley Forge, paid large dividends. It marked a turning point in the American War of Independence that, in retrospect, barring an unforeseen disaster, strongly increased the likelihood of an ultimate American victory. For these reasons alone, it would seem reasonable to expect that the battle would be commemorated with relish following the cessation of hostilities. This was not to be the case.

The battlefield at Monmouth Court House remained just another swath of sleepy farmland for decades after the war, its heroes unheralded and its importance uncelebrated. This reticence to glorify the past may have had its roots in local history. Monmouth County society suffered a profound schism during the course of the war, as factions with histories of disagreement aligned themselves with the patriot or Loyalist camp with the idea of settling old scores. As the Revolution in Monmouth devolved into a civil war, resulting in brazenly dishonorable acts and thuggish retaliation on both sides, residents from Allentown to Sandy Hook suffered immensely. The raw, personal, and even vicious character the war assumed within the county resulted in many incidents that must have seemed better left buried and forgotten after the last shot was fired. When some Loyalists who had fled to Canada came creeping back to their lands in the years following, citizens turned a blind eye. After the divisiveness of the war, it is actually rather remarkable that the populace transitioned so quickly and so completely into a normal peacetime way of life free from reprisals. There is no evidence of postwar violence in the area at all; in fact, although both sides were involved in extrajudicial killings during the conflict, the only lynching to take place in Monmouth County between 1783 and the present day was that of an African American man accused of rape who was hanged in the Eatontown jail doorway by a drunken mob in 1886. Perhaps the violence of the Revolutionary War years had gone so far that all concerned had lost their taste for it. Whatever the case, the generation that had lived through the war seems to have closed the book on it.[1]

Later generations, however, would come to find the Battle of Monmouth to be worth celebrating. The first recorded commemoration of the battle took place in 1828, a distant fifty years after the event and long enough for the misery and brutality that formerly defined the war for county residents to have softened into a retrospective vision that emphasized victory and patriotic sacrifice. In a history of New Jersey published in 1834, author Thomas F. Gordon wrote extensively about the battle, and deemed it an American victory in that the Continental army suffered fewer casualties and weakened Sir Henry Clinton's forces considerably during the engagement.[2]

Around this time, the soon-to-be most famous figure of the battle appeared in a soldier-memoirist's vivid depiction.

A woman whose husband belonged to the artillery and who was then attached to a piece in the engagement, attended with her husband at the piece the whole time. While in the act of reaching for a cartridge and having one of her feet as far before the other as she could step, a cannon shot from the enemy passed directly between her legs without doing any other damage than carrying away all the lower part of her petticoat. Looking at it with apparent unconcern, she observed that it was lucky it did not pass a little higher, for in that case it might have carried away something else, and continued her occupation.[3]

The anecdote, recorded many years after the battle by Joseph Plumb Martin, one of Colonel Cilley's picked men who fought in the Sutphin orchard, and included in his memoir published in 1830, is engineered to delight, to intrigue, and perhaps to mildly scandalize with its details of shorn undergarments and female brazenness. It seems to refer to the story of "Molly Pitcher," although it does not call its subject by that name, nor describe her as a water carrier.

The tale of Molly Pitcher has been told and retold in many variants, but the core story involves a camp follower and wife of an artilleryman who was charged with carrying water (hence the Pitcher appellation) to the men of Proctor's Artillery Battery during the Battle of Monmouth, and who jumped in to help fire a cannon when one of the artillerymen was wounded or killed. Most often the wounded or killed man is identified as her husband, William Hays. Does Molly Pitcher, whose legend has sifted down through the years to the present day unlike a thousand other atypical incidents witnessed during the war, represent a real person known to us only through a hodgepodge of her contemporaries' remembrances, or a tall tale woven together by old men seeking to amuse a younger generation with hyperbole? In the authors' opinion there is a real woman behind the myth, but in either case it is certain that the legend of her heroics coincided perfectly with the growing sense among New Jerseyans and Americans in general during the nineteenth century that the Battle of Monmouth represented the triumph of values

Americans enjoyed: resourcefulness, determination, courage, and willingness to meet the challenge of the hour.

To get a better sense of Molly Pitcher and the potential to identify her as a singular historical personage, it is important to understand the "camp follower" phenomenon, and the ways in which it brought eighteenth-century American women into contact with the battlefield. Molly is only the most famous of many women who endured the hardships of Revolutionary War campaigning alongside the soldiery of both sides. The so-called camp followers have been defamed as prostitutes by some writers, but it is illogical to categorize all women traveling with the army as such. Although prostitution was no doubt an in-demand service amongst Washington's soldiers, so was cleaning, cooking, washing, and nursing. In exchange for these valuable services, women and their children received rations, albeit in smaller portions than fighting men. As noted in a previous chapter, many camp followers were married to or in relationships with the men they accompanied, and even brought their children along, making for a frontline family unit that is quite unfamiliar in today's military or that of the recent past.[4]

As the camp followers trailed behind Washington's army, they experienced the war intimately, witnessing the results of conflict in real time. Some women took the next step; they participated in battle alongside enlisted men. The number of women who fought in the Revolution is not likely very great. Those who masqueraded as men were ejected from their units upon discovery, as in the case of Deborah Sampson, who served under the alias Robert Shurtleff. Sampson went to great lengths to successfully conceal her sex and did so despite being wounded several times, until a fever led her to be admitted to the infirmary; legend has it that the doctor in question agreed to keep her secret, but his lovesick nephew proceeded to reveal her true gender. If this revelation was intended to woo Sampson it seems to have failed, and once discharged she went on to marry a Massachusetts farmer and eventually took her astonishing story on the lecture circuit.[5]

The idea of a woman masquerading as a man in order to participate in battle was disquieting to the population at large and in

Top, Mary "Molly Pitcher" Hays was a common subject of nineteenth century illustrations. Bottom left, a popular Currier & Ives print. (*Library of Congress*) The apocryphal meeting between George Washington, bottom right, (here portrayed as he looked twenty years after the war), and "Molly Pitcher." (*Courtesy Dr. David Martin*)

general disapproved of; not only was there the matter of women becoming exposed to the bloodshed and risk of grievous bodily injury inherent in war, there was the issue of the social power a woman fraudulently obtained in living life as a man, as well as the disruption to society caused by her abandonment of womanly functions, such as managing the home and raising offspring. While living as a man was not culturally acceptable, briefly taking on certain male characteristics in the heat of battle in order to serve one's cause was. It was not unheard of for camp followers to be found at the front lines providing water to the men to relieve their thirst, or swabbing the artillery pieces between shots. There are documented cases of other women who, in the midst of engaging in standard camp follower duties, were compelled to take on an active fighting role due to circumstances. Margaret "Captain Molly" Corbin, who was wounded while helping operate a gun at the battle of Fort Washington on November 16, 1776, is a famous and well-documented example. Stories such as Corbin's add to the confusion over who may be identified as Molly Pitcher and whether she was a genuine person, or an imaginary figure incorporating elements of various events and individuals. Unfortunately Corbin's experience, probably owing to the similarity in names and actions, has become intertwined with the Molly Pitcher story over the years. Later anecdotes that were added to embellish the incident at the Battle of Monmouth, such as the story that she volunteered to man her husband's cannon in order to prevent it from being withdrawn from the field of battle, and that she was personally introduced to General Washington in the aftermath of the battle, are fictitious attempts to solidify Molly Pitcher's status as a brave and important Revolutionary figure. New Jersey schoolchildren of the 1890s were exposed to a wildly exaggerated and largely apocryphal account of Molly's adventures in a book by writer Frank Stockton titled *Stories of New Jersey*, which also included a similarly unsubstantiated essay on the man who had become by that time the villain of the battle, Charles Lee.[6]

A combination of factual confusion in stories related many years after the fact, and the popular veneration of Revolutionary heroes that took place during the mid-nineteenth century, have partially obscured the identity and actions of the real Molly Pitcher. All evidence indicates, however, that she was likely a bona fide person named Mary Hays McCauley. Residents of Carlisle, Pennsylvania, during the 1820's were familiar with a

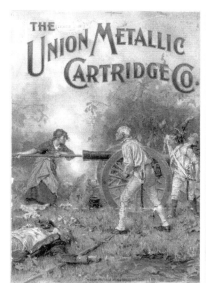

Two nineteenth-century advertisements featuring Molly Pitcher. (*Library of Congress*)

local figure who went by the nickname "Mollie Pitcher," and admonished young ladies: "You should have been with me at the Battle of Monmouth and learned how to load a cannon." In an unusual circumstance, this woman was granted a Revolutionary War pension in February 1822 by an act of the Pennsylvania legislature. Although it was not uncommon for women to appeal to the government for assistance based on their husbands' military service, the number of women granted pensions in their own right can be counted on one hand. It seems that Mary's martial reputation was a point of pride in Carlisle; a local man named Wesley Miles recollected in a piece published in the *Carlisle Herald* in 1876 that Mary McCauley, who once acted as his nursemaid, was buried with military honors upon her death.[7]

Miles's description of her as an "aged Irish woman" has contributed to confusion over Molly Pitcher's ethnic identity. Several nineteenth-century sources assert that Mary McCauley was of German or "Pennsylvania Dutch" descent and bore the maiden name Ludwig. Reverend C.P. Wing of Carlisle wrote a letter to the editor of the *Pennsylvania Magazine of History and Biography* in

1878 to claim that he had verified Mary McCauley's origins through a family Bible, but this source no longer exists and cannot be consulted. Dr. William H. Egle included Mary Ludwig in a genealogical study published in 1893; he provides a birth date and place and the name of Mary's father, but does not specify his source material. Conversely, Sally Smith Stafford, a schoolteacher born in Allentown, New Jersey, gave a statement in 1876 asserting that Molly Pitcher was really Mary Hanna, the daughter of an Irish Presbyterian named John Hanna and resident of Allentown. Although John Hanna's will does reference a daughter named Mary, and local lore has her married to a soldier named John Cavanaugh who was wounded at Monmouth, this information does not verifiably connect Mary Hanna to Mary Hays McCauley.[8]

Due to the paucity of vital records available to us from the mid-eighteenth century, it is impossible to establish Molly Pitcher's maiden name and ethnic heritage with any absolute degree of certainty. Although some of McCauley's Carlisle neighbors later recalled her Irish attributes, it must be kept in mind that their accounts were related some fifty-odd years after the fact, and drew on experiences they had had as children; in fact, Miles was only about five years old at the time McCauley worked for his family. There are those who argue strongly for the Ludwig name. McCauley's own granddaughter, Mrs. Polly McLeaster, was quoted as saying her grandmother was unmistakably German. It would seem logical to put more stock in family traditions than neighborhood lore, but ultimately neither case can be fully proved, although there is a case for the Ludwig birth name. At the time of the battle, however, "Molly" was Mary Hays, and when her husband died after the war (not on the field at Monmouth), leaving her with a son by him, she remarried, gaining the surname McCauley.

Whatever McCauley's heritage, it is clear that she participated heroically in the Battle of Monmouth. Primary sources, including Joseph Plumb Martin and a woman named Rebecca Clendenen, who in her pension application mentioned that her husband John often spoke about the hardships he endured during the Battle of

Monmouth and of a "Captain Molly" who was present carrying canteens of water to the soldiers, establish that a woman named Molly was engaged in transporting water to the front lines during the action, and that at one point she was involved in serving on an artillery crew. Mary Hays McCauley's pension, which cites the services she rendered during the war (but sadly does not specify what these services consisted of), indicates that McCauley contributed to the war effort in a manner outside the scope of the typical camp follower. Also, McCauley was widely reported to have reminisced about the battle and her role in firing the cannon as an older woman living in Carlisle. It was so widely recognized among the locals that she was the famed Molly Pitcher of the Battle of Monmouth that when she was buried, military honors were indeed afforded to her. Although fictional details were

Gravestone of Mary Hays McCauley in Carlisle, Pennsylvania. The stone was set in 1876, and the photo dates from June 28, 1905. (*Courtesy Bob Goodyear*)

added to her story at later dates in order to create a greater sense of drama and mythological power, her actions during the battle remain indisputable and worthy of recognition on their own merit. Those who doubt Molly Pitcher's existence point out that her story became prominent long after the war, at a time when war heroes were in high demand, and some were not above fabricating their accounts of great deeds; that the friends and neighbors who came forward to vouch for Mary McCauley as Molly Pitcher were recounting memories over fifty years old; and that there generally is not enough hard evidence to establish that Molly Pitcher was anything more than a tall tale or a conflation of several other people. Researchers of this era realize, however, that it is rare to locate a preponderance of contemporaneous doc-

Top, memorial monument to Mary Ludwig "Molly Pitcher" Hays McCauley erected in the cemetery in Carlisle, Pennsylvania, where she was buried in 1833. The statue was erected in 1916, with her face created from a composite of her great granddaughters. Bottom, relief sculpture on the monument of an imaginary Molly incident as she nurses a wounded infantryman at the front. (*Michael Waricher*)

umentary evidence when it comes to the lives of ordinary people. When examined in isolation, each piece of evidence identifying Mary McCauley as Molly Pitcher may not stand up to scrutiny, but taken together as a whole they create a substantive case in favor of this conclusion.[9]

The Molly Pitcher story, with its patriotic heroine, fits into a larger picture that involved the nineteenth-century movement to memorialize and glorify the Battle of Monmouth. As noted before, the 1820s and 1830s witnessed the deification of many Revolutionary figures; even today, George Washington is known more in popular culture as a saintly father figure rather than the tough-minded, active, and intelligent military and political strategist and tactician that he was. Monmouth County residents had an advantage when it came to lauding their forebears, actual and metaphorical; the Battle of Monmouth represented a crucial turning point in the war, and it was right in their backyards. In June of 1846, an advertisement appeared in the *Monmouth Inquirer* soliciting participation in a meeting to gauge the feasibility of erecting a monument on the battlefield. By now, the old wounds of the county's bitter wartime strife had apparently healed so completely that a placid nostalgia had taken their place. The meeting that resulted from the advertisement in the *Inquirer* resulted in the formulation of the following lofty goals, as set forth in the *Monmouth Democrat*'s July 2 issue.

> 1. Resolved, That it is the duty of a grateful posterity to commemorate not only in their hearts, but by suitable monuments, the noble deeds of their fathers, and the important events in their history.
>
> 2. Resolved, That among the important events of our Revolutionary struggle, the Battle of Monmouth should never be forgotten.
>
> 3. Resolved, That we believe the time has fully come when the citizens of Monmouth County should unite and erect a suitable monument to commemorate that important event.
>
> 4. Resolved, That the proceedings of this meeting be published in the Freehold papers.[10]

A subsequent meeting created the Monmouth Battle Monument Association and Commission, and in a public address to the people of Monmouth, printed and distributed in October

1846, the committee urged: "Be ready then, fellow-citizens, and when the Collectors call on you, in the course of the next six weeks, meet them with smiles and with a hearty welcome, and contribute at once as you are able, and send them on their way rejoicing." This earnest advice does not appear to have been heeded, because despite the burst of enthusiasm in which some residents made the push for a monument, nothing ever came of their efforts or their preliminary design of a sixteen-foot obelisk in Italian marble.[11]

The drive to erect a monument on the site was not the only way in which the importance of the battle was recognized by posterity; a number of notable anniversary celebrations and reenactments were held throughout the years. The earliest of these was apparently not very well received, at least by some, and may have been more of an opportunity for the organizers to promote certain political candidates than to venerate the glorious dead. The *True American* of Trenton posted a less than exhilarated review of the celebrations marking the fiftieth anniversary of the battle in 1828, calling the event "a complete failure," which hardly anyone of note in the state attended. A writer known only as "A Revolutionary Officer" wrote to the newspaper in a letter published on July 12 of that year complaining of the festivities, saying they "answered the expectation of no one" and noting that, "the authors of this celebration kept aloof, and the whole affair failed for want of friends and spirit to carry it on. I attended as an amateur, having fought in that field in the days of my youth, and was chagrined to find so brilliant a battle, so badly celebrated. But the object was known to be political—to build up the military candidate—and it failed." The "military candidate" for president in this era, when newspapers were blatant organs of political parties, was Andrew Jackson, who, in another column in the same paper, was described as having "no talents fit for the presidency," and a man whose election would "indeed be a curse to the country."[12]

In the 1850s, as the nation began to tear itself apart over slavery, interest in an earlier, seemingly more unified era grew. Although the *Monmouth Democrat* newspaper announced that "never, since the Revolution, has the patriotic spirit of the citizens of this county been so thoroughly aroused," a June 28, 1854, commemoration of the battle—organized by former assemblyman Joel Parker, then prosecutor of the pleas for Monmouth County, who was embarking on what would be a remarkably successful political career, and drew more than ten thousand people—proved somewhat disappointing, due largely to debilitating weather that rivaled that of June 1778. A "Sham Fight" reenactment (apparently the first such effort) of the battle by two thousand New Jersey and New York militiamen, planned as the day's centerpiece, was cancelled when the part-time soldiers scheduled to perform refused to do so after several participants collapsed from heatstroke, similarly to soldiers in the original battle. Subsequently,

Joel Parker (1816-1888), was a nineteenth century Monmouth County politician who twice served as governor of New Jersey (1863-1866 and 1870-1873) organized the 1854 commemoration of the battle and was responsible for the monument dedicated in 1884 that still stands today. (*John W. Kuhl*)

during a salute to the attending governor, Rodman M. Price, militiaman Abraham Coles of Newark had his left hand shattered by a misfiring artillery piece and was forced to undergo an amputation, while his compatriot James Johnson was burned on the face and arms. Elisa Smith of Freehold was not happy with the whole affair, which she thought "a strange way to show & feel our gratitude for our independence." Ms. Smith had plenty of visitors for the occasion, though, and she prepared a "sumptuous repast" for guests who went out to see the sham fight, "and sham it was," she concluded. Smith harrumphed to her cousin Sarah Waln that "their faces were burned to blisters. Tir'd and worn out with fatigue. Sat in a sunny field on a few sheaves of straw & some had to pay one shilling for a glass of water."[13]

In 1858, a large religious "camp meeting" held at "Tenant Church" also featured a tour of the battlefield, but the aura of conflict came back to Monmouth battlefield in reality during the Civil War. The state of New Jersey leased land from farmer Jacob Herbert along the Freehold and Jamesburg railroad line, which had laid tracks through the area in the early 1850s, to establish Camp Vredenburgh, named after prominent local judge Peter Vredenburgh. Construction began on temporary barracks on July 22, 1862, and they, along with tents, housed the recruits of three Union army regiments—the Fourteenth, Twenty-eighth, and Twenty-ninth New Jersey Volunteer Infantry—while those units were being organized and provided with rudimentary training later that summer. The Twenty-eighth was the last regiment to leave for the front, on October 2. After that regiment's departure, the camp lay unused until Company H of the Thirty-fifth New Jersey Infantry was organized there in August 1863. Company H, the last active-duty military unit to march across the Monmouth battlefield until the Third United States Infantry sent a ceremonial detachment to participate in the 1978 bicentennial reenactment, left to join the rest of its regiment in Flemington on September 24, 1863. In January 1864, the barracks were disassembled and moved by rail to Trenton, and the area reverted to agricultural use.[14]

No further progress was made on erecting a monument until 1877, when Joel Parker, by that time a two-term former governor, spoke at a celebration of the ninety-ninth anniversary of the battle. Using the occasion as a galvanizing event, several influential New Jerseyans, including Parker and Major James Yard, publisher of the *Monmouth Democrat*, created a new organization named the Monmouth Battle Monument Association and initiated fundraising efforts. Three dollars of the money donated came with an unusual story attached. According to a June 27, 1878, letter to the editor of the *Monmouth Inquirer* from Lincoln H. Hough of Brooklyn, New York, a dollar each was donated by James Conover Hough, Lincoln Hough, and Morrell Monmouth Hough, the great-grandsons of a Mary H. Rogers, "who was born in the old farm house on the battle field, and was three weeks old on the day of the Battle of Monmouth. On the day of the battle the mother hid herself and the babe in the woods all day long."[15]

On February 2, 1878, a piece of land near where the battle began was donated by the Schanck family to serve as the location of the monument. During the well-attended centennial celebrations in June 1878, the cornerstone of the monument was laid and the deed to the monument site was delivered to Parker, who acted as the president of the Monmouth Battle Monument Association. It would take another six years to raise the approximately $36,000 needed to complete the project, however. The dedication finally took place on November 13, 1884, revealing a tall column topped with a figure of *Columbia Triumphant.* The base of the monument is triangular, featuring a sculpture of a cannon at each angle. Five bronze reliefs on tablets depicting scenes related to the battle, and above the tablets the coats of arms of the original thirteen states are represented in bronze.[16]

The five scenes in bas relief depict, respectively, the Council of War at Hopewell; Lieutenant Colonel Ramsay (with his name spelled as "Ramsey") struggling

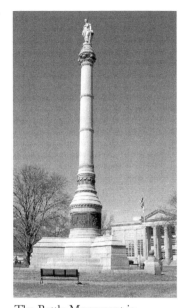

The Battle Monument in Freehold stands near the modern courthouse. The monument's cornerstone was laid during the centennial commemoration of the battle in 1878 and it was officially unveiled on November 13, 1884. Sculptor James E. Kelly created the relief sculptures of scenes from the campaign and the seals of the thirteen states on the monument itself. The statue of "Columbia Triumphant" atop the column was struck by lightning and seriously damaged in 1894 and replaced in 1896. (*Joseph Bilby*)

with a British dragoon during his rearguard action following the fight at the point of woods; Washington rallying Lee's retreating troops; Molly Pitcher manning her husband's cannon; and General Wayne leading the attack in the final fight at the hedgerow. New Yorker James Edward Kelly, chosen as the sculptor of the bronze reliefs, used his friend Thomas Edison as a

model for an artilleryman in the Molly Pitcher scene, and joked
that he caught the inventor in his "lean and hungry" stage before
his later financial successes, and thus preserved him in this state
for eternity. Kelly labored extensively over the panels, spending
three months alone on Molly Pitcher, although he had been initially allotted five months to complete the entire project; fortunately, the quality of his workmanship so impressed the association members that he was given an extension.[17]

The *New York Times* covered the unveiling event in an article
titled "Freehold's Great Day," the author describing a carnival-like
atmosphere that drew spectators from far and wide: "All the railroad trains that rolled into the village during the morning were
crowded out the platforms . . . the wagons began to arrive with
the country people very early, and every species of farm vehicle
stretched in long procession on every incoming road . . . in some
cases even the dog came in under the wagon to see the fun." The
Times estimated a crowd of twenty thousand people in attendance.
Mounted National Guardsmen pranced up and down the town's
main thoroughfare, Main Street, as vendors hawked street food
and souvenirs of dubious quality. A military parade ensued,
reviewed by then Governor George B. McClellan, along with former governors William A. Newell, Rodman M. Price, and Joseph
D. Bedle. Free enterprise not to be denied, the parade was closely
followed by "a gaudily painted wagon, heralding a newly invented magic soap, with boys throwing specimens to the crowd."[18]

Former Governor Parker, who had been so instrumental in the
creation of the monument, took the stage again to deliver an ora-
tion during the dedication ceremony. He noted the Continentals'
suffering and deprivation during their winter at Valley Forge,
made some unflattering comments regarding General Lee, whom
he characterized, not inaccurately, as "of a petulant disposition,
insubordinate, ambitious and vain," and went on to describe the
events of the battle in detail. At the conclusion of the speech,
Parker invoked more recent history as he made a correlation
between the spirit that drove the American struggle for independence, and the national force of will that kept the Union from permanently fragmenting during the course of the Civil War, when

Tennent Meeting House as it looked in 1868, before the deluge of commemorations of the battle. (*Courtesy Dr. David Martin*)

he had served as governor. He advised his audience that on this ground, "made sacred by the blood of our ancestors fighting for the freedom of our land, may we drink new inspiration, and resolve to stand by our country and maintain the Union in every crisis." His address was followed by a thirty-eight gun salute—one for every state then in the Union. Reunion was a constant theme with Parker. In 1874, while governor, he had sponsored an event at the battlefield where "North and South clasped hands over the bloody chasm" by inviting the governor of Maryland and a Maryland National Guard regiment to join hands with New Jerseyans to celebrate postwar national unity. Of course Maryland, while contributing soldiers to the Confederacy, never seceded, and recruited a number of men to serve in the Union army.[19]

It had taken the residents of Monmouth County, many of whom had spent the wartime years at each other's throats, generations before they were able to look back at the Revolution with a sense of national pride. Now, in the wake of the four-year-long struggle between the Union and Confederate armies and the assassination of a president, citizens clung to their first war and its legends and symbols even more tightly. The Revolution could even be used, as Parker used it, to de-emphasize the divisiveness of the Civil War, and reiterate the idea that all Americans were inextricably united by a common and unique character, forged during their crusade for independence from Great Britain, which made peaceful reunification possible after the Civil War. Although a strong supporter of the Union, Parker was a Democrat and political opponent—and sometimes caustic critic—of Abraham Lincoln during the war. Now he extolled the late martyred president as a symbol of the enduring American spirit.

> In his first inaugural address, President Lincoln, in alluding to the fraternal feelings produced by the knowledge that our forefathers fought in the American Revolution in and for a common cause, expressed the idea in one of the most beautiful and touching sentences in the language, when he said: 'The mystic chords of memory, stretching from every battle-field and patriot grave to every living heart and hearthstone all over this broad land, will yet swell the chorus of the Union, when again touched, as surely they will be, by the better angels of our nature.'[20]

After the 1884 monument dedication, commemoration ceremonies seemed to go more smoothly and continued to attract crowds. Special group outings to the battlefield were organized on occasion. In 1894, six hundred members of the Sons of the American Revolution from New Jersey, Pennsylvania, Delaware, and Maryland arrived in Freehold for a tour. The next major celebration marked the one hundred and twenty-fifth anniversary of the battle in 1903, which was held in "ideal" weather. Freehold was bedecked with banners and awakened by a sunrise twenty-one gun salute. Later in the day, visitors were treated to a choir of one hundred and sixty schoolchildren singing patriotic songs and a parade led by a National Guard honor guard. Governor Franklin Murphy, who presided, later recalled that "every house was covered with flags and bunting, every one desirous of using as many flags as possible evidently evincing a great interest in the day . . . the ladies and children could appear in their summer dresses and from beginning to end the celebration was a decided success."[21]

Like Parker before him, Murphy, a Civil War veteran, gave a

Left, the only known marker for a mass grave at the battle site, placed many years later, is outside the Tennent Meeting House front door. It marks the approximate site of burial for wounded soldiers who died while being tended in the church. Right, placed by the DAR during the monumentation era, in 1901, this plaque placed on the Tennent Meeting House commemorates the battle. (*Joseph Bilby*)

speech in which he attempted to connect the legacy of the battle to a topical political subject, in this case labor and immigration issues in a rapidly changing America. Owner of a Newark varnish plant, the governor hopefully opined that the "spirit of discontent" that arose so often between employers and their labor force in the industrialized American economy "can be allayed by mutual concessions and the recognition of mutual rights." Murphy struck a more alarmist tone when it came to immigration: "The quality of the average immigrant has distinctly lowered the last few years . . . The danger to the country, if there is any danger, will come from ignorance." From a modern perspective, Murphy's preoccupation with labor unions and fears of culturally distinct immigrant populations of the era, mostly from Southern and Eastern Europe, joining New Jersey's already historically diverse population does not seem to have much to do with the Battle of Monmouth. In Murphy's view, however, he recognized the eighteenth-century battle as a vindication of a unique American character, and he obviously saw organized labor, with its socialist stigma attached, and immigrant groups, with their "otherness," as threats to a particularly American ethos forged during the Revolution. In his concern, he, like Parker, overlooked the vicious intracommunity fighting of the war in New Jersey and Monmouth County. Murphy's speech reflected common anxieties of the time, however, which have surfaced periodically in similar forms before and since.[22]

The one hundred and fiftieth anniversary celebration in 1928 was another gala affair. Samuel C. Cowart, a Freehold attorney and descendent of an old local family, who had made the battle and its commemoration a personal cause, went to great lengths to put the sesquicentennial on the map. Cowart, who had organized the successful 1903 commemorations, appealed to each state to send a dignitary, and many national and local political figures attended, along with ten thousand of the general public. The day included a parade led by a military band, a reenactment of the battle, several addresses, and the reading of poems. Cowart reserved the centerpiece of the program for himself, giving a talk titled "Story of the Battle of Monmouth," which he had previously printed as a pamphlet. A lifelong Battle of Monmouth hobbyist, Cowart had also delivered the same speech to a group at the Tennent Meeting House in 1914.[23]

Commemorations of the battle continued with regularity throughout the twentieth century, but perhaps the most successful effort of all was that made for the bicentennial of the battle in 1978. The reenactment staged that day had been coordinated by the New Jersey Revolutionary War Bicentennial Commission and attracted participants from as far away as Ontario, Canada, and Florida. Although one journalistic estimate of forty thousand spectators seems high and may well be an exaggeration, there is no doubt that the bicentennial interest in the war attracted the greatest number of people to ever attend a Battle of Monmouth event to the field to witness the most authentic recreation of the battle ever staged. The bicentennial was also the occasion on which the newly created 1,519 acre Monmouth Battlefield State Park was formally dedicated by former Governor Robert B. Meyner.[24]

The struggle to make the battlefield into a historic park had been a long one, with origins in the creation of similar parks at Saratoga, New York, and Morristown, New Jersey, in the early 1930s. The effort was strongly supported by the Monmouth County Historical Association, whose members believed a park

Soldiers of the New Jersey National Guard's 114th Infantry Regiment parade down Freehold's main street during the battle's sesquicentennial commemoration in 1928. (*National Guard Militia Museum of New Jersey*)

would not only preserve important history, but serve as a WPA employment project in Depression-stricken America. Although Morristown National Historic Park—the first of its type in the nation—was dedicated on July 4, 1933, the proposal for Monmouth failed to materialize. The idea of land preservation for its own sake as well as history's became more pressing, as developers began to eye the open farmlands of the battle site in the relentless suburban expansion of the post-World War II era, however. In 1961, Dr. C. Malcolm B. Gilman, a Monmouth County resident and member of the Sons of the American Revolution, approached then Governor Meyner about the preservation of the battlefield. Dr. Gilman had recently approached the National Park Service for assistance, but none was forthcoming, a rather appalling state of affairs in retrospect, considering the historical importance of the battle. With the "Green Acres" land acquisition program on the state ballot for approval that November, however, there was hope that if the referendum passed, the battlefield could be purchased in the name of open space preservation. Meyner did not voice any opposition to the project, and his acting Chief of

State Parks, Joseph Truncer, became the park's greatest champion. In August 1963, the summer after the Green Acres bond issue was approved, a two-hundred-acre farm was acquired and set aside as park lands. Developers who owned the property on Combs Hill, where the current visitor center stands, resisted selling their lands to the state, as they had plans to construct high-rise senior citizen housing on the site. Fortunately, Truncer and his staff alerted the New Jersey Office on Aging to technical flaws in the development funding application, and that office in turn notified the Federal Department of Housing and Urban Development. The project was turned down, and, with the potential high rises no longer in the picture, the state was able to move forward on a slow but steady course to obtain ownership of the majority of the available battlefield acreage.[25]

Without the efforts of Truncer and the state government's Green Acres bond program that made these land purchases possible, it is certain that the site of one of the most important battles of the American Revolution would have been covered over with strip malls and housing developments, a fate that befell much of the once rural area surrounding it. In establishing and maintaining Monmouth Battlefield State Park, modern New Jerseyans, citizens of the most ethnically diverse state in the Union, symbolically fulfilled Joel Parker's hopes and allayed Franklin Murphy's fears for their state and country's future by uniting to save for posterity the historic land on which Continental soldiers of a long-gone world fought to create the nation they now enjoyed. In 2006, the battlefield became an official part of the Crossroads of the American Revolution National Heritage Area. One of only thirty-seven National Heritage Areas recognized by the president and Congress, the designated swath of New Jersey holds a particularly large number of sites associated with the American War for Independence, and will be promoted as a heritage tourism destination.

Monmouth Battlefield State Park encompasses 2,928 acres, which include the core area of the Battle of Monmouth Court House. During the 1990s, an extensive restoration project led to

The heat was as oppressive during the 1978 reenactment as during the actual battle or the failed 1854 reenactment. New Jersey National Guardsmen assist a regular army soldier of the Third U.S. Infantry's honor guard suffering from heat prostration off the field. The Third Infantry participated in the reenactment along with civilian reenactors. It is safe to say that the unit was better dressed than any of the original Continental units that fought at Monmouth in 1778. (*National Guard Militia Museum of New Jersey*)

the improvement of period buildings sitting on park lands, including the Craig farmhouse and Rhea-Applegate house, and the reconstruction of Revolutionary War-era lanes, fences, and a woodlot. The Monmouth County Historical Association has preserved other relevant sites in the vicinity. The battlefield is not identical to its appearance in 1778, owing largely to stands of trees that have grown in since then and the nineteenth-century draining of the "morasses." Portions of the battlefield remain working farm fields and orchards, managed by private families. Exhibits placed throughout the park along hiking trails help explain the course of the fighting, as well as local ecology, to visitors. An excellent brochure, complete with maps, explains the course of the battle, and specific guides keyed to each of the trails offer more detailed information. Tourists may also explore the visitor center, which features a showcase with excavated artifacts and other material culture, short films, a diorama, and a topographical relief map of the battle, as well as full-size artillery reproductions, but, unfortu-

Monmouth Battlefield State Park visitor center in March, 2010. (*Joseph Bilby*)

nately, is understaffed by the state. Part of the understaffing problem has been eased by the Friends of Monmouth Battlefield, PO Box 122, Tennent, NJ 07763, a nonprofit organization that supports the park with fund raising, an annual reenactment, and other event management and sponsorship, and a gift shop/bookstore. Another volunteer organization, the Deep Search Metal Detecting Club's Archaeological Committee, chaired by Dan Sivilich and Ralph Phillips, has made significant contributions to the understanding of the battle, as well as pioneering new archaeological techniques. Monmouth Battlefield State Park could easily be considered the "crown jewel" of New Jersey's park system, in both historical significance and as choice land saved from avaricious development.

The park, as with most historical sites, especially in New Jersey, would benefit from a larger operating budget, but unfortunately in the hard economic times coinciding with the writing of this book, funding for historical sites is a low-ranking priority for state lawmakers. Despite that reality, as of this writing, plans are in motion to build a new visitor center. Monmouth Battlefield State Park continues to divulge the secrets of the past to historians who mine the sources, archaeologists who work the site, and visitors who roam the fields where the ragged Continentals stood their ground and made a new nation possible, and will, happily, do so for generations to come.[26]

View from Combs' Hill from Wayne's artillery position. The bridge at the base of the hill crosses Spotswood South Brook, also known now as Wemrock Brook, and the site of the hedgerow line is in the field beyond. (*Joseph Bilby*)

In the midst of violence in 1778, Tennent Meeting House still stands, but in a peaceful setting in 2010. (*Joseph Bilby*)

Notes

Preface
1. The Saratoga disaster, although it had far-reaching consequences, was a unique event result, and did not involve Washington or his main army.

Chapter One
1. The names "Monmouth Court House" and "Freehold," the latter the current name of the town, were used interchangeably during the Revolution, but this account will use Monmouth Court House to avoid confusion.
2. Fleming, *New Jersey*, pp. 47–50; Lurie, "New Jersey: Radical or Conservative?" in Mitnick, *New Jersey in the American Revolution,* p. 41; Fowler, "These Were Troublesome Times Indeed," in Mitnick, *New Jersey in the American Revolution*, p. 21.
3. Fleming, *New Jersey*, pp. 59–60; Gerlach, "William Franklin," in Stellhorn and Birkner, *Governors of New Jersey,* pp. 75–76.
4. Lurie, "New Jersey: Radical or Conservative?" in Mitnick, *Governors of New Jersey,* p. 42; Fowler, "These Were Troublesome Times Indeed," in Mitnick, *New Jersey in the American Revolution*, p. 21.
5. Wright, *Continental Army*, pp. 255–56.
6. Boatner, *Encyclopedia*, pp. 797–98. Boatner gives Washington a paper strength of 28,500 men, but notes that actual "fit for duty" strength was around 19,000, with inadequate artillery and no cavalry.
7. Lundn, *Cockpit of the Revolution*, pp. 115, 122–27; Boatner gives Howe's paper strength as 32,625 with the number of "effectives fit for duty" at 24,464. Boatner, *Encyclopedia*, p. 798.
8. Captain Francis Hutcheson to General Frederick Haldimand, July 10, 1776, British Library, Additional Manuscripts no. 21680, folio 124. Copy courtesy of Gilbert V. Riddle; Lundn, *Cockpit of the Revolution*, pp. 115–19.
9. Lundn, *Cockpit of the Revolution*, pp. 149–51.
10. Ibid., pp. 142–45.
11. Ibid., pp. 160–61. For details on the course of the attempted Loyalist counterrevolution in Monmouth County, see chapter 2 of this work.
12. Lundn, *Cockpit of the Revolution,* p. 157; Cunningham, *Uncertain Revolution*, p. 13.

13. Hunter, *Journal of Gen. Sir Martin Hunter*, p. 27; "Reverend Alexander MacWhorter on British Brutality," in Gerlach, *New Jersey in the American Revolution*, pp. 296–97. Ironically, Nuttman was subsequently arrested by patriot militia as a Loyalist and jailed in Morristown. Frey, *British Soldier in America*, pp. 75–76; Cunningham, *Uncertain Revolution*, p. 183; Rees, "'We . . . wheeled to the Right to form the Line Of Battle,'" (Original Manuscripts, Israel Shreve Papers, Louisiana Tech University); Curtis, *Organization of the British Army*, p. 32.

14. Fischer, *Washington's Crossing*, pp. 346–48.

15. Lender, *New Jersey Soldier*, p. 23; Cunningham, *Uncertain Revolution*, pp. 182–85; Braisted, "Refugees and Others."

16. William Livingston to Philemon Dickinson, January 14, 1777. Neilson Family Papers, Alexander Library, Rutgers University; Ward, *General William Maxwell*, pp. 151; Fischer, *Washington's Crossing*, p. 349.

17. Cited in Scheer and Rankin, *Rebels and Redcoats*, p. 222; Fischer, *Washington's Crossing*, pp. 354–59.

18. Cited in Spring, *With Zeal and With Bayonets Only*, p. 278; *Pennsylvania Journal*, April 2, 1777.

19. Martin, *Philadelphia Campaign*, pp. 9–12; Jackson, *With the British Army in Philadelphia*, pp. 2–3.

20. Jackson, *With the British Army in Philadelphia*, pp. 2–3.

21. Ibid., p. 3.

22. Lundn, *Cockpit of the Revolution*, pp. 307–10.

23. Lundn, *Cockpit of the Revolution*, p. 314; Martin, *Philadelphia Campaign*, p. 21.

24. Lundn, *Cockpit of the Revolution*, pp. 307–10.

25. Martin, *Philadelphia Campaign*, pp. 24–26; Bailey, *Small Arms of the British Forces in America*, pp. 72, 181.

26. Ward, *General William Maxwell*, pp. 65–66.

27. Ibid., pp. 66–67. For a detailed study of the light infantry of both armies, including organization, tactics, and weapons, see chapters 3 and 4.

28. Jackson, *With the British Army in Philadelphia*, p. 7.

29. Ward, *General William Maxwell*, pp. 67–69; Ewald, *Diary of the American War*, pp. 76–79.

30. Wood, *Battles of the Revolutionary War*, pp. 94–97; Uhlendorf, *Revolution in America*, p. 107; Ward, *General William Maxwell*, pp. 70–71.

31. Ewald, *Diary of the American War*, p. 81; Yee, *Sharpshooters*, pp. 49–50; Bailey, *Small Arms of the British Forces*, p. 181. Bailey claims that Ferguson's company, originally one hundred men strong, were probably not all armed with the captain's breechloader, as "33 [Ferguson] rifles and 40 bayonets did not leave England until 22 June 1777, and Ferguson's unit sailed . . . south from New York on 20 July." Considering its reduced strength at Brandywine, however, it is likely that the remains of the company were all equipped with breechloaders.

32. Wood, *Battles of the Revolutionary War*, pp. 98–101. Ewald claims that the British loss was "nine hundred killed and wounded, among which were sixty-four officers," and that the American casualties were "fairly equal with ours," and included four hundred prisoners. Ewald, *Diary of the American War*, p. 87.

33. Boatner, *Encyclopedia*, pp. 828–29; Dann, *Revolution Remembered*, p. 149.

34. Jackson, *With the British Army in Philadelphia*, pp. 11–12; http://www.chaddsfordhistory.org/exhibits/path/path08.htm.

35. Martin, *Philadelphia Campaign*, pp. 149–51; Stryker, *Battle of Monmouth*, p. 2; Wright, *Continental* Army, p. 118; Boatner, *Encyclopedia*, pp. 426–30.

36. Martin, *Philadelphia Campaign*, pp. 152–55; Jackson, *With the British Army in Philadelphia*, pp. 92–93; Boatner, *Encyclopedia*, pp. 861–62.

37. Martin, *Philadelphia Campaign*, pp. 157–64.

38. Martin, *Philadelphia Campaign*, pp. 169–75; Stryker, *Battle of Monmouth*, p. 3; Risch, *Supplying Washington's Army*, p. 150.

39. Risch, *Supplying Washington's Army*, pp. 23–24, 208; "Reverend Nicholas Collin on the Ravages of War," in Gerlach, *New Jersey in the American Revolution*, p. 303; Ward, *General William Maxwell*, pp. 89–92.

40. Risch, *Supplying Washington's Army*, pp. 39, 221; Wright, *Continental Army*, p. 140; Lockhart, *Drillmaster of Valley Forge*, pp. 42, 203–4. Lockhart is ambivalent on Steuben's homosexuality. Although stating that "there is circumstantial evidence to suggest it," offering a story by a friend of the baron's that he once dropped a "miniature portrait of a beautiful young woman" as a counterargument. The circumstantial evidence to the contrary is far more substantial.

41. Wright, *Continental Army*, p.141.

42. Ewald, *Diary of the American War,* p. 121; Jackson, *With the British Army in Philadelphia*, pp. 97–98; "Reverend Nicholas Collin on the Ravages of War," in Gerlach, *New Jersey in the American Revolution*, pp. 302–3; Lundn, *Cockpit of the Revolution*, p. 376.

43. Lundn, *Cockpit of the Revolution,* pp. 388–89; "Colonel Elijah Hand to Colonel Charles Mawhood," in Gerlach, *New Jersey in the American Revolution*, p. 338; Ward, *General William Maxwell*, p. 93; Simcoe, *Simcoe's Military Journal*, p. 52.

44. *Pennsylvania Evening Post,* April 3, 1778, in Lee, *Documents Relating to the Revolutionary History of the State of New Jersey,* p. 146; "Reverend Nicholas Collin on the Ravages of War," in Gerlach, *New Jersey in the American Revolution*, pp. 303–4.

45. "Reverend Nicholas Collin on the Ravages of War," in Gerlach, *New Jersey in the American Revolution*, p. 304; Martin, *Philadelphia Campaign*, p. 179.

46. Stryker, *Battle of Monmouth*, pp. 9–10.

47. Risch, *Supplying Washington's Army*, p. 418.

48. Martin, *Philadelphia Campaign*, pp. 197–98.

49. Ward, *General William Maxwell*, pp. 93–95.

50. Jackson, *With the British Army in Philadelphia*, pp. 234–40.

51. New Jersey was often referred to as "the Jerseys," a reference to its former division into the colonies of East and West New Jersey, a division which many suggest still persists, although the divide today is described as a "north/south" one.

52. Jackson, *With the British Army in Philadelphia*, pp. 81–84, 89–90.

53. Boatner, *Encyclopedia*, pp. 844–45.

54. Ewald, *Diary of the American War*, p. 131; Fleming, *Washington's Secret War,* pp. 330–331.

CHAPTER TWO

1. Lurie and Mappen, *Encyclopedia of New Jersey*, pp. 528–29.

2. This story of cyclic violence serves as partial refutation of Van Buskirk's work, *Generous Enemies*, an interpretation of the wartime experience in the parts of New York and New Jersey near the British lines. Ms. Van Buskirk paints a picture of frequent passage back and forth between military lines, a healthy level of illegal trade between noncombatants and the enemy, and—most significantly—a lack of real animosity between those who came down on different sides of the fence. Although civilian travel between New York and New Jersey and illegal trade were undeniably frequent occurrences, a feeling of fellowship toward the enemy cannot be generally ascribed to the inhabitants of eastern New Jersey and New York City. The level of animosity between patriots and Loyalists, in Monmouth County in particular, was extreme. For a perspective on the violent and bitter nature of the Revolution in a different area of eastern New Jersey, see Leiby's seminal work on wartime Bergen County titled *The Revolutionary War in the Hackensack Valley.*

3. Cited in Lundn, *Cockpit of the Revolution*, p. 123.

4. Fowler, "Egregious Villains," (PhD diss., Rutgers University, 1987), pp. 56–57.

5. Ibid., p. 58.

6. Fowler, "Loyalist Insurrection," p. 1.

7. "Richard Stockton to Robert Ogden," in Gerlach, *New Jersey in the American Revolution,* p. 12.

8. Fowler, "Loyalist Insurrection," p. 2; Jamison, *Religion in New Jersey*, p. 58.

9. Jamison, *Religion in New Jersey,* p. 68.

10. Ibid., p. 68.

11. Ibid., pp. 67–68.

12. Fowler, Egregious Villains," pp. 66–67.

13. Ibid., p. 68.

14. Ibid., p. 69.

15. Lundn, *Cockpit of the Revolution*, pp. 160–61.

16. Fowler, "Egregious Villains," p. 81; Lundn, *Cockpit of the Revolution*, p. 163.

17. *Minutes of the Council of Safety of the State of New Jersey*, pp. 19–21.

18. Ibid., pp. 97–100.

19. Fowler, "Loyalist Insurrection," p. 2.

20. Pingeon, *Blacks in the Revolutionary Era*, p. 6.

21. Graydon, *Memoirs of His Own Time*, p. 247; "Ebenezer Hazard, Journey Thorough War-torn New Jersey," in Gerlach, *New Jersey in the American Revolution*, pp. 302–3.

22. Hodges, *Slavery and Freedom*, pp. 59–67.

23. Ibid., pp. 72, 91.

24. Ibid., pp. 92–93.

25. Petition from the Residents of Shrewsbury to the General Assembly, 1774, Manuscripts 1680s-1970s, box 14, no. 18, New Jersey State Archives, Dept. of Education, Bureau of Archives and History.

26. Hodges, *Slavery and Freedom*, p. 95.

27. Ibid., p. 98.

28. Ibid., p. 100.

29. Ibid., p. 102.

30. Ellis, *History of Monmouth County*, p. 214.

31. Hodges, *Slavery and Freedom*, p. 104; *New Jersey Gazette*, April 24, 1782.

32. *Minutes of the Provincial Congress and Council of Safety of New Jersey*, p. 497.

33. Adelberg, *"A Combination to Trample All Law"*, (unpublished manuscript, 1995). p. 4.

34. Court of General Quarter Sessions, 1760–1779, Series 3000, box 3, Monmouth County Archives, Court of Oyer and Terminer, 1752–1799, 1781, Series 2800.2, box 1, Monmouth County Archives.

35. Ellis, *History of Monmouth County*, p. 206.

36. Adelberg, *"A Combination to Trample All Law,"* p. 8.

37. Gérard, *Instructions and Despatches*, pp. 510–11.

38. Petition to the Legislature, Monmouth County, Collection MG14 (Ely), New Jersey Historical Society.

39. Adelberg, *"A Combination to Trample All Law,"* p. 9.

40. Adelberg, *"A Combination to Trample All Law,"* pp. 9–10; Adelberg, "They Do Rather More Harm Than Good," in *Impact*, p. 14; Lurie and Mappen, *Encyclopedia of New Jersey*, p. 283.

41. Weiss and Weiss, *Revolutionary Saltworks*, pp. 235–36.

42. Pierce, *Smuggler's Woods*, p. 14.

43. Ibid., p. 16.

44. Cherry Hall Papers, box 5, folder 9, Monmouth County Historical Association.

45. Pierce, *Smuggler's Woods*, p. 17.

46. Manuscripts 1680s-1970s, Numbered Manuscripts, box 103, folder 10948, New Jersey State Archives, Department of Defense, Adjutant General.

47. Adelberg, *"A Combination to Trample All Law,"* p. 21.

48. Ibid., pp. 25–26. The memorialization of extreme acts survived into the twentieth century. In 1927, the Daughters of the American Revolution and the descendents of Captain Samuel Allen placed a memorial plaque alongside New Jersey State Highway 70, just north of the Manasquan River, at "the spot where Capt. Allen executed six Tories and their chief," presumably on his own authority without benefit of trial. Allen served as a company commander in the Third Monmouth Militia Regiment from 1780 to 1783.

49. Pierce, *Smuggler's Woods*, p. 253.

50. Ellis, *History of Monmouth County*, pp. 208–9.

51. Adelberg, *"A Combination to Trample All Law,"* p. 22.

52. *New Jersey Gazette*, April 24, 1782.

53. Pierce, *Smuggler's Woods*, p. 254; *New Jersey Gazette*, May 15, 1782.

54. Pierce, *Smuggler's Woods*, p. 256.

55. Ibid., p. 257.

56. Ibid., p. 269.

57. Ibid., p. 275.

CHAPTER THREE

1. Willcox, "Sir Henry Clinton," in Billias, *George Washington's Generals and Opponents,* p. 73.

2. Ibid., pp. 78–79.

3. Willcox, "Sir Henry Clinton," in Billias, *George Washington's Generals and Opponents,* pp. 82–84; Morrissey, *Monmouth Courthouse 1778,* p. 15.

4. Rankin, "Charles Lord Cornwallis," in Billias, *George Washington's Generals and Opponents,* pp. 192–94.

5. Ibid., pp. 198–99.

6. Ibid., pp. 200–201, 220–21.

7. Morrissey, *Monmouth Courthouse 1778,* p. 16.

8. Boatner, *Encyclopedia,* pp. 588–89.

9. Shy, "Charles Lee," in Billias, *George Washington's Generals and Opponents,* pp. 22–25; Boatner, *Encyclopedia,* p. 605.

10. Shy, "Charles Lee," in Billias, *George Washington's Generals and Opponents,* p. 37.

11. Robert Mackenzie to Lord Percy, December 20, 1776. Manuscripts of Duke of Northumberland, vol. 150, Letters and Papers of the Percy Family, July 1774–December 1776, American War, Alnwick Castle, no. 50, 23/3. Copy courtesy of Gilbert V. Riddle; Shy, "Charles Lee," in Billias, George Washington's Generals and Opponents, p. 40.

12. Ibid., pp. 41–42. Ironically, Lee was also subject to the rumors of sexual preference that surrounded his rival Steuben. According to Shy, "There were hints, but no more than that, of [Lee's] homosexuality." The most significant Lee apologist is Alden, in his *General Charles Lee: Traitor or Patriot,* although Shy also takes a more nuanced view of the general.

13. Curtis, *Organization of the British Army,* pp. 51–66, 72–75; Holmes, *Redcoat,* p. 139; Conway, "The British Army."

14. Holmes, *Redcoat,* p. 139; Curtis, *Organization of the British Army,* p. 66.

15. Curtis, *Organization of the British Army,* pp. 3–9; Reid, *British Redcoat,* pp. 15–16; Howe to Viscount Barrington, May 8, 1776, David Library of the American Revolution, Microfilm Collection, P.R.O W.O. 1/2, pp. 393–96. Transcription by Gilbert V. Riddle.

16. Reid, *British Redcoat,* pp. 9–10; Sheppard, *Red Coat,* p. 24–25.

17. Jackson, *With the British Army in Philadelphia,* pp. 170–71. While most of these period barracks are long demolished, one, built in 1758 and used by Hessian troops during the Revolutionary War and then as an American barracks and hospital afterward, survives in Trenton, New Jersey. Old Barracks Museum Web site, http://www.barracks.org.

18. Jackson, *With the British Army in Philadelphia,* p. 262; Uhlendorf, *Revolution in America,* p. 89; Ewald, *Diary of the American War,* p. 132.

19. Ewald, *Diary of the American War,* pp. 129, 144.

20. Reid, *British Redcoat,* pp. 12–14; Curtis, *Organization of the British Army,* p. 31; Hagist, "Women of the British Army," pt. 1; "Women of the British Army," pt. 2; Burgoyne, "Women with the Hessian Auxiliaries," pt. 1; Chartrand, "Notes

Concerning Women"; Sir Henry Clinton (British Army Headquarters) Papers, William L. Clements Library, University of Michigan, 36:5. Transcription by Gilbert V. Riddle.

21. Quoted in Whisker, "African–American Gunsmiths."

22. Hodges, *Slavery and Freedom*, p. 94. Quarles, *Negro in the Revolution*, p. 150. Dunmore's suggestion to raise regular black regiments was never really adopted, although he was still proposing it as late as 1782 in Charleston. It is most interesting that free black New Jerseyans (and possibly even some slaves) were apparently able to possess firearms at the time.

23. Quarles, *Negro in the Revolution*, p. 157; Hodges, *Root and Branch*, p. 146.

24. "A Look at some British Soldiers"; Hodges, *Root and Branch*, p. 148; Quarles, *Negro in the Revolution*, p. 135. "Pioneers" were the eighteenth-century equivalent of combat engineer units in a modern army.

25. Hodges, *Slavery and Freedom*, p. 92. In 1778, Corlies was expelled from the Shrewsbury Meeting of the Society of Friends for refusing to manumit his slaves.

26. Hodges, *Root and Branch*, p. 159. Not all of the more than three thousand African-Americans who left New York were from the area. Many were enslaved before the war in the South, and at least five hundred African-American Virginians came to New York under British escort in 1779. Quarles, *Negro in the Revolution*, pp. 115, 173.

27. Wright, *Continental Army*, pp. 29–40.

28. Ibid.

29. Ibid., p. 111.

30. Rees, "The Greate Neglect in Provideing Cloathing," pt. 1.

31. Higginbotham, *War of American Independence*, pp. 389–91; Bolton, *Private Soldier Under Washington*, pp. 44–72.

32. Ibid., pp. 392–94.

33. Wright, *Continental Army*, p. 150.

34. Ibid.

35. Rees, "New Material Concerning Female Followers," pt. 1 of 2; Rees, "An Examination of the Numbers of Female Camp Followers"; Rees, "New Material Concerning Female Followers," pt. 2 of 2; DePauw, "Women in Combat."

36. Mahon, *History of the Militia and the National Guard*, p. 22; Green, "The Negro in the Armed Forces"; Bolton, *Private Soldier Under Washington*, p. 22; Rees, "New Material Concerning Female Followers," pt. 2.

37. Higginbotham, *War of American Independence*, pp. 394–95; Quoted from New Jersey Statutes in Gough, "Black Men and the Early New Jersey Militia."

38. Lender, *New Jersey Soldier*, pp. 17–18; Walling, *Men of Color*, pp. 15–16; Dann, *Revolution Remembered*, pp. 390–99; Quarles, *Negro in the Revolution,* p. 185.

39. Lender, *New Jersey Soldier*, p. 20; Schleicher and Winter, "Patriot and Slave," 30–43.

40. Walling, *Men of Color*, p. 14.

41. Ewald, *Diary of the American War*, p. 131; Walling, *Men of Color,* pp. 7–9.

42. Wright, *Continental Army*, p. 146.

43. Stryker, *Battle of Monmouth*, p. 49.

44. Stryker, *Battle of Monmouth*, pp. 31–32, 50; Ewald, *Diary of the American War*, pp. 132–33.

45. Stryker, *Battle of Monmouth*, p. 50; Simcoe, *Simcoe's Military Journal*, p. 6.

46. Stryker, *Battle of Monmouth,* p. 50; William Maxwell to Philemon Dickinson, 19 June 1778, cited in Rees, "What is this you have been about to day?" http://www.revwar75.com/library/rees/monmouth/MonmouthToc.htm.

47. Trevelyan, *American Revolution*, p. 371; Stryker, *Battle of Monmouth*, pp. 51–52; Ewald, *Diary of the American War*, p. 133; Cited in Rees, "What is this you have been about to day?"

48. Riddle, "Lessons from the Courts"; Bell, "Copy of a Journal."

49. Stryker, *Battle of Monmouth*, pp .52–54; Cited in Rees, "What is this you have been about to day?"; Uhlendorf, *Revolution in America*, p. 185.

50. Papers of John Peebles of the Forty-second Foot, 1776–1782, Scottish Record Office, Edinburgh, copy in Monmouth County Historical Association (MCHA) Battle of Monmouth Collection; Wilkin, *Some British Soldiers in America*, p. 263; Morris, "The Hessians at Monmouth"; Unidentified newspaper clipping, copy in MCHA Battle of Monmouth Collection; Martin, *Memoir of a Revolutionary Soldier*, p. 70.

51. A good account of the adventures of a New Jersey militiaman during the British march across the state is that of William Lloyd of Upper Freehold, detailed in Dann, *Revolution Remembered*, pp. 123–25.

52. Simcoe, *Simcoe's Military Journal*, p. 67.

53. Martin, Bloomfield, and Lender, *Citizen Soldier*, p. 136.

54. Morris, "The Hessians at Monmouth," MCHA Battle of Monmouth Collection; Dr. Garry W. Stone (Monmouth Battlefield State Park Historian), in discussion with the author, January 2010.

55. Martin, *Philadelphia Campaign*, p. 205; Martin, Bloomfield, and Lender, *Citizen Soldier*, p. 135. Congress passed legislation authorizing the nine-month militia draft to Continental service in February 1778. Many of the men raised by the act, however, were actually paid substitutes for draftees.

56. Fleming, *Washington's Secret War,* p. 311; Stryker, *Battle of Monmouth*, pp. 59–62; Martin, *Philadelphia Campaign*, p. 205–6; Ward, *General William Maxwell*, p. 97.

57. Anburey, *Travels Through the Interior Parts of American,* p. 380; Ward, *General William Maxwell*, p. 99.

58. Ward, *General William Maxwell*, p. 97.

59. Stryker, *Battle of Monmouth*, p. 72.

60. Ibid., pp. 77–78.

61. Dearborn, *Journals of Henry Dearborn,* p. 15; Stryker, *Battle of Monmouth*, pp. 70–71; Trevelyan, *American Revolution*, p. 373; Morrissey, *Monmouth Courthouse 1778*, pp. 85–86. Morrissey attempts to sort out the organization of Washington's ad hoc units of "picked men," which some other authors have confused with formal organized regiments.

62. Martin, *Memoir of a Revolutionary Soldier*, p. 70.

63. Stryker, *Battle of Monmouth*, pp. 79–80; Higginbotham, *Daniel Morgan*, p. 88.

64. Boatner, *Encyclopedia*, p. 718.

65. Hagist, "The Women of the British Army," pt. 3.

66. Ibid. Female looters were apparently a perennial problem with British forces in America, and in his 1781 Southern campaign, Cornwallis decried his women camp followers as "the source of the most infamous plunder," cited in Frey, *British Soldier in America*, p. 76.

Chapter Four

1. Curtis, *Organization of the British Army*, p. 3; Wilkin, *Some British Soldiers in America*, p. 223.
2. Hughes, *Firepower*, pp. 94–98; Nosworthy, *Anatomy of Victory*, p. 347.
3. Reid, *British Redcoat*, pp. 27–28. For a detailed description and analysis of the variety of "firings" a British unit was theoretically capable of in the 1770s, see Harding, *Small Arms of the East India Company*, pp. 266–69.
4. Nosworthy, *Anatomy of Victory*, p. 345; Fuller, *British Light Infantry*, p. 47.
5. Reid, *British* Redcoat, p. 31; Fuller, *British Light Infantry*, pp. 86–90.
6. Holmes, *Redcoat*, p. 42; Fuller, *British Light Infantry*, pp. 124–25; Curtis, *Organization of the British Army*, p. 4; "General Howe's Manoeuvres for the Light Infantry" are reprinted in Fuller, *British Light Infantry*, pp. 247–52.
7. Fuller, *British Light Infantry*, pp. 247–52. Fuller reproduces the Howe manual as an appendix.
8. Padelford, *Colonial Panorama 1775*, pp. 43–44.
9. John Montressor to Lord Townsend, June 19, 1775, typescript copy supplied by Gilbert V. Riddle, W.O. 73/21; Fuller, *British Light Infantry*, pp. 126–27.
10. Fuller, *British Light Infantry*, p. 127; James Abercrombie to Sir Jeffrey Amherst, June 20, 1775, Amherst Manuscripts, U1350 080/3, Centre for Kentish Studies, Sessions House, County Hall, Maidstone, UK. Typescript copy courtesy of Don Hagist and Gilbert V. Riddle; Babits, *A Devil of a Whipping*, p. 18; Loftus Cliffe to "My Dr Jack," September 21, 1776, Loftus Cliffe Papers, William Clements Library, University of Michigan. Typescript copy courtesy of Gilbert V. Riddle. Fuller's objectivity may be questioned. A World War I veteran, he described Hessian troops as "probably like most German soldiers . . . addicted to pillage and drunkenness." He also attributed British losses on the retreat from Lexington and at Bunker Hill to the American use of rifles, for which there is no evidence. Massachusetts militiamen were armed with smoothbore muskets.
11. Fuller, *British Light Infantry*, pp. 135–36.
12. Boatner, *Encyclopedia*, p. 634; Wright, *Continental Army*, pp. 149, 151, 167.
13. Peter Force Papers, Orderly Book of Capt. Hatfield, 43rd Regiment, Grenadier company, Feb. 7 to March 15, 1776, Library of Congress; Journal of Ensign Thomas Glyn, Princeton University Library Manuscript Collection; Reid, *British Redcoat*, pp. 31–32; Howe to Barrington, May 8, 1776, Microfilm Collection, W.O. 1/2, pp. 393–96, 163, David Library of the American Revolution. Transcriptions courtesy of Gilbert V. Riddle.
14. Lockhart, *Drillmaster of Valley Forge*, pp. 109–11.
15. Reid, *British Redcoat*, pp. 54–55; May and Embleton, *British Army in North America*, pp. 44–45; Simcoe, *Simcoe's Military Journal*, p. 20.
16. Rees, "The Greate Neglect in Provideing Cloathing," pt. 1, pp. 163–70.

17. Rees, "The Great Neglect in Provideing Cloathing, pt. 2, pp. 12–20; Stryker, *Officers and Men of New Jersey*, p. 333.

18. Boatner, *Encyclopedia*, p. 485. Hanger (1751–1824), to be kind, failed to distinguish himself while in temporary command of the Loyalist British Legion in the south in 1780. His postwar career was checkered, and included a term in debtor's prison and a subsequent stint as a carousing partner of his wartime buddy Banastre Tarleton and the profligate Prince of Wales.

19. Quoted in Harding, *Small Arms of the East India Company*, p. 291. Harding cites the original source of the quote as Hanger's *A Letter to Lord Castlereagh from Colonel George Hanger* (1808).

20. Ibid., p. 291.

21. Often confusing to the modern reader is the period reference to the frizzen as the "hammer." To avoid such confusion, modern terms will be used in the text.

22. Harding, *Small Arms of the East India Company,* p. 219–20, 222, 229.

23. Bailey, *British Military Longarms*, pp. 11–12.

24. Ibid., pp. 15–16.

25. Ibid., pp. 17–18.

26. "Extract from the Review return of the King's Regiment and the 6th Regiment of Dragoons for 1774," David Library of the American Revolution Microfilms, P.R.O. W.O. 4/92, 172. Transcription by Gilbert V. Riddle; Griffith, *Forward into Battle*, p. 29; Dann, *Revolution Remembered*, pp. 124–25.

27. *Minutes of the Council of Safety of the State of New Jersey,* p. 207.

28. Flayderman, *Flayderman's Guide,* pp. 725–30.

29. Bury, *Manual of Rifling and Rifle Sights*, p. 2; Trench, *A History of Marksmanship*, p. 199; Lugs, *Firearms Past and Present*, pp. 35–36; Carman, *A History of Firearms*, pp. 105–6; Bailey, *British Military Flintlock Rifles*, p. 7.

30. Griffith, *Forward into Battle*, pp. 44–48; Bailey, *British Military Flintlock Rifles,* p. 21; Boatner, *Encyclopedia*, pp. 934–35.

31. Bailey, *British Military Flintlock Rifles*, p. 21.

32. Flayderman, *Flayderman's Guide*, p. 660.

33. Ibid., pp. 11, 12, 15.

34. Ibid., pp. 64–67.

35. Ibid., pp. 21, 59.

36. Ibid., pp. 27–34.

37. Ibid., p. 35.

38. Bailey, *British Military Flintlock Rifles*, p. 20; Ross, *From Flintlock to Rifle,* p. 33.

39. *Lady's Magazine. Copy courtesy of Gilbert V. Riddle.*

40. Bailey, *British Military Flintlock Rifles*, pp. 38–39.

41. War Office Order dated "6th March, 1777," David Library of the American Revolution, Microfilm Collection P.R.O.W.O. 4/99 109. Transcription courtesy of Gilbert V. Riddle, pp. 42–43.

42. Bailey, *British Military Flintlock Rifles*, pp. 49–50.

43. Ibid., pp. 53–54.

44. War Office Order dated "6th March, 1777," David Library of the American Revolution, Microfilm Collection P.R.O.W.O. 4/99 217. Transcription courtesy of Gilbert V. Riddle.

45. Moore, *Weapons of the American Revolution*, p. 62.

46. Bilby, "A Soldier of Military Distinction and Honor."

47. Blackmore, *British Military Firearms*, pp. 86–87; Bailey, *British Military Flintlock Rifles*, pp. 55–58.

48. Lockhart, *Drillmaster of Valley Forge*, p. 155.

49. Coates, Kochan, and Troiani, *Don Troiani's Soldiers in America*, pp. 19, 55; Rees, "Shoulder Arms of the Officers"; Martin, Bloomfield, and Lender, *Citizen Soldier*, pp. 124, 127; "Notes on the Battle of Monmouth."

50. Harding, *Small Arms of the East India Company*, p. 220; Curtis, *Organization of the British Army*, p. 21; Bailey, *Small Arms of the British Forces*, pp. 253–54.

51. Bailey, *Small Arms of the British Forces*, p. 245. A dram is 27.5 grains and there are 7,000 grains in a pound.

52. Lewis, *Small Arms and Ammunition,* pp. 24–27, 167.

53. Batchellor, *Ranger Service in the Upper Valley,* p. 22; Bolton, *Private Soldier Under Washington*, p. 122; Lewis, *Small Arms and Ammunition*, p. 108; Peterson, *Book of the Continental Soldier*, pp. 60–61; "Notes on the Battle of Monmouth"; Dr. Garry W. Stone, in discussion with the author, January 2010.

54. Bailey, *Small Arms of the British Forces,* p. 250; Hagist, "Lessons from the Courts."

55. Bailey, *Small Arms of the British Forces*, pp. 246–49, 139. These musket balls, originally discovered in storage in Nepal, were purchased by the author from International Military Antiques, Gillette, New Jersey, in June 2008; Veit, *Digging New Jersey's Past*, p. 87; Stone, Sivilich, and Lender, "A Deadly Minuet."

56. Bailey, *Small Arms of the British Forces*, pp. 260–63.

57. Bailey, *Small Arms of the British Forces*, pp. 257–59; Coates, Kochan, and Troiani, *Don Troiani's Soldiers in America*, p. 53.

58. Harding, *Small Arms of the East India Company,* pp. 412–18. Harding disputes the result of the 1846 trials, convincingly maintaining that "point blank" range against large targets could be as great as 200 yards depending on aiming point.

59. Yee, *Sharpshooters*, p. 89.

60. Boatner, *Encyclopedia*, p. 680; Griffith, *Forward into Battle*, p. 37.

61. Boatner, *Encyclopedia*, p. 680.

62. Fuller, *British Light Infantry*, p. 47; Bailey, *Small Arms of the British Forces*, pp. 273–75.

63. Padelford, *Colonial Panorama 1775,* p. 44.

64. Bailey, *Small Arms of the British Forces*, p. 276.

65. Curtis, *Organization of the British Army*, p. 19.

66. Quoted in Fischer, *Washington's Crossing*, p. 355.

67. Ward, *General William Maxwell*, p. 66; Wright, *Continental Army*, p. 141.

68. Simcoe, *Simcoe's Military Journal*, p. 65.

69. The tests were conducted at the Monmouth County Rifle and Pistol Club, Howell Township, New Jersey, on January 11, 2010.

70. Webster, *American Socket Bayonets*, pp. 7–8; Presidential Papers of George Washington, Orderly Book of the First Battalion Light Infantry (British) Aug. 4 through Oct. 13, 1778, Library of Congress, Series 6b, vol. 6, p. 62. Copy courtesy of Gilbert Riddle; Curtis, *Organization of the British Army*, pp. 20–21.

71. Boatner, *Encyclopedia*, pp. 1062–67; Peterson, *Arms and Armor in Colonial America*, p. 200.

72. Quoted in Haythornthwaite, *Weapons and Equipment of the Napoleonic Wars*, p. 27; Carrington, "Familiar Hints to Indiana Soldiers Taking to the Field," undated newspaper clipping from the Greencastle, Indiana, *Putnam Republican Banner*.

73. Peterson, *Round Shot and Rammers*, pp. 33, 41.

74. Manucy, *Artillery Through the Ages*, pp. 63–70.

CHAPTER FIVE

1. Ward, *General William Maxwell*, p. 102.

2. Stryker, *Battle of Monmouth*, pp. 109–10.

3. Stone et al., "Lee's Advance Force," Monmouth Battlefield State Park Collection. Copy courtesy of Dr. Garry W. Stone; Stryker, *Battle of Monmouth*, pp. 115–16; William Maxwell testimony, in Lee, *Proceedings of a General Court-Martial*; Martin, *Philadelphia Campaign*, p. 211; Ward, *General William Maxwell*, p. 103. The actual units composing Lee's force have also been confusing historians since the time of the battle. His command included the special "picked men" detachments Washington had been creating out of existing units and sending forward during the previous week, as well as certain regular regiments and brigades. Sometimes officers were in command of "picked troop" units rather than their usual regimental and brigade formations, which has added to the confusion.

4. Pepe, *Freehold*, p. 19; Salter, *A History of Monmouth and Ocean Counties*, p. 90; Smith, *Battle of Monmouth*, 1964, pp. 7–8. The Covenhoven house still stands, maintained by the MCHA, at 150 West Main Street in Freehold, NJ; Di Ionno, *A Guide to New Jersey's Revolutionary War Trail*, pp. 133–34; Dr. Garry Wheeler Stone, e-mail message to author, January 8, 2010; Morris, "The Hessians at Monmouth"; "The Battle of Monmouth: A Contemporaneous Visit to the Battlefield," undated and unidentified newspaper clipping reprinting "The Cave of Vanhest," from the *United States Magazine*, 1779, MCHA Battle of Monmouth Collection.

5. Gordon, *A Gazetteer of New Jersey*, p. 145; Lossing, *Pictorial Field Book of the Revolution*, p. 358; Lynn, "Annals of the Buffalo Valley," p. 72, http://files.usg-warchives.net/pa/union/history/lynn/l126166.txt; Stryker, *Battle of Monmouth*, p. 114; Martin, *Private Yankee Doodle*, p. 116. The terms "morass" and "ravine," along with actual names, have often been used interchangeably to describe the various brooks and ancillary wetlands crossing the battlefield. For the purpose of clarity and consistency, this work will use the terms used by Dr. Garry W. Stone in his maps of the battlefield.

6. Stone et al., "Lee's Advance Force"; Stryker, *Battle of Monmouth*, pp. 118–19.

7. Lundn, *Cockpit of the Revolution*, p. 399; Fleming, *Washington's Secret War*, p. 313.

8. Stryker, *Battle of Monmouth*, p. 122; Reprint of John Laurens letter of July 2, 1778, in "The Battle of Monmouth," *Monmouth Democrat*, n.d., MCHA Battle of Monmouth Collection; Simcoe, *Simcoe's Military Journal*, pp. 68–72; Lockhart, *Drillmaster of Valley Forge*, pp. 154–55.

9. Martin, *Philadelphia Campaign*, p. 211.

10. Callahan, *Daniel Morgan*, pp. 164–65.

11. Martin, *Philadelphia Campaign*, p. 212

12. The hill on which Clinton established his headquarters was called Briar Hill in the nineteenth century, but was not called that in the eighteenth. Dr. Garry W. Stone, e-mail message to author, January 8, 2010; Dr. Garry W. Stone, in discussion with the author, January 15, 2010.

13. Anonymous officer, First Battalion British Grenadiers, to Lord Amherst, Amherst Papers, David Library of the American Revolution, text-fiche, W.O. 34/111, p. 71. Transcribed 1993 by Dr. Garry Wheeler Stone, Gilbert Riddle, and Mark Lender. Transcription provided by Gilbert Riddle.

14. John Laurens to Henry Laurens, July 2, 1778, Lee Papers; Maxwell and Lafayette testimony, in Lee, *Proceedings of a General Court-Martial*; Dr. Garry W. Stone, in discussion with the author, January 2010.

15. Oswald testimony, in Lee, *Proceedings of a General Court Martial*.

16. Martin, *Private Yankee* Doodle, p. 115; Cited in Higginbotham, *Daniel Morgan*, p. 90; Anthony Wayne to wife, 1 July 1778, Lee Papers. Bracketed word added by Rees in sources for "What is this you have been about to day?"

17. Wilkin, *Some British Soldiers in America,* p. 257.

18. Dr. Garry W. Stone, discussion, January 2010; Pepe, *Freehold*, p. 42.

19. Testimony of Lieutenant-Colonels Harrison and Tilghman, in Lee, *Proceedings of a General Court-Martial*.

20. Wilkin, *Some British Soldiers in America*, p. 258; Martin, *Private Yankee Doodle,* p. 115.

21. Martin, *Private Yankee Doodle,* p. 116; James Jordan pension deposition (W8225), Revolutionary War Pension Applications, National Archives, cited by Rees, http://www.revwar75.com/library/rees/monmouth/MonmouthI.htm; Testi-mony of Lieutenant-Colonels Tilghman and Brooks, in Lee, *Proceedings of a General Court-Martial*.

22. Smith, *Battle of Monmouth*, 1964, p. 19.

23. Dr. Garry W. Stone, e-mail message to author, January 8, 2010; *Monmouth Democrat,* July 6, 1854.

24. Anonymous officer, First Battalion British Grenadiers, to Lord Amherst, Amherst Papers, David Library of the American Revolution, text-fiche, W.O. 34/111; Smith, *Battle of Monmouth*, 1964, pp. 17, 19; Martin, *Philadelphia Campaign*, pp. 222–23.

25. Stone, Sivilich, and Lender, "A Deadly Minuet; Henry B. Livingston to Robert Livingston, June 31, 1778, Rutgers University Special Collections and Archives, Alexander Library, Accession no. 3097, copy in MCHA Battle of Monmouth Collection; Wilkin, *Some British Soldiers in America*, pp. 258–59, 263; Testimony of Captain-Lieutenant John Cumpston, Third Continental Artillery and Brigadier General Knox, in Lee, *Proceedings of a General Court Martial;* Anonymous officer, First Battalion British Grenadiers, to Lord Amherst, Amherst Papers, W.O. 34/111; Wilkin, *Some British Soldiers in America*, p. 258; "Notes on the Battle of Monmouth" [*London Chronicle* newspaper]. It seems possible, but increasingly less likely, that Monckton was killed later in the battle. Morrissey, *Monmouth Courthouse 1778*, p. 70, is ambivalent on the site and time of

Monckton's death. It should be noted that Monmouth Battlefield State Park historian Dr. Garry Wheeler Stone, who is more familiar with the details of the battle than anyone else, is of the opinion that Monckton died at the time of the earlier hedgerow fight, as is Dr. David Martin. Dr. Garry W. Stone, e-mail message to author, January 8, 2010; Dr. Garry W. Stone, discussion, January 2010; Dr. David Martin, e-mail message to author, January 28, 2010.

26. Dr. Garry W. Stone, discussion, January 2010.

27. Lockhart, *Drillmaster of Valley Forge*, pp. 160–61.

28. Dr. Garry W. Stone, discussion, January 2010; Stone, Sivilich, and Lender, "A Deadly Minuet."

29. Wilkin, *Some British Soldiers in America*, p. 260; Ironically, the British artillery was in part manned by members of the Loyalist Second Battalion New Jersey Volunteers, detailed to artillery service in 1777. The battalion was originally raised by Lieutenant Colonel John Morris from among Monmouth County Loyalists, some no doubt from the Tory stronghold of Upper Freehold Township, in 1776. "A History of the 2nd Battalion, New Jersey Volunteers," http://www.royalprovincial.com/military/rhist/njv/2njvhist.htm; Callahan, "Henry Knox, American Artillerist," pp. 252–53; Martin, *Private Yankee Doodle*, pp. 96–97. For the full story of "Molly Pitcher," see chapter 6.

30. Callahan, "Henry Knox, American Artillerist," p. 253; Dr. Garry W. Stone, discussion, January 2010.

31. Stone, Sivilich, and Lender, "A Deadly Minuet."

32. Stone, Sivilich, and Lender, "A Deadly Minuet." A detailed description of the archaeological study of this fight can be found in Veit, *Digging New Jersey's Past*, pp. 83–87. It should be noted that the Forty-second was issued some of the 1776 Pattern British rifles, so the smaller balls found in the archaeological dig may have been dropped or fired by rifle-armed Highlanders, although the .58 ball is smaller than the usual British carbine size. Bailey, *Small Arms of the British Forces*, p. 179; Wright, *Continental Army*, p. 150.

33. Stone, Sivilich, and Lender, "A Deadly Minuet."

34. Barber and Howe, *Historical Collections*, p. 341; Dr. Garry W. Stone, discussion, January 2010.

35. Barber and Howe, *Historical Collections,* pp. 341, 347; Lossing, *Pictorial Field Book of the Revolution*, p. 363; Lossing, *Potter's American Monthly,* pp. 262–63; *Frank Leslie's Illustrated Newspaper*, July 12, 1878.

36. In retrospect, much of the movement at Monmouth was probably at a slower pace than would usually be the case due to the heat. This fact may well have facilitated disengagements for both sides.

37. Cited in Stone, Sivilich, and Lender, "A Deadly Minuet"; Ewald, *Diary of the American War*, pp. 136–37; "The Memorial of Lieutenant Colonel Thomas Rogers late of the Georgia Loyal Militia." David Library of the American Revolution. Transcription by Gilbert Riddle.

38. Andrew Bell, "Copy of a Journal."

39. Lee, *Documents Relating to the Revolutionary History of the State of New Jersey,* pp. 273–74; Andrew Bell, "Copy of a Journal."

40. Wilkin, *Some British Soldiers in America*, p. 260; Hunter, *Journal of Gen. Sir Martin Hunter and Some Letters*, p. 42; Uhlendorf, *Revolution in America*, pp. 185–87; Van Dyck, "A Report of the No. slain buried in the Field of Battle near Monmouth Court Ho. 29th. June 1778," George Washington Papers, Presidential Papers Microfilm (Washington, DC: 1961), Series 4, reel 50, cited by Rees in "What is this you have been about to day?"; Montross, *Rag, Tag, and Bobtail*, p. 287; "George Washington to John Washington, July 4, 1778," in Gerlach, *New Jersey in the American Revolution*, pp. 307–8; Martin, *Philadelphia Campaign*, p. 233; Ewald, *Diary of the American War,* pp. 135–37; Dr. Garry W. Stone, discussion, January 2010.

41. "Personal Narrative of the Services of Lieutenant John Shreve," p. 570; Diary of Surgeon Samuel Adams, New York Public Library, copy in MCHA Battle of Monmouth Collection.

42. Gibbes, "Reminiscences of Dr. William Read, Arranged from Notes and Papers," in *Documentary History of the American Revolution*, pp. 256–57.

43. Col. Otho Williams to Dr. Phil Moore, June 29, 1778, General Otho Williams Papers, Maryland Historical Society. Transcribed by Dr. Garry W. Stone, copy courtesy of Gilbert V. Riddle; Israel Shreve to "Dear Polly," Historical Society of Pennsylvania, Dreer Collection, "Soldiers of the Revolution," box 4, Series 52:2, vol. 4, copy in MCHA Battle of Monmouth Collection; Barber and Howe, *Historical Collections*, p. 343; David Vanderveer Perrine memoir, n.d., copy in MCHA Battle of Monmouth Collection.

44. Barber and Howe, *Historical Collections*, pp. 341–42; Perhaps surprisingly, Revolutionary War battlefield burial sites, save at Princeton, are not readily identified today, and unlike Civil War burials, reinterments were apparently rare. A marker at Princeton notes that bodies of the slain were buried nearby, and nineteenth-century construction in Trenton came across what were apparently the remains of Hessians killed at the battle there. Archaeologists have only made one discovery of a Revolutionary War postcombat burial location in New Jersey, the site of the September 1778 "Baylor Massacre" of several Continental dragoons by a British foraging party from New York. Hunter and Burrow, in "The Historical Geography and Archeology of the Revolutionary War in New Jersey," in Mitnick, *New Jersey in the American Revolution*, p. 187; Journal of Enos Barnes (Fifth Connecticut Regiment), Morristown National Historical Park, copy in MCHA Battle of Monmouth Collection; Stryker, *Battle of Monmouth*, p. 229–30; Beekman, *Early Dutch Settlers,* p. 85. The gravesite in Freehold, according to Dr. David Martin, who has studied the matter, was "buried in an empty lot a block from the courthouse"; Dr. David Martin, e-mail message to author, January 31, 2010. Dr Martin made his unpublished study, "Burial of the Slain at Monmouth," available to the author.

45. Cited in Bilby, *Three Rousing Cheers,* p. 82.

46. General Orders Head Quarters Brunswick Landing July 3rd 1778, Washington Papers, Alderman Library, University of Virginia, copy courtesy of James Raleigh, MCHA Battle of Monmouth Collection; "Lieutenant Thomas Blake's Journal," in Kidder, *History of the First New Hampshire Regiment,* p. 43.

47. Fleming, *Washington's Secret War*, p. 327; Testimony of Wayne, Scott, Meade, and Lafayette, in Lee, *Proceedings of a General Court-Martial*. An excellent synopsis of the Lee court-martial is provided in Fleming, "Military Crimes."
48. Fleming, "Military Crimes."
49. Fleming, *Washington's Secret War*, p. 328; Testimony of Laurens and Hamilton, in Lee, *Proceedings of a General Court-Martial*.
50. Testimony of Mercer and Wikoff, in Lee, *Proceedings of a General Court-Martial*.
51. Fleming, "Military Crimes." Fleming advised that although he would not be quite so damning in his opinion of Lee today, he nonetheless thought it best for the country that the general was removed from active duty. Thomas Fleming, e-mail message to author, January 24, 2010.
52. For a detailed account of the Battle of Springfield, see Fleming, *Forgotten Victory*; Martin, Bloomfield, and Lender, *Citizen Soldier*, pp. 136–37; Bell, "Copy of a Journal"; Ewald, *Diary of the American War*, p. 136.
53. J. Huntington to father, June 30, 1778, John Rees Collection, Valley Forge NHP, copy in MCHA Battle of Monmouth Collection; Henry Knox to brother, July 3, 1778, Henry Knox Papers, vol. 4, item 117 (reel 4), Massachusetts Historical Society, copy in MCHA Battle of Monmouth Collection; Higginbotham, *War of American Independence*, p. 247.
54. Lee, *Documents Relating to the Revolutionary History of the State of New Jersey*, p. 561–68; General Sir Henry Clinton to H.F.C. Pelham-Clinton, 2nd Duke of Newcastle, July 11, 1778, University of Nottingham (UK) Manuscripts and Special Collections. Copy courtesy of Gilbert V. Riddle; Samuel Johnson to Lord Amherst, 13 July 1778, Kent County [England] Archives, Amherst Manuscripts U1350 079/22, transcribed February 1995 by Lee Boyle and Garry Stone from a copy in the library, Valley Forge NHP, copy in MCHA Battle of Monmouth Collection.
55. Conway, "The British Army."
56. Ferling, "Myths of the American Revolution."

CHAPTER SIX
1. Bilby and Ziegler, *Asbury Park*, p. 55. This lynching was actually the only such crime in the whole state of New Jersey from the Revolution to the present day, although Monmouth County sheriff Clarence Hetrick foiled a threatened lynching of an innocent man accused of murdering a child in Asbury Park in 1910.
2. Gordon, *History of New Jersey*, p. 274
3. Martin, *A Molly Pitcher Source Book*, p. 1. Martin thoroughly researches the various Molly myths and his conclusions remain the current last word on the subject.
4. Ibid., pp. 247–48.
5. Ibid., pp. 252–53.
6. Ibid., pp. 251–53; Stockton, *Stories of New Jersey*, pp. 186–92.
7. Smith, *A Molly Pitcher Chronology*, p. 7.
8. Martin, *A Molly Pitcher Sourcebook*, pp. 244–46.
9. Smith, *A Molly Pitcher Chronology*, p. 4; Documents supplied to the authors by

Robert Goodyear, a direct descendent of Mary Ludwig Hays McCauley, strongly support the identity of "Molly Pitcher" as noted here.

10. Pepe, *Freehold*, pp. 117–19.

11. "Address to the Citizens of Monmouth County on the Subject of Raising a Monument to Commemorate the Battle of Monmouth," New Jersey Historical Society, New Jersey Pamphlets, N040 N42 N.1 no. 13, 1846.

12. *The True American*, Trenton, NJ, July 2 and 12, 1828, MCHA Battle of Monmouth Collection.

13. Wright, "Joel Parker," in Stellhorn and Birkner, *Governors of New Jersey*, p. 132; *Monmouth Democrat*, June 22, July 6, 1854, MCHA Battle of Monmouth Collection; Elisa Smith to Sarah Waln, June [?] and July 6, 1854, MCHA Battle of Monmouth Collection.

14. *Monmouth Inquirer*, September 18, 1858, copy in MCHA Battle of Monmouth Collection; Martin, "The Story of Camp Vredenburgh," in Martin, *Monocacy Regiment*, pp. 195–209.

15. *Monmouth Inquirer*, Freehold, NJ. June 27, 1878, MCHA Battle of Monmouth Collection.

16. *Monmouth Inquirer*, Freehold, NJ. July 4, 1878, MCHA Battle of Monmouth Collection; Pepe, *Freehold*, p. 120.

17. Styple, *Tell Me of Lincoln*, pp. 154–62.

18. *New York Times*, November 14, 1884; *Monmouth Democrat*, July 5, 1878.

19. Text of Joel Parker speech in Monmouth Battle Monument dedication pamphlet, MCHA Battle of Monmouth Collection; Unidentified newspaper clipping dated "June 4, 1903," in MCHA Battle of Monmouth Collection. Parker was the first New Jerseyan to serve two terms as governor, and went on to also serve as attorney general and a judge on the state's Court of Errors and Appeals (Supreme Court). Hoch, "Joel Parker," in Bilby, *New Jersey Goes to War*, p. 95.

20. Excerpt from Parker speech in "Monmouth Battle Monument Dedication."

21. Undated newspaper clipping, MCHA Battle of Monmouth Collection; Olsen, *A Billy Yank Governor*, p. 173.

22. *New York Times*, June 28, 1903. Despite his last name, which might suggest it, Murphy was not of Irish-Catholic immigrant heritage, but came from an old, established and wealthy New Jersey protestant family. He was actually a moderate progressive, and, in an age of robber baron capitalism, paid his workers a living wage and granted them retirement pensions. As governor, he introduced introducing child labor laws and instituted civil service reforms. Olsen and Burke, "Franklin Murphy," in Bilby, *New Jersey Goes to War*, p. 88. Growing concern about the potential perils of immigration from eastern and southern Europe increased after World War I, when some immigrants were viewed as potential Bolsheviks. The predominantly Catholic and Jewish religious orientation of the immigrants of the era was also viewed as a threat to a Protestant America by many. These fears proved a boon to the revived Ku Klux Klan, which, in the 1920s, directed much of its efforts at immigrants, Catholics, and Jews. Monmouth County became a stronghold of the Klan in New Jersey, and the "Tri-State Konklave" held at its headquarters in long Branch from July 2–4,

1924, was the largest such gathering in the state. By 1940, weakened by political and sexual scandals and with concerns with the Depression and impending war coming to the fore, the Klan had, however, virtually disappeared from public view, even in Long Branch. Bilby and Ziegler, *Asbury Park*, pp. 65–70.

23. "Sesquicentennial of the Battle of Monmouth," *Quarterly Journal of the New York State Historical Association* 9, p. 279.

24. *New York Times*, June 26, 1978.

25. Cunningham, *Uncertain Revolution*, p. 327; Newark *Sunday Call*, September 5, 1936; Gary Wheeler Stone, "The Right Time, the Right Place, and the Right Man: Joe Truncer and the Preservation of Monmouth Battlefield" (oral presentation at the Friends of Monmouth Battlefield Living History Day Program, February 20, 1994). Transcript in Monmouth Battlefield State Park collection.

26. Monmouth Battlefield State Park Web site, http://www.state.nj.us/dep/parksandforests/parks/monbat.html.

BIBLIOGRAPHY

BOOKS, ARTICLES, AND COMPILATIONS

Adelberg, Michael S. *"A Combination to Trample All Law Underfoot": The Association for Retaliation and the American Revolution in Monmouth County.* Unpublished manuscript, 1995. Monmouth County Historical Society.

____. "'They Do Rather More Harm Than Good': An Examination of Continental Soldiers in Revolutionary Monmouth County." In *Impact: Papers Presented at a Symposium on the Impact of the War of Independence on Civilian Populations.* Morristown, NJ: Morristown National Historical Park, 1995.

Ahearn, Bill. *Muskets of the Revolution and the French and Indian Wars.* Lincoln, RI: Andrew Mowbray, 2005.

Alden, John Richard. *General Charles Lee: Traitor or Patriot.* Baton Rouge: Louisiana State University Press, 1951.

[Anburey, Thomas]. *Travels Through the Interior Parts of America: In a Series of Letters by an Officer,* Vol. 1. London: William Lane, 1789.

Anderson, Fred. *A People's Army: Massachusetts Soldiers and Society in the Seven Years' War.* Chapel Hill: University of North Carolina Press, 1984.

Babits, Lawrence E. *A Devil of a Whipping: The Battle of Cowpens.* Chapel Hill: University of North Carolina Press, 1998.

Bailey, De Witt. *British Military Flintlock Rifles, 1740–1840.* Lincoln, RI: Andrew Mowbray, 2002.

____. *British Military Longarms, 1715–1865.* London: Arms and Armour Press, 1986.

____. *Small Arms of the British Forces in America, 1664–1815.* Woonsocket, RI: Andrew Mowbray, 2009.

Barber, John W. and Henry Howe. *Historical Collections of the State of New Jersey, Containing a General Collection of the Most Interesting Facts, Traditions, Biographical Sketches, Anecdotes, Etc. Relating to its History and Antiquities, with Geographical Descriptions of Every Township in the State.* Newark, NJ: Benjamin Olds, 1844.

Batchellor, Albert Stillman. *The Ranger Service in the Upper Valley of the Connecticut and the Most Northerly Regiment of the New Hampshire Militia in the Period of the Revolution.* Concord, NH: Rumford Press, 1903.

Beekman, George C. *Early Dutch Settlers of Monmouth County, New Jersey*. 2nd ed. Freehold, NJ: Moreau Brothers, 1915.

Bell, Andrew. "Copy of a Journal, by Andrew Bell, Esq., At one time Confidential Secretary of General Sir Henry Clinton. Kept during the march of the British Army through New-Jersey, in 1778." *New Jersey Historical Society Proceedings* 6, 1852.

Benninghoff, Herman O. II. *Valley Forge: A Genesis for Command and Control, Continental Army Style*. Gettysburg, PA: Thomas Publications, 2001.

Bilby, Joseph G. "Brown Bess." *Military Heritage Magazine* (December 1999).

_____, ed. *New Jersey Goes to War: Biographies of 150 New Jerseyans Caught Up in the Struggle of the Civil War, including Soldiers, Civilians, Men, Women, Heroes, Scoundrels— and a Heroic Horse*. Ridgewood: New Jersey Civil War Heritage Association, 2010.

_____. "'A Soldier of Military Distinction and Honor': The Story of Pattie Ferguson and His Rifle." *Dixie Gun Works Blackpowder Annual*, 2004.

_____. "Sole Survivor." Pt. 1. *Muzzle Blasts* (April 1985).

_____. "Sole Survivor." Pt. 2. *Muzzle Blasts* (May 1985).

_____. *Three Rousing Cheers: A History of the Fifteenth New Jersey from Flemington to Appomattox*. Hightstown, NJ: Longstreet House, 1993.

Bilby, Joseph, and Harry Ziegler. *Asbury Park: A Brief History*. Charleston, SC: History Press, 2009.

Bill, Alfred Hoyt. *New Jersey and the Revolutionary War*. Princeton: D. Van Nostrand, 1964.

Billias, George Athan. *George Washington's Generals and Opponents: Their Exploits and Leadership*. New York: Da Capo Press, 1994.

Blackmore, Howard L. *British Military Firearms, 1650–1850*. London: Herbert Jenkins, 1961.

Boatner, Mark M. III. *Encyclopedia of the American Revolution*. Mechanicsburg, PA: Stackpole Books, 1994.

Bolton, Charles Knowles. *The Private Soldier Under Washington*. New York: Charles Scribner's Sons, 1902.

Braisted, Todd W. "Refugees and Others: Loyalist Families in the American War for Independence." Pt. 1. *Brigade Dispatch* 26, no. 4 (Winter 1996).

Bray, Robert, and Paul Bushnell, eds. *Diary of a Common Soldier in the American Revolution, 1775–1783: An Annotated Edition of the Military Journal of Jeremiah Greenman*. DeKalb: Northern Illinois University Press, 1978.

Burgoyne, Bruce E. "Women with the Hessian Auxiliaries during the American Revolutionary War. Pt. 1. *Brigade Dispatch* 26, no. 1 (Spring 1996).

Bury, Lt. Col. Viscount M.P. *Manual of Rifling and Rifle Sights for the National Rifle Association, 1864*. London: Longman, 1864.

Callahan, North. *Daniel Morgan: Ranger of the Revolution*. New York: Holt, Rinehart, and Winston, 1961.

____. "Henry Knox, American Artillerist." In Billias, *George Washington's Generals and Opponents*.

Carman, W.Y. *A History of Firearms from Earliest Times to 1814*. London: Routledge and Kegan Paul, 1955.

Carrington, Henry B. "Familiar Hints to Indiana Soldiers Taking to the Field." Undated newspaper clipping from the Greencastle, Indiana, *Putnam Republican Banner*.

Casterline, Greg. *Colonial Tribulations: The Survival Story of William Casterline and His Comrades of the New Jersey Blues Regiment, French and Indian War, 1755–1757*. Self-published, 2007.

Chartrand, Rene. *Colonial American Troops 1610–1774*. Vol. 2. Oxford: Osprey, 2002.

____. "Notes Concerning Women in the 18th Century French Army." *Brigade Dispatch* 25, no. 3 (Autumn 1995).

Clinton, Henry. *Narrative of Lieutenant-General Sir Henry Clinton, Relative to His Conduct During Part of His Command of the King's Troops in North America*. London: J. Debrett, 1783.

Coakley, Robert W., and Stetson Conn. *The War of the American Revolution: Narrative, Chronology, and Bibliography*. Washington, DC: U.S. Army Center of Military History, 1975.

Coates, Earl J., James L. Kochan, and Don Troiani. *Don Troiani's Soldiers in America, 1754–1865*. Mechanicsburg, PA: Stackpole Books, 1998.

"Colonel Elijah Hand to Colonel Charles Mawhood." In Gerlach, *New Jersey in the American Revolution*.

Conway, Stephen. "The British Army, 'Military Europe,' and the American War of Independence." *William and Mary Quarterly* 67, 3rd ser., no. 1 (January 2010).

Cowart, Samuel Craig. *Address, Battle of Monmouth and Poem, Patriot Sires of Monmouth by Samuel Craig Coward, Old Tennent Church, June 24th, 1914, Welcoming Washington Pilgrimage*. Hightstown, NJ: Longstreet House (1998 reprint).

Cunningham, John T. *The Uncertain Revolution: Washington and the Continental Army at Morristown*. West Creek, NJ: Cormorant, 2007.

Curtis, Edward E. *The Organization of the British Army in the American Revolution*. New Haven: Yale University Press, 1926.

Dann, John C., ed. *The Revolution Remembered: Eyewitness Accounts of the War for Independence*. Chicago: University of Chicago Press, 1980.

Darling, Anthony D. *Red Coat and Brown Bess*. Bloomfield, Ontario: Museum Restoration Press, 1971.

Dawson, Henry W. *Battles of the United States by Sea and Land: Embracing Those of the Revolutionary and Indian Wars, the War of 1812 and the Mexican War; With Important Official Documents*. New York: Johnson, Fry, 1858.

Dearborn, Henry. *Journals of Henry Dearborn, 1776–1783*. 1886. Reprinted from the Proceedings of the Massachusetts Historical Society. Cambridge, MA: John Wilson and Son University Press, 1887.

DePauw, Linda Grant. "Women in Combat: The Revolutionary War Experience." *Armed Forces and Society* 7, no. 2 (Winter 1981).

Di Ionno, Mark. *A Guide to New Jersey's Revolutionary War Trail for Families and History Buffs*. New Brunswick: Rutgers University Press, 2000.

"Ebenezer Hazard, Journey Thorough War-torn New Jersey." In Gerlach, *New Jersey in the American Revolution*.

Ellis, Franklin. *History of Monmouth County*. Philadelphia: J.B. Lippincott, 1886.

Ewald, Johann. *Diary of the American War: A Hessian Journal*. Edited by Joseph P. Tustin. New Haven: Yale University Press, 1979.

Ferling, John. "Myths of the American Revolution." *Smithsonian Magazine* (January 2010).

Fischer, David Hackett. *Washington's Crossing*. New York: Oxford University Press, 2004.

Flayderman, Norm. *Flayderman's Guide to Antique American Firearms and Their Values*. Iola, WI: Gun Digest Books, 2007.

Fleming, Thomas J. *Forgotten Victory: The Battle for New Jersey, 1780*. Pleasantville, NY: Reader's Digest Press, 1973.

_____. *New Jersey: A History*. New York: W.W. Norton, 1977.

_____. "'The Military Crimes' of Charles Lee." *American Heritage* 19, no. 3 (April 1968).

_____. *Washington's Secret War: The Hidden History of Valley Forge*. New York: Smithsonian Books, 2005.

Fowler, David J. "Egregious Villains, Wood Rangers, and London Traders: The Pine Robber Phenomenon in New Jersey During the Revolutionary War." PhD diss., Rutgers University, 1987.

_____. "Loyalist Insurrection in Upper Freehold Township, 1776: The Woodward Episode." *Monmouth County Historical Association Newsletter* 13, nos. 1 and 2 (Fall 1984/Winter 1985).

_____. "These Were Troublesome Times Indeed." In Mitnick, *New Jersey in the American Revolution*.

Frey, Sylvia R. *The British Soldier in America: A Social History of Military Life in the Revolutionary Period*. Austin: University of Texas Press, 1981.

Fuller, Colonel J.F.C. *British Light Infantry in the Eighteenth Century*. London: Hutchinson, 1925.

"George Washington to John Washington, July 4, 1778." In Gerlach, *New Jersey in the American Revolution*.

Gérard, Conrad Alexandre. *Instructions and Despatches of Conrad Alexandre Gerard, 1778–80*. Baltimore: Johns Hopkins University Press, 1939.

Gerlach, Larry R., ed. *New Jersey in the American Revolution, 1763–1783: A Documentary History*. Trenton: New Jersey Historical Commission, 1975.

____. "William Franklin." In Stellhorn and Birkner, *Governors of New Jersey, 1664–1974: Biographical Essays*.

Gibbes, Robert Wilson. *Documentary History of the American Revolution*. New York: D. Appleton, 1857.

Gooding, James S. *An Introduction to British Artillery in North America*. Ottawa: Museum Restoration Service, 1965.

Gordon, Thomas F. *A Gazetteer of New Jersey*. Trenton: Daniel Fenton, 1834.

____. *The History of New Jersey from its Discovery by Europeans to the Adoption of the Federal Constitution and Gazetteer of New Jersey*. Trenton: Daniel Fenton, 1834.

Gough, Robert J. "Black Men and the Early New Jersey Militia." *New Jersey History* 88, no. 4 (Winter 1970).

Graydon, Alexander. *Memoirs of His Own Time with Reminiscences of the Men and Events of the Revolution*. Edited by John Stockton Littell. Philadelphia: Lindsay and Blakiston, 1846.

Green, Lorenzo. "The Negro in the Armed Forces, 1619–1783." *Negro History Bulletin* (October 1951).

Griffith, Paddy. *Forward into Battle: Fighting Tactics from Waterloo to the Near Future*. Novato, CA: Presidio Press, 1991.

Hagist, Don N. "Lessons from the Courts: A Safe Guard Hits His Target." *Brigade Dispatch* 24, no. 2 (Spring 1993).

____. "The Women of the British Army: A General Overview; Living Conditions." Pt. 1. *Brigade Dispatch* 34, no. 3 (Spring 1993).

____. "The Women of the British Army: A General Overview; Living Conditions." Pt. 2. *Brigade Dispatch* 34, no. 4 (Autumn 1993).

____. "The Women of the British Army: A General Overview; Living Conditions." Pt. 3. *Brigade Dispatch* 25, no. 1 (Spring 1995).

Hamilton, Alexander, and William Irvine. "The Battle of Monmouth: Letters of Alexander Hamilton and General William Irvine, Describing the Engagement Author(s): Alexander Hamilton and William Irvine." *Pennsylvania Magazine of History and Biography* 2, no. 2 (1878), pp. 139–48.

Harding, David F. *Small Arms of the East India Company, 1600–1856*. Vol. 3. *Ammunition and Performance*. London: Foresight Books, 1999.

Harper, Robert W. *Old Gloucester County and the American Revolution, 1763–1778*. Woodbury, NJ: Gloucester County Cultural and Heritage Commission, 1986.

Haythornthwaite, Philip. *Weapons and Equipment of the Napoleonic Wars*. London: Arms and Armor, 1996.

Hicks, James E. *Notes on U.S. Ordnance, 1776–1941*. Vol. 2. Greens Farms, CT: Modern Books and Crafts, 1971.

Higginbotham, Don. *Daniel Morgan: Revolutionary Rifleman*. Chapel Hill: University of North Carolina Press, 1961.

_____. *The War of American Independence: Military Attitudes, Policies and Practice, 1763–1789*. New York: Macmillan, 1971.

Hoch, Edward S, "Joel Parker." In Bilby, *New Jersey Goes to War*.

Hodges, Graham Russell. *Root and Branch: African Americans in New York and East Jersey, 1613–1863*. Chapel Hill: University of North Carolina Press, 1999.

_____. *Slavery and Freedom in the Rural North: African-Americans in Monmouth County, New Jersey, 1665–1865*. Madison, WI: Madison House, 1997.

Holmes, Richard. *Redcoat: The British Soldier in the Age of Horse and Musket*. New York: W.W. Norton, 2001.

Hughes, Major General B.P. CB, CBE. *Firepower: Weapons Effectiveness on the Battlefield, 1630–1850*. New York: Sarpedon, 1997.

Hunter, Martin. *The Journal of Gen. Sir Martin Hunter and Some Letters of His Wife Lady Hunter. . . .* Edinburgh: Edinburgh Press, 1894.

Hunter, Richard W. and Ian C.G. Burrow. "The Historical Geography and Archaeology of the Revolutionary War in New Jersey." In Mitnick, *New Jersey in the American Revolution*.

Hurwitz, Mark. "The Third New Jersey Regiment, Maxwell's Brigade, and the Campaign of 1778," *Brigade Dispatch* 27, no. 4 (Winter 1997).

Jackson, John W. *With the British Army in Philadelphia, 1777–1778*. San Rafael, CA: Presidio Press, 1979.

Jamison, Wallace N. *Religion in New Jersey: A Brief History*. Princeton, NJ: D. Van Nostrand, 1964.

Karels, Carol, ed. *The Revolutionary War in Bergen County: The Times That Tried Men's Souls*. Charleston, SC: History Press, 2007.

Katcher, Philip. *Armies of the American Wars, 1755–1815*. New York: Hastings House, 1975.

Kidder, Francis. *History of the First New Hampshire Regiment*. Albany, NY: Joel Munsell, 1868.

Lady's Magazine; or, Entertaining Companion for the Fair Sex, appropriated solely to their Use and Amusement for June, 1776.

Lee, Charles. *Proceedings of a General Court-Martial, Held at Brunswick in the State of New-Jersey by Order of His Excellency General Washington, Commander in Chief of the Army of the United States of America for the Trial of Major-General Lee. July 4th, 1778. Major-General Lord Stirling, President*. New York: privately printed, 1864.

Lee, Francis B., ed. *Documents Relating to the Revolutionary History of the State of New Jersey: Extracts from American Newspapers, 1778*. Vol. 2. Trenton, NJ: John L. Murphy, 1903.

Lee Papers, 1776–1778. Collections of the New-York Historical Society for the Year 1872. Vol. 2. 1776–1778. New York Historical Society. New York, 1873.

Leiby, Adrian. *The Revolutionary War in the Hackensack Valley: The Jersey Dutch and the Neutral Ground*. New Brunswick, NJ: Rutgers University Press, 1980.

Lender, Mark Edward. *The New Jersey Soldier*. Trenton: New Jersey Historical Commission, 1975.

____. *One State in Arms: A Short Military History of New Jersey*. Trenton: New Jersey Historical Commission, 1991.

Lewis, Berkeley R. *Small Arms and Ammunition in the United States Service, 1776–1865*. Washington, DC: Smithsonian, 1956.

"Lieutenant Thomas Blake's Journal." In Kidder, *History of the First New Hampshire Regiment*.

Lockhart, Paul. *The Drillmaster of Valley Forge: The Baron de Steuben and the Making of the American Army*. New York: Harper Collins, 2008.

"A Look at some British Soldiers." *Brigade Dispatch* 22, no. 2 (Summer 1991).

Lossing, Benson J. *The Pictorial Field Book of the Revolution*. Vol. 2. New York: Harper and Brothers, 1850.

____, ed. *Potter's American Monthly: The American Historical Record and Repertory of Notes and Queries Concerning the History and Antiquities of America and Biographies of Americans*. Vol. 3. Philadelphia: John E. Potter, 1874.

Lugs, Jaroslav. *Firearms Past and Present: A Complete Review of Firearm Systems and their Histories*. Vol. 1. London: Grenville, 1975.

Lundn, Leonard. *Cockpit of the Revolution: The War for Independence in New Jersey*. N.p.: Lundn Press, 2007

Lurie, Maxine N. "New Jersey: Radical or Conservative?" In Mitnick, *New Jersey in the American Revolution*.

Lurie, Maxine N., and Marc Mappen, eds. *The Encyclopedia of New Jersey*. New Brunswick: Rutgers University Press, 2004.

Lurie, Maxine N., Peter O. Wacker, and Michael Siegel. *Mapping New Jersey: An Evolving Landscape*. New Brunswick, NJ: Rivergate Books, 2009.

Lynn, John Blair Lynn. *Annals of the Buffalo Valley*, http://files.usgwarchives.net/pa/union/history/lynn/l126166.txt.

Mahon, John K. *History of the Militia and the National Guard*. New York: Macmillan, 1983.

Manucy, Albert. *Artillery through the Ages: A Short History of Cannon, Emphasizing Types Used in America*. Washington, DC: U.S. Government Printing Office, 1949.

Martin, David G. Martin. *Burial of the Slain at the Battle of Monmouth*. Unpublished monograph.

____. *A Molly Pitcher Source Book*. Hightstown, NJ: Longstreet House, 2003.

____, ed. *The Monocacy Regiment: A Commemorative History of the Fourteenth New Jersey in the Civil War, 1862–1865*. Hightstown, NJ: Longstreet House, 1987.

____. *The Philadelphia Campaign: June 1777–July 1778*. Cambridge, MA: Da Capo Press, 1993.

____. "The Story of Camp Vredenburgh." In *The Monocacy Regiment*.

Martin, James Kirby, Joseph Bloomfield, and Mark E. Lender, eds. *Citizen Soldier:*

The Revolutionary War Journal of Joseph Bloomfield. Newark: New Jersey Historical Society, 1982.

Martin, Joseph Plumb. *Memoir of a Revolutionary Soldier: The Narrative of Joseph Plumb Martin*. Mineola, NY: Dover, 2006.

_____. *Private Yankee Doodle, Being a Narrative of Some of the Adventures, Dangers and Sufferings of a Revolutionary Soldier*. Edited by George F. Scheer. Boston and Toronto: Little, Brown, 1962.

May, Robin, and Gerry Embleton. *The British Army in North America, 1775–1783*. Revised *ed.* Cambridge: Osprey, 1997.

McHenry, Dr. James. "The Battle of Monmouth." *Magazine of American History* 3. Pt. 1. 1879.

Milsop, John. *Continental Infantryman of the American Revolution*. Cambridge: Osprey, 2004.

Minutes of the Council of Safety of the State of New Jersey. Jersey City, NJ: John H. Lyon, 1872.

Minutes of the Provincial Congress and Council of Safety of New Jersey. Naar, Day, and Naar, Trenton, NJ: 1879.

Mitnick, Barbara J., ed. *New Jersey in the American Revolution*. New Brunswick: Rivergate Books, 2005.

Montross, Lynn. *Rag, Tag, and Bobtail: The Story of America's Continental Army*. New York: Harper and Brothers, 1952.

Moore, Warren. *Weapons of the American Revolution*. New York: Promontory Press, 1967.

Morrissey, Brendan. *Monmouth Courthouse 1778: The Last Great Battle in the North*. Cambridge: Osprey, 2004.

Nosworthy, Brent. *The Anatomy of Victory: Battle Tactics, 1689–1763*. New York: Hippocrene Books, 1990.

"Notes on the Battle of Monmouth." *Pennsylvania Magazine of History and Biography* 14, no. 1 (April 1890).

Olsen, Bernard. *A Billy Yank Governor: The Life and Times of New Jersey's Franklin Murphy*. West Kennebunk, Maine: Phoenix, 2000.

Olsen, Bernard and Thomas Burke Jr. "Franklin Murphy." In Bilby, *New Jersey Goes to War*.

Padelford, Phillip, ed. *Colonial Panorama 1775: Dr. Robert Honyman's Journal for March and April*. San Marino, CA: Huntington Library, 1939.

Pepe, Barbara. *Freehold: A Hometown History*. Charleston, SC: Arcadia, 2003.

Peterson, Harold. *Arms and Armor in Colonial America*. Harrisburg, PA: Stackpole Books, 1956.

_____. *Book of the Continental Soldier*. New York: Bonanza Books, 1977.

_____. *Round Shot and Rammers: An Introduction to Muzzle-loading Land Artillery in the United States*. New York: Bonanza Books, 1969.

Pierce, Arthur D. *Smugglers' Woods*. New Brunswick, NJ: Rutgers Unversity Press, 1960.

Pingeon, Francis D. *Blacks in the Revolutionary Era*. Trenton: New Jersey Historical Commission, 1975.

Plaster, John L. "Riflemen of the Revolution." *American Rifleman* (May 2009).

Quarles, Benjamin. *The Negro in the Revolution*. Chapel Hill: University of North Carolina Press, 1961.

Rankin, Hugh F. "Charles Lord Cornwallis: Study in Frustration." In Billias, *George Washington's Generals and Opponents: Their Exploits and Leadership*, pp. 193–94.

Rees, John, ed. "An examination of the Numbers of Female Camp Followers with the Continental Army." Pt. 1. *Brigade Dispatch* 23, no. 4, (Autumn 1992).

_____. "'The Greate Neglect in Provideing Cloathing. . . .': Uniform Colors and Clothing in the New Jersey Brigade During the Monmouth Campaign of 1778." *Military Collector and Historian* 46. Pt. 1, no. 4 (Winter 1994).

_____. "'The Great Neglect in Provideing Cloathing. . . .': Uniform Colors and Clothing in the New Jersey Brigade During the Monmouth Campaign of 1778." Pt. 2. *Military Collector and Historian* 47, no. 1, (Spring 1995).

_____. "New Material Concerning Female Followers With Continental Regiments." Pt. 1 of 2. *Brigade Dispatch* 27, no. 1 (Spring 1998).

_____. "New Material Concerning Female Followers With Continental Regiments." Pt. 2 of 2. *Brigade Dispatch* 28, no. 2 (Summer 1998).

_____. "Shoulder Arms of the Officers of the Continental Army; With Some Mentions of Bayonets and the Lack Thereof." *Brigade Dispatch* 23, no. 1 (Winter 1992).

_____. "'We . . . wheeled to the Right to form the Line Of Battle': Colonel Israel Shreve's Journal of 1777." *Brigade Dispatch* 22, no. 1 (Spring 1991).

Reid, Stuart. *British Redcoat, 1740–1793*. Cambridge: Osprey, 1996.

"The Reverend Alexander MacWhorter on British Brutality." In Gerlach, *New Jersey in the American Revolution*.

"The Reverend Nicholas Collin on the Ravages of War." In Gerlach, *New Jersey in the American Revolution*.

"Richard Stockton to Robert Ogden." In Gerlach, *New Jersey in the American Revolution*.

Riddle, Gilbert V. "Lessons from the Courts," *Brigade Dispatch* 25, no. 2 (Summer 1995).

Risch, Erna. *Supplying Washington's Army*. Washington, DC: Center of Military History, U.S. Army, 1981.

Ross, Steven. *From Flintlock to Rifle: Infantry Tactics, 1740–1866*. Rutherford, NJ: Fairleigh Dickinson University Press, 1979.

Ryan, Dennis P. *New Jersey's Loyalists*. Trenton: New Jersey Historical

Commission, 1975.

Salter, Edwin. *A History of Monmouth and Ocean Counties.* . . . Bayonne, NJ: E. Gardner and Son, 1890.

Scheer, George F., and Hugh F. Rankin. *Rebels and Redcoats: The Living Story of the American Revolution.* New York: World, 1957.

Schleicher, William, and Susan Winter. "Patriot and Slave: The Samuel Sutphen Story." *New Jersey Heritage Magazine* 1, no. 1 (Winter 2002).

Sheppard, E.W. *Red Coat: An Anthology of the British Soldier During the Last Three Hundred Years.* London: Batchworth Press, 1952.

Shreve, John. "Personal Narrative of the Services of Lieutenant John Shreve of the New Jersey Line of the Continental Army." Pt. 2. *Magazine of American History with Notes and Queries* 3, 1879.

Shy, John W. "Charles Lee: The Soldier as Radical." In Billias, *George Washington's Generals and Opponents.*

Simcoe, John Graves. *Simcoe's Military Journal: A History of the Operations of a Partisan Corps Called the Queen's Rangers, Commanded by Lieut. Col. J.G. Simcoe During the War of the American Revolution.* New York: Bartlett and Welford, 1844.

Smith, Samuel Stelle. *The Battle of Monmouth.* Monmouth Beach, NJ: Philip Freneau Press, 1964.

_____. *The Battle of Monmouth.* Trenton: New Jersey Historical Commission, 1975.

_____. *A Molly Pitcher Chronology.* Monmouth Beach, NJ: Philip Freneau Press, 1972.

Spring, Matthew H. *With Zeal and With Bayonets Only: The British Army on Campaign in North America, 1775–1783.* Norman: University of Oklahoma Press, 2008.

Stember, Sol. *The Bicentennial Guide to the American Revolution: The Middle Colonies.* Vol. 3. New York: Saturday Review, 1974.

Stellhorn, Paul A. and Michael J. Birkner, eds. *The Governors of New Jersey, 1664–1974: Biographical Essays.* Trenton: New Jersey Historical Commission, 1982.

Stockton, Frank. *Stories of New Jersey.* New York: American Book, 1896.

Stone, Garry W., Mark Lender, John U. Rees and Brendan Morrissey. "Lee's Advance Force." Monmouth Battlefield State Park Collection.

Stone, Garry W., Daniel M. Sivilich, and Mark Edward Lender. "A Deadly Minuet: The Advance of the New England 'Picked Men' against the Royal Highlanders at the Battle of Monmouth, 28 June, 1778." *Brigade Dispatch* 26, no. 2 (Summer 1996).

Stryker, William S. *The Battle of Monmouth.* Edited by William Starr Myers. 1927. Reprint, Tennent, NJ: Friends of Monmouth Battlefield, 1999.

_____. *Officers and Men of New Jersey in the Revolutionary War,* Vol. 2. Trenton: William T. Nicholson and Son, 1872.

Styple, William, ed. *Tell Me of Lincoln: Memories of Abraham Lincoln, the Civil War and Life in Old New York by James E. Kelly.* Kearny, NJ: Bellegrove Press, 2009.

Trench, Charles Chenevix. *A History of Marksmanship*. Chicago: Follett, 1972.

Trevelyan, George Otto. *The American Revolution*. Vol. 4. New York: Longmans, Green, 1922.

Uhlendorf, Bernhard A., ed. *Revolution in America: Confidential Letters and Journals 1776–1784 of Adjutant General Major Baurmeister of the Hessian Forces*. New Brunswick: Rutgers University Press, 1957.

Van Buskirk, Judith L. *Generous Enemies: Patriots and Loyalists in Revolutionary New York*. Philadelphia: University of Pennsylvania Press, 2002.

Veit, Richard. *Digging New Jersey's Past: Historical Archeology in the Garden State*. New Brunswick: Rutgers University Press, 2002.

Wade, David R., "Washington Saves the Day at Monmouth." Special issue, *Great Battles: Turning Points in the American Revolution*, 2005.

Walling, Richard. *Men of Color at the Battle of Monmouth, June 28, 1778*. Hightstown, NJ: Longstreet House, 1994.

Ward, Harry M. *General William Maxwell and the New Jersey Continentals*. Westport, CT: Greenwood Press, 1997.

Webster, Donald B. Jr. *American Socket Bayonets, 1717–1873*. Alexandria Bay, NY: Museum Restoration Service, 1967.

Weiss, Harry B., and Grace M. Weiss. *The Revolutionary Saltworks of the New Jersey Coast*. Trenton, NJ: Past Times Press, 1959.

Whisker, James B. "African–American Gunsmiths," *Gun Report* (September 1991).

Whitehead, William A. *Documents Relating to the Revolutionary History of the State of New Jersey, Extracts from American Newspapers*. Vol. 2. Trenton, NJ: John L. Murphy, 1903.

Wilkin, W.H., ed. *Some British Soldiers in America*. London: Hugh Rees, 1914.

Willcox, William B. "Sir Henry Clinton." In Billias, *George Washington's Generals and Opponents:*, pp. 83–84.

Wood, W.J. *Battles of the Revolutionary War: 1775–1781*. Chapel Hill: Algonquin Books, 1990.

Wright, Robert K. Jr. *The Continental Army*. Washington, DC: Center of Military History, U.S. Army, 1989.

Wright, William C. "Joel Parker." In Stellhorn and Birkner, *The Governors of New Jersey*.

Yee, Gary. *Sharpshooters: 1750–1900; The Men, Their Guns, Their Story*. Broadmoor, CA: Sharpshooter Press, 2009.

Zlatich, Marko, and Peter F. Copeland. *General Washington's Army, 1775–1778*. Vol. 1. Cambridge: Osprey, 1994.

MANUSCRIPTS

Cherry Hall Papers. Battle of Monmouth Collection. Monmouth County Historical Association, Freehold, New Jersey.

Court of General Quarter Sessions 1760–1779, 1779. Court of Oyer and Terminer 1752–1799, 1781. Monmouth County Archives.

Duke of Northumberland Manuscripts. Letters and Papers of the Percy Family. Library of Congress, Washington, DC.

Manuscripts 1680s-1970s. New Jersey State Archives, Dept. of Education, Bureau of Archives and History.

Microfilm Collection of Revolutionary War documents and pension records. David Library of the American Revolution. Washington Crossing, Pennsylvania.

Numbered Manuscripts. Department of Defense, Adjutant General. New Jersey State Archives, Dept. of Education, Bureau of Archives and History.

Washington, George. Presidential Papers. Library of Congress, Washington, DC.

Williams, General Otho. Papers. Maryland Historical Society, Baltimore, Maryland.

INTERNET SOURCES

The On-Line Institute for Advanced Loyalist Studies. "A History of the Second Battalion, New Jersey Volunteers."
http://www.royalprovincial.com/military/rhist/njv/2njvhist.htm

Rees, John U. "'What is this you have been about to day?': The New Jersey Brigade at the Battle of Monmouth."
 http://www.revwar75.com/library/rees/monmouth/MonmouthToc.htm

INDEX

Abercrombie, James (Captain), 139
Abercromby, James (General), 158
abolitionism, 59
Ackerman, Phil, *151ph*
Adams, John, 26, 144, 156–157
Adams, Samuel, 224
Additional Continental regiments, 186
agriculture, 188–189
Aiken's Tavern Road, 27
Alexander, William "Lord Stirling"
  casualties reported by, 217
  following Lee, 125
  at Hopewell, 128
  at Metuchen, 24–25
  at Monmouth Court House, *211map*
  on Perrine Ridge, 212
Allen, Samuel, *78ph*, 267n48
Allentown, New Jersey, 122, 129
Allentown Road, 123
Alloways Creek, 38
Amboy road, 200
ambushes
  description of, 2
  Ferguson and, 29
  at Quinton's Bridge, 38
American Indians, 115
American Volunteer corps, 164
Amherst, Lord, 161, 232
ammunition
  artillery and, 183
  boxes for, 173
  buckshot, 170, 177–179, *178ph*
  cartridges, 169–171, 173, 177, *178ph*
  diameter of, 171
  distribution of, 196
  flints and, 168–169
  handguns and, 166
  lack of, 199
  loading of, 171–173
  marksmanship training and, 175–176
  for muskets, 148
  range and, 173–174
  testing of reproduction weapons and,
    177–179; *see also* weapons
Andre, John, 80–81, 120
Anspach regiments, 101
Antill, John, 131
Armed Boat Company, 106

Arnold, Benedict, 81, 125
artillery
  British regiment for, 99
  Continental, 110–111
  exchange on Perrine Ridge, 214–215
  overview of, 181–184
  picked men and, 216–217
  reproduction "four pounder," *183ph*
  see also Pitcher, Molly; weapons
Asgill, Charles, 80–81
Associated Loyalists. *see* Board of
  Associated Loyalists
Association for Retaliation
  Board of Associated Loyalists and, 78
  cycle of violence and, 47, 82
  Forman and, 53, 65
  founding of, 68–69
  methods of, 72–75
  motivation of, 76
  recognition petition and, 70–71, 72
Association to Oppose the Return of
  Tories, 75–76
Assunpink Creek, 12

baggage train
  Clinton on, 232
  Knyphausen and, 89, 117, 122, 181,
    220
  see also supplies
Bailey, De Witt, 158, 165
Baldwin, Daniel, 13
Barber, James, 219
Bard, Samuel, 69
Barker, Mathias, 162
Barren Hill, 42–43, 115
Basking Ridge, New Jersey, 11, 92
battalion box, 173; *see also* ammunition;
  cartridges
battle formations. *see* military formations
Bauermeister, Carl von, 120, 222–223
Baylor Massacre, 277n44
bayonets
  description of, 179–181
  on Long Island, 157, 180
  Maxwell's forces and, 28
  at Paoli, 30–31
  at point of woods, 208
  reproduction of, *151ph*

Acknowledgments

Unlike the craft of a novelist, that of a historian is not a lonely exercise. No history comes to print without the assistance of numerous people and institutions. Although it lasted but a day, Monmouth Court House is a very complicated battle, as confusing to its participants, their recollections often colored by partisan causes, as to historians trying to unravel it centuries later. Establishing the correct time line for various incidents within the general action is a particularly difficult task, and the authors wish to profusely thank Dr. Garry Wheeler Stone, Dr. David Martin, and James Raleigh, who know the battlefield better than anyone, for their on-site clarifications, manuscript review, advice, explanation, and corrections where necessary. Gilbert V. Riddle acted as a research assistant extraordinaire, drawing upon his own extensive collection of primary sources, and ferreting out new material. The collections of battle-related sources in the Monmouth County Historical Association, and in the files of Monmouth Battlefield State Park also proved invaluable, as did the well-researched and sourced articles on Revolutionary War material culture in the Brigade of the American Revolution's journal *The Brigade Dispatch*. Others whose valuable assistance helped make this a much better book include Peter Culos, Steven Garratano, Bob Goodyear, Don Hagist, Kevin Marshall, Don Troiani, Michael Waricher, Jeff Williams, Bill Winslow, and Eric Wittenberg. If we have forgotten anyone, forgive us. Needless to say, any errors are those of the authors.